Good Behavior

Good Behavior

*Being a Study of
Certain Types of Civility*

Harold Nicolson

To Juliet, aged one

Axios Press
P.O. Box 118
Mount Jackson, VA 22842
888.542.9467   info@axiospress.com

Distributed by NATIONAL BOOK NETWORK.

Library of Congress Cataloging-in-Publication Data

Nicolson, Harold, 1886–1968.
      Good behavior : being a study of certain types of civility / Harold Nicolson.
            p. cm.
      Originally published: London : Constable, 1955.
      ISBN 978-1-60419-010-6 (pbk.)

      1. Conduct of life. I. Title.
      BJ1601.N5 2009
      177'.1—dc22

                                          2009004430

Contents

List of Photos
& Illustrations

Introduction

Good Behavior is not as Harold Nicolson explains "a manual on etiquette" as the title may lead one to believe. Nor did his first grandchild, aged one at the time of publication, and to whom this book is dedicated, benefit from a life-long lesson in exemplary manners. In fact as a grandfather Harold was, to our delight, an incorrigible advocate of rather bad behavior, always the first to jump into our paddling pool with his shoes and socks on, daring us to jump off perilously high, crumbling walls at Sissinghurst, and igniting our candy cigarettes with his pocket lighter.

Good Behavior is one of a series of twelve interconnecting essays in which Harold Nicolson examines "the varying types of civility produced during the last two thousand years." He hoped to write an amusing, cultural account of behavioral shifts over the preceding centuries, looking at the patterns of conduct of a sequence of notable, noble (and some less noble) minorities and individuals. In so doing he elevated the concept of good behavior into a heroic subject. While applauding the values of decency with which he had grown up, Harold was fascinated and sometimes appalled by the ever evolving social tastes and habits of those who helped define their age.

Writing remained a constant throughout Harold Nicolson's life and he is probably best known now for his published diaries that span more than half a century. After an early career in the Foreign Office and then as a Member of Parliament, he lost his Liberal seat shortly after the Second War. By 1948 as, in his friend and biographer James Lees Milne's words, a "god-given" substitute for politics, Harold's writing took a central professional role and his literary versatility resulted in works of biography, history, criticism and fiction. In 1952 Lees Milne described the public response to his official biography of *George V* as one of "unwonted interest and enthusiasm" and the book earned the occasionally diffident Harold an ambivalently welcome knighthood. That book was in some ways the apex of his literary career and a faint scent of the contrived hovers over some of the books that followed. Harold's evident but detached amusement at his subject sometimes came at a cost to substance and commitment.

Nicolson begins his study of manners by discussing the early Chinese and Japanese civilizations, and the twin classical societies of Homeric Athens and pre-Christian Rome. His globe embracing cultural history lesson then moves through a period of deep, dark-aged decline before civility or "manners" emerge again. The somewhat absurd chivalric posturing in France and the knightly elitism of Chaucerian England precedes an extended look at the philosopher Erasmus's humanist writings and influence. Luther, Shakespeare, Dr. Johnson and Goethe all play a part in Nicolson's idiosyncratic history while a chapter on respectability includes a wonderful section on manners in Jane Austen's novels. Harold eventually arrives at the present day (well, the present of over fifty years ago) pausing to describe the metamorphosis of the public school system and the increasing shame attached to men who cry in public. Nelson, Wellington and Tennyson used frequently to "sob passionately" (as in fact did Harold) but by the time of Queen Victoria's death the practice was considered "feminine or provincial or foreign."

By the middle of the twentieth century when the convention of kissing on greeting had become so spontaneous, Harold suggests that the more naturally reserved English might soon rebel altogether and begin meeting and parting "with nothing more than a stylized grunt."

When he began writing, the clarity of the concept of *Good Behavior* evaded him, but fourteen months after he had first started thinking about the book, he recorded in his diary of 8 December 1953 that he had woken up "to find that the plan of my book on manners has suddenly become quite clear in the night. This is unconscious celebration."

Harold gave three reasons for writing this book. He had always been interested in human behavior. He had already accumulated much material with his long adopted habit of noting references to "manners" on the flyleaf of every book he read. Finally he had the "good fortune" to possess an extensive library at Sissinghurst, with its special tomato red collapsible ladder up which, on his instruction, we children would race to retrieve a book from the top shelf. *Good Behavior* was written at the same wide planked wooden desk that overlooks the yellow and orange, gold and red Cottage Garden from which these words of mine also come.

Despite the further precious resource of what James Lees Milne called "his well stocked mind" there remained gaps in Nicolson's wide ranging historical and cultural learning and even in his extensive travel experience.

But perhaps the biggest missing ingredient was a failure to be open minded towards the subject. Admitting to the writer James Pope Hennessy that he "found the civilization of the East unfamiliar and unsympathetic" he was repelled by the extravagant nonsenses of the court of Louis XIV, although the passages on the French court are some of the funniest in the book.

Harold was essentially a man of eighteenth century sensibilities, his feelings rooted in a classical temperament that abhorred the fascistic extremes of behavior and belief that had marked the twentieth century. His responses mirrored those of the eighteenth century classicists that he admired so much and who had in turn rejected the passionate excesses of the century that preceded them. In recognizing the advancing importance of American culture, Harold was honest enough to admit that while he had many personal American friends, he found the behavioral influences from across the Atlantic difficult to accept. A gently implicit resistance to the present and the future is made taut by the reassurance and convictions that Harold derived from the certainties of the past.

In tandem with this tug of classical sympathies went a rejection of the self-indulgent. His marriage to the writer Vita Sackville West had fallen into crisis immediately after the First War when Vita had fallen in love with Violet Trefusis, an old childhood friend. During the scorching intensity of the affair, Vita had considered abandoning her husband and two small children forever. The story of Vita and Violet's passion for one another and the hiatus it caused in Vita and Harold's otherwise long and mainly happy partnership has been described in my father Nigel Nicolson's *Portrait of a Marriage.* By the time of the writing of *Good Behavior,* the affair had been over for thirty years, but Harold's loathing for excessive romantic desire and posturing that destroys things that are simple and good remained with him. In *Good Behavior* he condemns the French courtly "service of love" which "created a wholly false relationship between the sexes" and which he believed to have been in practice "an abominable wastage of time and emotion."

However, this book goes some way to diluting accusations of snobbery that have been thrown at Harold both during and after his lifetime. He did not advocate the benefits of an intellectual elite as a model for leadership in society. He was far more supportive of the role of the individual, and of personal merit. Nigel Nicolson believed that his father rated "liveliness of mind" as the most important of all intellectual attributes. The pursuit of individuality rather than conformity and hereditary habits was, Harold Nicolson believed, the better choice.

In June 1954 Harold confided to the privacy of his diary new doubts about the progress of the book. He had just become a grandfather and was feeling "old, deaf, and stupid" and devoid of ideas, and he regretted ever embarking on the project.

But by the time the book was published in September 1955, he admitted to James Lees Milne that he felt it to be "among his best" and was disappointed by the paucity of attention and praise it received compared to the coverage usually given to his work. Perhaps the reticence was due to a recognition that the book was in some respect hobbled by the prejudices of the writer. Even so the *Times Literary Supplement* called Harold "an acknowledged master of the essay." S. P. B. Mais, the distinguished writer and original broadcaster of the BBC Radio's "Letter from America" believed *Good Behavior* to be among Harold's best and that master of prose style Patrick Leigh Fermor thought it "an excellent book."

In 1955, just before *Good Behavior* was published, Vita loyally wrote to Harold, "the texture of your prose is now so tight, so economical and yet at moments so lyrical." She added that she considered the new book "a Hadji book" the adjective being her private name for her husband, but the whole phrase reassuring him that *Good Behavior* was both original and highly entertaining—an unmistakeably Harold Nicolson type of book.

—JULIET NICOLSON

Chapter 1
The Necessity of Manners

This book is not either a social history or a manual on etiquette, but a study of successive types of civility—The importance of variation—Some code of manners observed by all living creatures—Patterns of behavior among birds—Greeting and courting postures—Dancing and self-display—Snobbishness among hens—The savage—His tribal organization—Civility initiated by minorities—The progress from egoism to unselfishness—My twelve types of civility—China-Greece-Rome—The early Christians—Chivalry—Erasmus—Castiglione—The French courtier—The English gentleman—The German bourgeois—Respectability—The public school spirit—Reasons why I have not included the United States—Some reflections on American civility—Their sense of "service" and their natural kindness.

One

THIS BOOK IS neither a social history nor a manual on etiquette. It is an endeavor to depict certain patterns of behavior which, at different dates and in different places, have been evolved by minorities as representing the culture of their time. The varying types of civility produced during the last two thousand years reflected, not material conditions only, but also what was regarded as most admirable by contemporary thinkers and idealists. Every society invents for itself a type, a model, an exemplar, of what the perfect member of that society ought to be. These heroes and heroines are much more than the products of existing social and economic conditions: they are myths which repeat the legends of the past and enhance the dreams of the future. In a materialistic age it is salutary to remind ourselves of such fictions.

In an epoch, moreover, when egalitarianism is quickly expanding, when the whole earth is menaced by uniformity, it is comforting to recall that mankind has progressed owing to difference rather than to sameness, owing, not to similitude, but to variation. It is fissure rather than attachment that has furthered evolution; it has been from dissimilarity rather than similarity that the richest cultures have emerged. Even in the most monotonous or regimented community it has been the exceptional rather than the ordinary individual who has assumed leadership and invented progress. Warmly as I advocate equality of opportunity, I do not believe that all men are created equal or that a society based upon such a fallacy will advance very far in the pursuit of happiness. To me it appears wholly insufficient to construct a system by which the individual will be protected against fear and want. The ideal society, while providing safety, should also furnish opportunities for the expression of idiosyncrasy, the enjoyment of differing pleasures, and the embellishment of life. Those types of civility which seek to further such purposes are "good" types: whereas those which seek to forbid or cramp such opportunities are "bad." Our social conscience, our hatred of social injustice, are admirable innovations: it would be sad were they to make us dull. The study of manners may correct or delay this tendency.

I do not wish it to be supposed that this book is the product of any specialized research. It is the result of three almost fortuitous circumstances. First, that all my life I have been much interested in human behavior. Secondly, that for years I have adopted the practice of marking my books and writing my own index on the fly leaf. Always there has been a special heading under the word "Manners," with the corresponding references attached. Thirdly, I have had the good fortune to possess a house in the country containing sufficient space to accommodate what has become quite an extensive library. I have had to do little more than collect these references and place them in some sort of order. I am aware that to the reader they may seem numerous and irrelevant.

I trust also that it will not readily be assumed that I am writing from a reactionary, feudal, aristocratic, or esoteric point of view. I am not in the least ashamed of preferring polite people to rude people, cultivated people to uncultivated people, or the gifted to the dumb. I am confident that in coming generations the proportion of uninteresting people will be much diminished, whereas the proportion of interesting people will increase. I do not think that we shall sink to the level of a beehive or that in the classless State there will be no more cakes and ale. I should wish this book to be read in the mood of inquisitive and benevolent optimism with which it has been written. I believe that civility, however much it may alter its shape and coloring, is based upon reason and affection, which, in spite of recent evidence, are eternal.

Two

Good manners are inevitable also since they result primarily from one of the oldest and most enduring instincts possessed by living creatures, namely the instinct for self-preservation. The antiquity of this instinct and the customs and ritual that it produces can be recognized in beasts and birds. Although among most animals and savages the survival of the individual is closely connected with the survival of the herd or tribe, there are certain groups, even among the lesser animals, in which individualism, initiative, vanity, snobbishness and class distinctions can be traced.

We are assured that animal life in some form has existed upon this globe for a hundred million years.

It was but half a million years ago that a creature similar to man evolved in Lemuria, a now submerged continent between Madagascar and Ceylon. The reason why animals have remained comparatively static whereas man has developed quickly is that we possess the capacity for abstract thought and they do not. The fact that the emotional processes of animals are often akin to our own has led some people to imagine that their mental processes must also be similar. This anthropomorphic treatment of animals is inaccurate in itself and highly irritating to biologists. To contend for instance that the Eberfeld horses could master square roots in five months was nonsense. "Clever Hans" was not endowed with any gift for equations: he merely responded to imperceptible inflexions of Herr von Osten's voice and body. Pavlov discovered that of the three primary instincts—hunger, sex and self-preservation—the first two were the more potent; a dog suffering from lack of food, or sex excitement, can stand more pain than would be tolerable if these two instincts had been satisfied. As for the "conditioned reflexes," or acquired habits, they were immediately inhibited once the three primary instincts became operative: thus when, on September 23, 1924, the Leningrad floods invaded his kennels, the dogs forgot all about their conditioned reflexes in the face of immediate danger. Although animals do not possess our powers of reasoning, their sensory faculties are more acute and they have a more immediate awareness of need. Thus minnows (who are not highly endowed intellectually) are five hundred times more sensitive than are human beings to the presence of salt or sugar. The bombicidae butterflies can smell their mates from enormous distances; hens are possessed of astonishing eyesight; and a dog is endowed with a gift for orientation which is independent of sight or smell. I mention these facts in order to indicate that my discussion of animal behavior is not affected by the fallacy that bees possess thoughts.

Yet among their many instincts there certainly exists an instinct for social behavior which often takes the most elaborate forms. "The basis for human social conduct," writes Lloyd Morgan, "is unquestionably to be traced in the social behavior of animals, in inherited tendencies to cooperation and mutual help, in the bonds of sympathy arising through the satisfaction of impulses towards such behavior, and perhaps, to some extent, in the influence of tradition."

The need of self-protection often creates among animals what we should call institutional arrangements. Antelopes, for instance, post sentries to guard the herd against unheralded attack, these sentries being relieved at regular intervals. The Adelie penguins have similar institutions to prevent their eggs being stolen by the Skuas; and we can all remember having seen rabbits stamp their little legs to warn their comrades of the approach of danger. Animals have also derived a method of assuring their friends that they are prepared to be amicable and not hostile. They have a "recognition posture" which varies according to the species. The mandrill will expose his canines; the less ferocious baboons merely smack their lips in greeting.

Birds, as is well known, adopt all manner of display movements. These attitudes represent what Armstrong has called "the ritualization of activities." They constitute movements, sounds, and postures, generally of a conventional kind, which evoke responses in other birds.

They include gaping, billing, fencing, bowing and just showing off.

"A bird," writes Armstrong, "enjoys ceremonial, not only to express its emotions but to influence the emotions and control the behavior of other birds. What we may regard as an elaborate pattern of ceremonial signalling has been evolved in order that the rhythms of male and female might be synchronised and the perpetuation of the race assured."

Dancing among birds is defined as "a type of posturing with an emotional basis but not concerned with the satisfaction of hunger." Some of the bird dances are solo dances, some are conducted with a partner; some take place within a ring of spectators, and some, as with partridges, amount to figure dances. Many human dances are directly copied from these bird dances, such as the "dance of the white cranes" in China, or the crane dance performed by Theseus on his return from Crete.

The processes of sex selection among birds also entail conduct which we should regard as individualistic.

Darwin believed that the bird who had the gayest feathers or could sing the loudest exerted greater sexual attraction than the bird whose plumage was bedraggled or whose voice was hoarse. Most animals are indifferent to incest, but I have been assured that the Egyptian goose is most sensitive on the subject and deplores mating between members of the same family. The Kasarka geese, on the other hand, have developed an eccentric practice according to which it is the female who courts the male. Selous has recorded that the love displays of the great crested grebe and the red-throated divers are so elaborate as to amount to ceremonial. Occasionally their courting ceremonies take the form, not of coition motions, but of those of nest building or rearing young. During these rituals they "adopt a constrained expression or appearance, as though they were discharging a duty rather painful than otherwise but which they owed to themselves and to society." Professor Julian Huxley goes so far as to assert that these rituals become so intricate and prolonged that they are "self-exhausting" and that the birds are thereby rendered too tired for copulation. Such, as we learn also from St. Simon, is the depressing result of etiquette once it becomes an end rather than a means.

Interesting also are the class distinctions which some animal communities impose. Until I had read Schjelderup-Ebbe's *Beiträge zur Sozialpsychologie des Haushuhns,* I had believed that in any given poultry-run all hens were created equal. This was an ignorant assumption. Some hens, owing to resolution of character rather than strength of physique, become more important than their fellows. Thus hen A pecks hens B, D, F and G; hen B pecks hens C, D, E, F; hen E pecks hen F only, whereas hen F is pecked by everyone and never does any pecking herself. It has been observed that the hens of the highest aristocracy peck their subordinates less brutally than do those of the middle class; thus hen D is far more unkind to hens E and F than hen A ever is to hens B and D. Moreover a hen, when pecked, does not peck back but discharges her anger upon a hen of lower social status. Hen D, if pecked by hen B, will peck hen G. This, if we may speak anthropomorphically, is a most human characteristic.

Similar class distinctions have been examined in other groups, such as crows, lapwings, lizards, seals, mice and monkeys. Some relation seems to exist between the establishment of these social hierarchies and the condition of the endocrine glands. Mr. Shoemaker, for instance, noted the pecking order of six female canaries and then injected the lowest grade with a solution of male hormones. At once they started to sing gaily and before long had risen to the top class in the pecking order.

Such are some of the variations of behavior even in what at first sight may appear a homogeneous community. We can well believe that, in a perfect classless society such as has been achieved by the USSR, similar pecking orders must exist.

It is not my intention, in this study of types of civility, to go back to the Pithecanthropus Erectus who lived upon this earth some half a million years ago. I fear also that I know but little about the manners of our Cromagnon ancestors who, in about 35,000 BCE, hunted in packs along the valleys of the Lot and the Dordogne and spent their evenings drawing pictures of bison and little horses on the walls of their caves. It is best to start after the Iron Age and to consider the "savage" about whom the anthropologists have had so much to say.

The old eighteenth century theory was that the noble savage lived an ideal existence untrammeled by the usages of society. This fiction was succeeded by the idea that he was little better than a wild beast, spending his days in cannibalism and rapine. There followed the period when we believed that he was governed by too many, rather than by too few, rules and that his existence was fettered by a mass of superstitions imposed upon him by the medicine men and the shamans. Malinowski has since taught us that savage ritual is based, not so much upon tribal superstitions, as upon perfectly reasonable considerations of mutual advantage. He found when working in the Trobriand Islands northeast of New Guinea that the fisher folk were dependent for their vegetables on the cultivators of the inland, who in their turn depended on the fishermen for their fish. The reciprocal advantage thereby created was elaborated into a custom, which might be mistaken for a ritual. The perfect manners with which the ceremony of exchange is conducted are accompanied "by keen self-interest and watchful reckoning." Good manners are observed by the Trobrianders, since any departure from them would cause the individual to appear "ridiculous, clumsy and socially uncouth." At the same time the ritual observed does not preclude the pleasures of self-display. "In giving of gifts," writes Malinowski, "in the distribution of their surplus, they feel a manifestation of power and an enhancement of personality." The social instincts among these primitive islanders would thus seem to predominate over the aggressive instincts, and Locke's conception of the state of nature being a state of good nature, seems closer to reality, either than Hobbes' wolf-like society, or to the contention of Freud that kindly feelings are no more than "derivations" of frustrated aggression.

Sensible though the Trobrianders may be, the fact remains that there persist in human beings many vestigial instincts that derive from palaeolithic ancestors. Darwin argued that even as there are some eighty parts of the human body, such as the appendix and the ear and tail muscles, which no longer perform any function, so also there remain in us many instincts dating from Cromagnon days. To these vestigial instincts he attributes the persistence of immorality among the higher peoples. He cites eight of such instincts, namely fear, pugnacity, the desire to hunt, herd instinct, play instinct, imitative instinct, revenge instinct, selfishness instinct, and the instinct for sloth. I have observed that in many civilized individuals these instincts could not invariably be described as vestigial. But Darwin fortifies his argument by stating that savage tribes only very rarely possess in their languages terms to express such concepts as justice, chastity, sympathy, temperance, modesty, gratitude, forgiveness, remorse or conscience. On this analogy we reprove the Germans for not possessing any word equivalent to our word "fair." On the whole I do not regard the language test as an unjustifiable method of assessing standards of good manners.

The distinction between undeveloped and highly developed types of civility has never been better defined than by Clive Bell on page 163 of his *Civilization:* "The first step towards civilization," he writes, "is the correcting of instinct by reason; the second, the deliberate rejection of immediate satisfactions with a view to obtaining subtler. . . . From these primary qualities, Reasonableness and a Sense of Values, may spring a host of secondaries: a taste for truth and beauty, tolerance, intellectual honesty, fastidiousness, a sense of humor, good manners, curiosity, a dislike of vulgarity, brutality and over emphasis, freedom from superstition and prudery, a fearless acceptance of the good things of life, a desire for complete self-expression and for a liberal education, a contempt for utilitarianism and philistinism, in two words: sweetness and light."

The stages by which mankind progresses towards reasonableness and a sense of values is not a stairway of continual ascent. There are frequent relapses. Yet this ascent is initiated and aided by the existence of enlightened and active minorities:

"Any society," writes Ruth Benedict, "selects some segment of the arc of possible human behavior and in so far as it achieves integration its institutions tend to further the expression of its selected segment and to inhibit opposite expressions."

It is again the variety, rather than the uniformity, of primitive culture that Ruth Benedict emphasizes. She examines the Dobuans of Melanesia, the Zuni of New Mexico, and the Kwakiutl of the North West, as examples of this differentiation. Why should some be so sedative and affable whereas others, such as the Dobuans, are dour, suspicious and consumed with jealousy? Simply because variety is a constant element in all patterns of culture.

The development from egoism to consideration for others, which as I hope to show is the foundation of all good manners, can be illustrated by taking a simple single element in civility, such as personal cleanliness. Originally, as Frazer has contended in the *Golden Bough,* such cleanliness as existed among savages was not based upon any conception of decency, but due to fear lest personal attributes (such as hair or nail parings) might be stolen by some enemy and used for magic. In Tana, for instance, it was believed that house refuse, or Nahak, might be employed by magicians or "disease makers" to cast a spell. Yet it would be an error to suppose that human beings became more cleanly as they became more civilized. In Greece and Rome baths were a constant feature of daily life; in the Middle Ages public baths existed in every city and constant washing was considered excellent for the health; yet by the sixteenth century baths had come to be regarded, not only as indecent and immoral, but also as focuses of infection. Thus Doctor Guillaume Bunel in a pamphlet published in 1513 on the best means of avoiding the plague advised people:

> Estuves et bains je vous en prie
> Fuyez les, ou vous en mourrés.

In succeeding centuries cleanliness was no longer regarded as immoral or dangerous, but it was held that cold water was bad for the skin and caused neuralgia. Thus it was only in the nineteenth century that men and women started again to wash frequently and without fear. Their attitude, as many contemporary manuals insist, was dictated not by selfish reasons but by consideration for others.

This development from selfishness to consideration will, I trust, become apparent from the chapters that follow.

I have taken, one by one, twelve main types of civility. Each type represents the human being whom, in different ages, a minority of cultivated people admired and sought to imitate. Sometimes, as at Urbino or in Devonshire House, this minority represented but a minute segment of the community: sometimes, as in the cult of respectability that became so universal in the nineteenth century, it embraced almost the whole of the upper and middle income groups. Sometimes these minorities were wholly intellectual, as at Athens, or when Erasmus came to Oxford and discussed the theological import of the *Epistle to the Romans* with Colet, Linacre and More. Sometimes they were composed exclusively of courtiers, as under Louis XIV; and sometimes they represented a mutual admiration society of devoted friends, inheriting a great tradition. At other periods it was a bourgeois minority that set the tone, whether purely domestic as were the Germanies before 1870, or commercial and evangelical as the mighty class that arose in England with the machines of the Industrial Revolution. Different though they were from each other, these twelve types possessed a common belief in their own formulas, and a common conviction that their own pattern of behavior was that best adapted to rendering the converse between human beings pleasurable, righteous, or instructive.

Each of these emphasized certain facets of conduct which appeared important as expressive of the contemporary ideal, whether that happened to be seriousness, or sanctity, or abstract speculation, or romance, or grandeur, or decorated ease. Each of them ignored those elements in contemporary society which did not conform to their own theology and predilections, or which appeared liable to diminish their certitudes. If we could combine together all that was most valuable in each of these designs, we should be able to construct the complete or perfect man. Conversely, it would be possible, without destroying the mould, to extract from each successive type enough vices to create a Caliban of grossness, a De Sade of cruelty, or a Louis XV of imperturbable egoism.

The Chinese ideal of the superior man was a conception which conferred great benefits upon the human race. Over a vast area of Asia, and at a period when life had only recently been brutish and short, it taught men to control their passions, to cultivate moderation, and to aim at honorable efficiency. It has to its credit superb achievements in philosophy, in scholarship, in art, literature and science. At a time of barbarism it instructed people how to behave with consideration to each other and how to observe the decencies of converse. Yet in the end the Chinese theory of good manners degenerated into a theory of etiquette; century after century men continued to repeat the same words and genuflexions, until the whole structure of society seemed to revolve round buttons, peacock feathers and jade sceptres. The intricate machine came to a standstill; the wheels no longer revolved; and it was swept away, as if in a single night, with all its worm-eaten columns and its decaying balustrades.

The Greek ideal of the beautiful and the good, although it was realized for no more than eighty short years, has left behind it an imperishable memory. We may deplore their indifference to suffering and untruthfulness, yet it was they who discovered and bequeathed the bliss of abstract speculation and aesthetic delight. The treacheries and tragedies that marred the dominance of Athens are to our minds barbaric. Yet still she shines for us, violet crowned and unblemished, serene and formidable, across two thousand years of fog and strife.

The Roman cult of dignity may to us seem ponderous, even as their enjoyments were obscene. Yet their genius for equity and order has left its impress upon their former subjects, and those countries and areas which never experienced Roman conquest and administration have never since succeeded in becoming wholly European. There was much in the Roman type of civility that was clumsy and gross: yet they left behind them a lapidary respect for law, contract, and faithfulness.

It may be that the early Christian Church, in its insistence on holiness, ignored many aspects of civilization and culture. It may be that the early Fathers and their disciples displayed much self-righteousness, little tolerance and an exaggerated lack of refinement. Yet, after all, if manners are ever to be more than etiquette they must be founded on a lively consideration for others, and that consideration can spring only from gentleness and humility. It would be foolish, and indeed improper, to contend that, because the early Christians happened to prefer monastic cells to wrestling schools and hair shirts to silken underwear, they did not change for ever the relationship between man and man. As a humanist and an apostate, I may have been unfair to the early Church in the chapter that I have devoted to her manners. I am irritated by her pharisaism and iconoclasm: but I regard her ultimate teaching with respect.

Similarly I may have shown too great an affection for what I admit were the silly phantasies of the age of chivalry. I see them all in light colors of blue and pink, picked out with gold; and in my ears there echo the voices of the troubadours and the sound of lutes. Absurd though they were, they did accord emphasis to the virtues of courage, loyalty and love. I know that it was no more than a day dream; yet how sunny a dream it was!

I have always been fascinated by the divergence between the development of civility in England and on the continent. Erasmus, who in spite of ill treatment on the part of our customs officials, was naturally pro-British, stands out as the hero and saint of humanism and as a man who by his personality raised the tone of our universities. But in spite of Erasmus we progressed in our own eccentric way. The sons of our nobility were set to perform menial tasks away from home, and were soundly beaten if they erred. They acquired by these methods a staunch independence of character and a contempt for intellectual and aesthetic pursuits.

The solemnity of theological Europe was much relieved by the teaching of Baldassare Castiglione, who reminded people that civility is apt to become ponderous once it ceases to be gay. He taught the useful lesson that good manners are but a means of agreeable intercourse and should never become an end in themselves. This important lesson was never correctly absorbed by the courtiers of Louis XIV, who ignored the wide tapestry of life in order to concentrate their acute minds upon the tiny embroideries of etiquette. They thus allowed the fine conception of the *honnête homme* to degenerate into the thin ideal of the man of the world.

Slavishly did some of our aristocrats, such as Lord Chesterfield, strive to emulate the manners of France. Yet the rural, the country gentleman, habit was too strong for them. The neat candles of Parisian deportment were puffed out by the gigantic sense of Samuel Johnson and the genial guffaw of Charles James Fox. In place of Marly and Versailles we had the Devonshire House circle, who with their humor, their elegance, their affectionate sentimentality, and their sincere although hopelessly vague liberalism, represent perhaps the most attractive type of civility that our island has yet produced. Then came the Industrial Revolution. The old stratification of society became dislocated in every country. The rise of the middle class produced, in Germany the rather charming habit of *Gemütlichkeit,* and in England the cult of respectability. All this earnestness culminated in Thomas Arnold and in the priggish, snobbish but so healthy schoolboys who set the tone of British civility until 1939.

Diverse indeed are the beads that I have strung together. The thread that connects them is hidden by their disparity, their glitter or their opaqueness. Yet it is in fact a simple thread, being no more than the conviction that, since men and women have to live together in communities, it is well that there should exist a changing ritual of intercourse, expressing in ever varying form the essential doctrine that good manners are founded on consideration for others, which in its turn is a matter of heart.

It may seem strange that at a time when Europe has lost its dominance I should, except for a brief and diffident excursus into the wisdom of the East, have confined my consideration to European types of civility. Why is it that, apart from incidental references, I have ignored the mass manners of the United States, which, as I believe and hope, will in the end set the tone for the whole free world?

There are three reasons for this reticence. First, because manners in America change nervously, so that what might be true in 1955 may by 1956 have become irrelevant. Secondly, because, although I have lived and traveled much in the United States, and although I count many Americans among my closest friends, I have not the arrogance to suppose that I understand them, in the sense that I understand the Athenians of

2500 BCE. To me they appear to belong, not to a different race merely, but to a different planet. It is a constantly renewed surprise to me that when an American catches a cold in his head his symptoms should be indistinguishable from those which afflict me in a similar predicament. In the third place, I am aware that the Americans are more than sensitive, more than touchy: they suffer from hyperesthesia, a malady which induces them to interpret the kiss of a butterfly (especially if he be an English butterfly) as the sly stab of a penknife in the shoulder, or a knuckle blow upon the cheek. I am fond of Americans: I do not wish to cause them pain.

Yet I must at least indicate what is the type of civility which in the United States I so deeply admire. They call it "service," but we should describe it as a universal gift for being unfailingly helpful, hospitable and polite. It is not a virtue confined to any class; it comes as naturally to a porter at a railway station as it does to the president of a fresh water university. At the end of our very first day in America, when once the telephone has ceased to shrill, we retire to bed feeling lapped in the luxury of a universal welcome; feeling that here at last we have discovered the legendary beauty of the classless State and found it to be kindness, kindness all the way; feeling that, in contrast to this sweet equality, the distinctions and servitudes of Europe are cruel and outmoded; feeling that here is no artificial pattern of courtesy, but the warm and steady pulsation of a gigantic human heart.

If the visitor leaves the Eastern seaboard and plunges into the interior of the continent, he will find this type of civility everywhere inculcated and admired. The difference between the several provinces of the United States, which to our forefathers appeared so marked and curious, is not today apparent. The visitor will, it is true, notice some slight variations in accent between Virginia and Illinois, and even, if he possess a delicate ear, between Texas and New Hampshire. Yet what will impress him far more than any variations of culture is the amazing uniformity of the whole. It will seem to him that his hostess in Houston and his hostess in Dayton possess the same perfect manners, have identical subjects of conversation, read the same magazines, are inspired by similar ideals and convictions, and even adopt the same schemes of decoration in their homes.

Why, it may well be asked, should this fine standard of life and living be incomprehensible to the humanist? I agree that with all this side of American civility I find myself in the most comfortable harmony. Yet there are certain elements in American civilization which, as a European, I find it impossible to understand. I shall cite but three examples.

It seems strange to me, for instance, that whereas American adults sometimes seem to be inhibited by conventions which have long been discarded in the Old World, American children and adolescents are accorded a license without bond or bound. The adulation accorded to children and young boys and girls is to our minds bewildering. The pert, pampered and loud-voiced infants of the Great Republic are for us almost as incomprehensible as the bunching, petting, date-seeking boys and girls of the universities and colleges. We fail to understand.

A second cause of incomprehension is the position of privilege and power claimed by, and accorded to, the American woman. It is not merely that American mothers and grandmothers expect and obtain a level of worship comparable only to that established among the primitive matriarchal societies of the Malabar coast. It is that American wives assume a contemptuous attitude towards their husbands, whom they exploit economically and to whom they adopt an attitude of cultural superiority. To those who have been nurtured in the Graeco-Roman tradition such arrogances and exactions are not comprehensible.

There is again the curious indifference to, or disregard of, what to us is one of the most precious of all human possessions, namely personal privacy. To them, with their proud belief in equality, with their rather ignorant affection for the pioneer spirit, privacy denotes something exclusive, patronizing, "unfolksy," and therefore meriting suspicion. Thus they leave their curtains undrawn at dusk, have no hedges separating their front gardens, and will converse amicably with strangers about private things. How can a European dare to discuss the manners of a people who seem to ignore, or to be unconscious of, what to him is civilization's most valued heritage? Let me not venture upon any such impertinence.

I am devoted to Americans. I cannot hear an American voice in the streets of London without wishing to repay by some courtesy the lavish kindness that I have received over there. I love their energy, their intelligence, their central heating, their virtue, the way they do their hair, their excellent small feet, their homesickness, their invention, their good manners, their efficiency, and their delicious alternations between ecstasy and despair. But, as I have said, I do not really understand their type of civility and do not desire to hurt their feelings.

Chapter 2
Chou-Li

Manners should not stagnate—In the East there is a tendency for manners to degenerate into etiquette—The Turkish Selamlik in the days of the Caliph—A Persian coronation—Spanish court ceremonial—In China ceremonial became a moral precept—The Kowtow—The high value of Chinese civilization—But the type of civility it created cannot become a pattern for the Western World—The *Confucian Analects*—Confucius' theory of the Superior Man—His rules of deportment—The I-Li and the Li-Chu—The book of etiquette written by Father Simon Kiong—Japanese conception of *Bu-shi-do* and *On*—Lady Murasaki compared to Earl Tostig—My ignorance of such matters.

One

I T IS DIFFICULT to distinguish between manners and customs, if only for the reason that the manners of one generation become the customs of the next. Again and again, when we study the evolution of manners, do we find that certain patterns of deportment devised by an élite, for the purpose of differentiating its members from the classes below them, are before long imitated by the lower strata, and therefore abandoned by the elite which originally invented them. This process is salutary and creative. It means no more than that the middle, and eventually the lower, classes acquire by processes of imitation ever more polite standards of living. Nothing but praise should be accorded to those societies where this process of renewal is continuous and mobile. The third generation of an aristocracy, observing that the manners and even the shibboleths of their grandfathers have now been acquired by the bourgeoisie, invent new formulas, which, when their own grandchildren come of age, will in their turn have been absorbed by the community. In this process of transference much that was snobbish, futile, extravagant or artificial in the manners of an older generation is discarded; only those formulas are retained which facilitate rather than impede intercourse between human beings. Without this continual reabsorption and transformation, good manners would become static and therefore bad.

In certain oriental societies manners did in fact become inextricably entwined with customs, and the latter in their turn acquired an almost religious sanction. The type of civility most admired was an exclusive type, governed by conventions both so intricate and so invariable that the circulation of manners was impeded. For those of us who believe that good manners should be expansive rather than restricted—easily understood and therefore imitable rather than esoteric or confined—these rigid patterns of behavior are both exasperating and dull. For those of us again who think that a liberal society should aim at the maximum extension of the individuality of its members—should never become a static pool but should be renewed continuously by fresh waters entering from diverse tributaries—the stagnancy of oriental manners during so many centuries appears in no sense a triumph of intelligence. Ancestor worship is to our minds an unprogressive form of religion. We prefer multiform myths.

I am aware that there is some prejudice, and much ignorance, in this point of view. Although I have spent many years of my life in the Near and Middle East, I have never visited Japan or China and my knowledge of their customs is superficial only, being derived from books. Moreover any appreciation of manners is essentially a subjective appreciation, reflecting personal affections or dislikes. I am conscious, for instance, that my temperamental impatience renders me unduly intolerant of conventions that entail what, to me, seems an unnecessary wastage of time. It would appear also that the acute self-consciousness so often found in people who have enjoyed a British education renders them perhaps foolishly ill-adapted to the charades entailed by the apparatus of oriental ceremony. And I realize that I am myself unusually sensitive to any forms of deportment that appear to impose on human beings a denial of their individual dignity, or to entail gestures or postures that seem humiliating and grotesque. To me, the goose-step of the Prussian regiments, even the drill that I occasionally witness in barrack squares at home, is not an exhilarating spectacle, but one that makes me sad. I have been assured by men whose judgment I value that there is in fact a pleasure, which is akin to an aesthetic pleasure, that can be derived from the perfect synchronization of movement experienced by those who form part of a well-drilled company or a carefully trained team. Long ago I derived at least some intimations of this pleasure when I rowed for a few weeks in one of my college boats. I then understood that difficult conjoint rhythm can in itself become an intoxicant, or rather a narcotic. This was but a fleeting and I fear incompetent experience: in general it is painful for me to observe human beings being obliged to behave like automata. It maybe that this disinclination derives from my most distant past.

Two

When I was a very little boy, I was taken by my father to witness the ceremony of the Selamlik, performed by the then Ottoman Sultan, Abdul Hamid. The diplomatists and their guests were accommodated for the occasion in the upper room of a small kiosk looking down upon the strip of road which separated the park of Yildiz from the Hamidieh Mosque. The space between the gate of the park and the steps of the mosque was packed with soldiers guarding the short lane through which the Sultan was to drive. We were given coffee and sweetmeats while we waited and frequent courtesies were exchanged between the diplomatists and the Court officials by whom they were being entertained. As I munched my macaroon, I was startled by the blare of trumpets and by the brisk triple sound of soldiers presenting arms. The iron gates that led from the park were swung open by servitors in scarlet liveries; in front of the gate were grouped the members of the Turkish Cabinet, arrayed in heavy uniforms with frontages of gold. A neat little victoria emerged from the arch of the gate and seated in it was a hunched figure, whose dyed hair and beard were the color of mahogany and whose haggard cheeks were white under a scarlet fez. The troops yelled in unison: "Many years to our Padishah;" the bands burst into some metallic tune; and the victoria at a smart trot proceeded towards the steps of the mosque some two hundred yards distant. It was then that I noticed that the members of the Cabinet had each taken a strap or cord attached to the carriage and were running beside it, their legs moving rapidly. Middle-aged they were most of them, and a few were demonstrably old. I was shocked by this exhibition and enquired of my father whether it was right that elderly gentlemen should be expected to run beside the carriage of the Caliph. He assured me that it was not right. And thus, when twenty years later, I was again in Constantinople and happened to catch sight of Abdul Hamid pacing the terrace of Beylerbey as a prisoner under heavy guard and looking like a crushed rook, my sympathy was not as acute as that which ought to be aroused by fallen greatness or by aged monarchs under duress.

I have since discovered that the strange sight that I witnessed outside the park gates of Yildiz had behind it a long Oriental, and even Roman, tradition. Did not Assur-Beni-Pal boast in many lapidary inscriptions that he had forced eight captive kings to run beside his chariot? And did not the Emperor Caligula reintroduce the practice and force even *togatos,* even Senatorial patricians, to run for several hundred yards beside him as he drove? I share with Suetonius the horror that such a spectacle must have aroused in every Roman heart.

I have witnessed other oriental ceremonies of a less atrocious character. The coronation of Reza Shah Pahlevi was not accompanied by the humiliation of others. Blazing with diamonds this ex-trooper of the Cossack Brigade, took his seat upon the Peacock Throne and like Napoleon crowned himself with slow propriety as King of Kings. The cabinet ministers and courtiers stood around him, wearing their robes of honor, keeping their hands and forearms tucked neatly within their sleeves, and composing their features to an expression of beatific servitude. They were not made to run beside a carriage or to creep along the floor. And when, on his birthday, we would all gather before him under the high portico, the Shah would sit there motionless as an image, looking impersonally furious, and listening with sullen disgust to the court poet intoning an interminable eulogy to the sound of fountains splashing in alabaster pools.

I have observed a similar convention of regal impassivity, of hierophantic inattention, in the ceremonial of the Spanish Court. Alfonso XIII was young and naturally exuberant; Queen Victoria Eugénie was beautiful and urbane. Yet when, at an official reception, they would seat themselves upon the great thrones of Aragon and Castille, raised high upon a dais, each step to which was flanked by a golden lion pawing a golden globe, they would assume an expression of being unaware that there were people around them. They would gaze with vacant eyes upon the clouds that drifted, white upon blue, beyond the great windows, down from the Guadarrama towards the south. The grandees of Spain were grouped behind them: the diplomatists, embassy by embassy, were aligned with their backs to the windows: along the avenue thus left in front of the throne, the Ministers, the officers of State and finally the members of the Cortes filed in slow procession, bowing to their sovereigns as they passed. These salutations were not returned. The eyes of Alfonso and Victoria Eugénie continued to gaze with languid inattention at the floating clouds. Yet when the last deputy had shuffled past, then the palace guards would rap their halberds sharply upon the parquet flooring, the royal effigies would leap suddenly to life, would cross to the waiting Ambassadors and engage with charm and animation in the ordeal known as doing *cercle.* Then off Los Reyes would go together, hand in hand, and one would hear further halberds rapping on distant floorings as they passed from room to room.

It is tempting to suggest that the degree of civilization achieved by any given community can be assessed according to the amount and nature of the inconvenience or indignity imposed upon individuals by etiquette and especially by court ceremonial. Such an argument would be misleading. Thus, although under the Bourbon kings court etiquette was as intricate as three dimensional chess, the ordinary subjects of Louis XIV, Louis XV or Louis XVI were allowed to wander almost unimpeded about the palaces and royal gardens, to stare at their sovereign while he ate his dinner, and to make the most irreverent remarks aloud. It was Napoleon who first closed the Tuileries and its garden to the public; until then the famous terrace with its orange tubs had been used as a communal latrine. Moreover, although to this day the Pope is borne aloft in the *sedia gestatoria,* surrounded by guards arrayed in uniforms designed by Michael Angelo, the ceremonial of the British court is reduced to the bare necessities of decorum, and the courtiers bow to their sovereign with no more than an abrupt inclination, an *exiguum clinamen,* of the head. It is this difference in degrees of obeisance that, more than any other form of etiquette, marks the distinction between Europe and the East.

Three

The word "kowtow" is derived from the Chinese expression "*k'o-t'eu,*" meaning "to knock the head upon the ground." Among the ancient Egyptians there existed a similar gesture, entitled "*senta*" which implied that an inferior on approaching a superior was expected to kiss the ground. The habit of prostration became universal throughout the East. When Alexander the Great in his dazzling rush through Asia observed how the Persians groveled on the ground before him, he thought that it would be an excellent idea to impose a similar obeisance or *proskunesis* upon the Macedonians and his Greek allies. It was Callisthenes, an individualist, who voiced the opposition:

"In this matter of the *proskunesis,*" records Plutarch, "Callisthenes, by refusing sturdily and in a manner worthy of a philosopher to perform the act, by standing up alone and explaining in public the reasons for the indignation which the Macedonians cherished in secret, saved the Greeks from a great disgrace and Alexander from a greater."

This incident well illustrates the division, I might almost say the point of rupture, between European individualism and the more subservient manners of the East. Etiquette is perhaps inevitable; ceremonial can be as superb as is desired; but neither should at any moment be permitted to transgress an underlying principle of personal independence.

I may at this stage be accused of undervaluing what has been called "the eternal dignity of the East." There is always something dignified about the static and until quite recent years the East, in its religion, customs and ideas, was fully petrified by the past. I agree that, in gait, in stance, in diction, in gesture and in expression no person can possibly be more dignified than a Bedouin or an educated Moor. I am aware also that for an Englishman to express any lack of admiration for the Arabs, or the Moslems generally, is indicative of ignorance, effeminacy and bad taste. Yet I cannot regard a type of civilization that has preserved unchanged the customs and prejudices recorded in the eighteenth chapter of Genesis as an inspired civilization. I do not rate dignity of demeanor very high in my list of virtues; nor do I disagree with Østrup's suggestion that the entrancing hospitality of the Arabs, and particularly of the Bedouin, is largely to be ascribed to their incapacity for reflection and the utter boredom of their monochrome lives.

The uneasiness caused to sensitive people by Oriental manners is due to the fact that they create two highly unpleasant situations. In the first place, they confront the stranger with a code of behavior which he is anxious not to transgress, but with which, in that it derives from a totally different background, he is wholly unfamiliar. In the second place, they entail what, even for a patient person, is an exacting waste of time. I look back with pain on the hours I have consumed in exchanging compliments with a succession of pashas, valis, mutessarifs, mudirs, kaimakams, bimbashis, sheikhs, kadhudas and chapachibashis. In every Eastern country in which I have resided I have found that it is regarded as most discourteous to go straight to any point. I have known people who regard those otiose arabesques, those endless postponements, the succession of unwanted cups of coffee, as providing a certain languid grace, an exotic charm. To me they have seemed merely irritating, senseless and essentially impolite.

Yet if we are to realize the fundamental gulf that opens between European manners and those of the East, it is desirable to examine in some detail the etiquette prevailing, even in my own lifetime, among the Chinese. Here surely manners have been devised to cause the utmost inconvenience to all concerned.

I am in no danger of underestimating the beauty and seriousness of Chinese civilization as a whole. The manner in which for centuries they were able to maintain their own view of life wholly uncontaminated by extraneous influences, and to preserve their identity against all alien infiltration proves a deep authenticity of culture. Nothing can be more impressive than the mysterious force that for centuries imposed upon a continent, possessing such variations of climate, language and race, a uniform pattern that can be recognized as a distinctive Chinese pattern. Something most important must have been reverenced to weld chaos into unity over such vast stretches of time and space.

Nor should any slighting reference be made to the Chinese, or more specifically the Confucian, passion for learning, although to the European humanist their recurrent examinations appear to have assumed too rigid and literal a shape. Yet a civilization in which the aristocratic element was provided by the scholar rather than by the soldier, in which membership of the elite was not hereditary but acquired by individual talent and effort, is assuredly a civilization which we should all examine and emulate. Moreover, in reflecting upon the etiquette imposed by any pattern of civilization, it would be foolish to ignore the fact that art and literature are also the direct reflections of standards of civility. A culture, such as the Chinese culture, which can produce such masterpieces of poetry and art, must obviously be based upon an attitude towards life that is profoundly intelligent and wise.

Were I Chinese, I should I suppose choose Tao as my way of life, seeking to find in the delights of natural beauty and in the seclusion of deliberately induced contentment, alternatives to the disappointments of ambition and the dangers of indulgence. Yet in this study I am not considering either aesthetics or ethics. I am considering successive types of civility with the desire to reach at least a few conclusions as to what elements in old patterns of behavior should be adopted by the classless society towards which Europe and America are now tending. To this purpose, the elaborate and formidable conventions established by the Chinese and the Japanese are wholly irrelevant, since they arose out of conditions that will never again occur. Their value to me is that they indicate how inapplicable to future society will be the codes of other intelligent but utterly remote civilizations. Incidentally also they illustrate the bad effects upon individualism of all systems that are based on too deep a veneration for the past and too static a conception of the future.

Four

The principles of behavior advocated by the Confucian canon stretch back beyond the Chou civilization into the mists of pre-history that preceded the dynasties of Shang and Hsia. So vast seems the ravine that separates our European conception from the ideology of the Chinese, that it is with a shock of surprise that we realize that Confucius died but eight years before the birth of Socrates. It is not only that we are faced by a wholly different theory of human relationships; it is that, when we approach the subject, we encounter utterly dissimilar minds. I can understand, although not admire, the patriarchal dignity of a Bedouin, the old contemptuous courtesy of an Ottoman, the dawdling grace of a Moorish patrician, or the decorative digressions practiced by Iranians of the school of Nasr-ed-Din or Fath-Ali Shahs. But the Chinese scheme of things seems to me both as beautiful, and as alien, as the mating of macaws.

The philosopher Kung Futze, known to the western world as Confucius, shared with Plato the illusion that the ideal state might be created if only some ruler, or even tyrant, could be taught the principles of virtue and wisdom. Plato retired from the court of Syracuse before his disillusion became absolute, believing to the day of his death that the conception of the philosopher-king need not, given the right individual and the right conditions, be dismissed as a fantasy. Confucius was less fortunate. Having proved both his virtue and his capacity when serving as chief magistrate of the city of Chung-tu, he was chosen by the provincial tyrant, or Marquis, as his Minister of Crime. Nobly did he endeavor to suppress brigandage and to establish central authority over the robber barons of the provinces. Yet after four years he discovered that despots could not after all be turned into philosophers. He resigned his office, and thereafter wandered about collecting disciples and talking much. "No intelligent ruler," he finally proclaimed, "arises to take me as his master. My time has come to die."

We must accept the fact that Confucius was a remarkable philosopher and that the disciples whom he gathered around him were, as he claimed, "scholars of extraordinary ability." Certainly he left on Chinese thought and learning an impact that lasted for more than two thousand four hundred years. Yet we possess none of his own writings and the works of his grandson Tze-sze and his pupil Tsang Sin can provide us with the shadow only of his personality and doctrine. His apophthegms, which were collected under what the Chinese call the Lun-Yii, and we call the "analects of Confucius," create but a meager impression on the European mind.

Confucius was the first philosopher to inculcate the truly golden rule that a man should always do unto others what he would wish were done to himself. He taught that the wise man should be indifferent to physical comforts, and that a scholar who was concerned with the quality of his clothes or his food should not be taken seriously by any right-minded person. Yet we, perhaps in our ignorance of his real background, of the then prevailing climate of opinion, cannot escape the impression that his teaching was conservative and superficial rather than original or profound. "It is better," he taught, "to be mean than insubordinate." "The study of strange doctrines," he remarked, "is indeed harmful." "Filial piety," he insisted, "and fraternal submission—are they not the root of all benevolent actions?" "A youth," he said, "when at home should be filial and respectful to his elders. He should be earnest and truthful. He should overflow with love to all, and cultivate the friendship of the good. When he has time and opportunity, after the performance of these things, he should employ them in polite studies."

When we consider Confucius' picture of "the superior man," it seems incredible that his teaching should be contemporaneous with the Socratic discussions on the nature of the beautiful and the good. The superior man, according to Confucius, should be a scholar abstemious in all things, he should keep himself "under the restraint of the rules of propriety;" he should be above party politics; in his language he should avoid lowness or impropriety; "in deportment and manner he should keep from heedlessness and violence;" and he should preserve "the elegant regulations of antiquity." He should not be so unsporting as to fish with a net or shoot sitting birds. He should refrain from wearing purple or puce colored clothes. He should be "affable but not adulatory," should be slow and cautious in his speech, and should cultivate "dignified ease without pride." The superior man is "virtuous and thus free from anxieties—wise, and thus free from perplexity—courageous, and thus free from fear." It is not sufficient for the superior man to be firm in all his dealings: he must be "correctly firm" as well. He should be accurate and precise in his diction. When asked what would be the first thing he would do if entrusted with the government of a province, Confucius replied: "I should first rectify names." When invited to explain this cryptic utterance he replied: "If names be not correct, then language is not in accord with the truth of things and affairs cannot be successfully administered. The superior man is careful to use names appropriately." Warmly as I agree with Sir Alan Herbert and Mr. Henry Strauss in their contention that democracy suffers from an overindulgence in incorrect nomenclature, I do not feel that in a society as corrupt and cruel as was the China of the fifth century BCE semantics should form the first preoccupation of the philosopher king. It is difficult, I confess, to resist the impression that Confucius in his teaching attached less importance to substance than to form.

He himself displayed many idiosyncrasies which his disciples recorded with puzzled awe. His nightshirt was longer than the customary Chinese nightshirt; when out driving he refrained from looking round and in his opinion it was vulgar, in any circumstances, to point. If his mat were not at an exact right angle with the wall he would refuse to sit on it, disliking all asymmetric things. His behavior at court was such as to remain for long in the memory of observers. After speaking to his sovereign, Confucius did not permit himself to assume "a satisfied expression" until he had descended the first step of the throne. "When," we are told, "he had reached the last of the steps, he would hurry to his place, with his arms stretched out on each side of his body as if they were wings." On resuming his seat his manner and facial expression indicated "respectful uneasiness." On the rare occasions when his master, the Marquis, was so kind as to allow Confucius to carry the royal sceptre, his deportment became odd indeed. "His countenance," we are told, "seemed to change and to become apprehensive. He dragged his feet one after the other, as if they were tied by something to the ground."

Not thus did Plato conduct himself at the court of Dionysius or Socrates face his judges in the Stoa of Zeus.

Five

I should not have devoted space to a theme as remote as the Analects of Confucius had it not been that his precepts affected Chinese behavior until 1912. The continuity of the formulas that he inherited and transmitted provides a perfect example of how manners, once their true function and purpose became overlaid, degenerate into etiquette; and how etiquette in its turn can become fossilized with ceremonial.

The Chinese possess many classics on the subject of the proper observance of ceremonial, the most important of which are the I-Li, the Chou-Li, and the Li-Chu, "Li" being the Chinese word for etiquette. I quote some of the observances recommended by these manuals, if only for the purpose of demonstrating how horrible are the theatricals imposed on human beings once ceremonial becomes static.

The ceremony of the "capping," or as we should say the "coming-of-age," by an officer's son furnishes a useful example. Instructions are provided as to how the guests should be dressed, how their hair should be done, whether they should stand facing east or facing west, and how often they should each bow to the other. On reaching the steps of the pavilion in which the ceremony is to be held, the guests should "mutually yield precedence three times." The following false dialogue is prescribed between the father of the youth and the friend whom he has chosen as godfather or conductor of ceremonies:

Father: "I, so and so, have a son, so and so, who is about to be invested with the black cloth cap. I hope that your honor will instruct him by presiding at this ceremony."

Guest: "I am not a clever man, and I am afraid that I may mismanage the business and thereby expose your honor to shame."

Father: "I still hope, none the less, that your honor will give my son the benefit of your exalted instructions."

Guest: "Since your honor has repeated your commands, dare I do other than consent?"

Such unnecessary abasements, such mock humility, such hollow compliments, are devised for every occasion. It never seems to have dawned upon the Chinese that this ritual represented an artificial code of manners and entailed an unpardonable wastage of time.

Here, to take another and even more abhorrent example, is the formula prescribed for the visit of one officer to another. The following dialogue is prescribed:

Host: "You, Sir, are demeaning yourself by coming here. I pray that your honor will return home, where I shall hasten to present myself before you."

Guest: "I cannot bring disgrace upon you by obeying this injunction. Be good enough to end by granting me this interview."

Host: "I do not dare to set an example as to how a reception of this kind should be conducted, and I must therefore persist in asking your honor to return to your own house where I shall call upon you without delay."

Guest: "It is I who do not dare to make a precedent. I therefore must persist in asking you to grant me an interview."

Host: "As for me, as I have failed to obtain your permission to refuse this honor, I shall press my objection no further. But I hear that your honor is offering me a present, and this at least I must decline."

Guest: "Without a present I dare not venture into your presence."

Host: "I am not a sufficient expert in such ceremonies and I must persist in declining."

Guest: "Without the support and confidence given me by my gift, I have not the courage to pay this visit. I must persist in my request."

Host: "I am also decided in declining. Yet, as I cannot secure your consent that I should visit you in your house, how dare I not now respectfully obey?"

The present regarding which this silly dialogue was conducted was generally a goose, with its legs tied together, its body enclosed in a colored cloth and its head protruding "to the left." When the present is of silk, the donor should not approach his host with "great strides" but should walk trippingly so as to display uneasiness. If it be jade that is given, the donor should "step carefully, lifting his toes and dragging his heels." When visiting a superior, it is permissible to ask leave to retire when the host either yawns, stretches himself, looks at his watch or "begins to eat leeks or garlic as a cure for sleepiness." One should never look a superior in the eyes, except at the moment of arrival and departure; for the rest of the interview the eyes should concentrate upon the center of the great man's chest.

Even more elaborate is the protocol laid down for the conduct of Ambassadors. The Ambassador (not of course a European ambassador, but an ambassador from some tributary state of the Chinese Empire) arrives carrying with him a "symbol of authority" made of jade and enclosed in a cloth of red or blue silk. On reaching the palace he is instructed to adopt a most artificial deportment:

> He enters the palace gate with an impressive air: he ascends the steps in a deferential manner: when he is about to hand over his symbol of authority he looks purposeful and moves quickly. On handing over his credential he should assume the expression of a

man watching to seize an advantage, when
he descends the steps of the throne he should
adopt the manner of a person escorting
someone else. Once he has reached the bot-
tom of the steps he can let his breath go and
can take things easily. He lifts his feet two or
three times, and thereafter steps out naturally. When he gets to the door he resumes
his correct demeanor. And then he and his
staff leave the palace like a flock of wild geese,
one following behind the other.

Even more stringent are the regulations enjoined
on an ambassador when invited to a state banquet in
his honor:

The Ambassador, sitting down between the
principal dishes and the extra ones, takes the
bowl of millet porridge in his left hand and
the Grand Soup in his right and then goes
down. The Prince declines to permit this, so
the Ambassador faces west, sits down, and
lays them on the western steps. Then, facing
east, he replies consenting. Then, facing west,
he sits, and, taking them up, rises and strides
up the steps two at a time, faces north, and
replaces them.

Even in my early days, the Lord Chamberlain's office
at Vienna, the most ceremonial of all European courts,
did not impose upon ambassadors so exacting a ritual.
Yet I suppose that when I was a boy the I-Li was still

observed in the Forbidden City or at the Summer Palace and that when a Governor of some remote province visited Peking he was obliged to observe at least the vestige of this extraordinary liturgy. I suppose that in my lifetime there existed mandarins who, when meeting their equals or inferiors, went through one of the six different forms of greeting, either the *kongcheou* used with intimates, which entailed no more than raising the two sleeves to the level of the mouth, or the full *k'o-t'eu* or grovel, employed only in the presence of the Emperor or when listening to the reading of an imperial rescript.

So recently as 1906 Mr. Simon Kiong, S. J., published his *Quelques Mots* designed to instruct Europeans on the deportment regarded as essential by the pre-revolution Chinese. According to him, the body should be inclined slightly forward, but never to the right or the left. When advancing to meet a guest the gait should be rapid, when bidding farewell to a guest the host should drag his footsteps. Inferiors, when in the presence of their superiors, should sit at the edge of the chair, keep their hands tucked in their sleeves, never cross their feet or their legs, never rest their elbows on anything, and avoid wearing spectacles. At meals guests should always go through the ceremony of not daring to sit down till pressed to do so, they should not help themselves to any dish before the chief guest, they should always refuse to touch the last course offered, and they should drink in little sips only, never emptying their glasses. It was customary for a host to offer tidbits to his guests, but they were not obliged to swallow these morsels unless they so desired. The problem of precedence was so terrible, that Father Kiong advises a host to seat his guests, not at a long table when degrees of honor would be emphasized, but at a series of small round tables, when the order of precedence can be disguised.

Even more incomprehensible to the European mind is the elaborate ceremonial practiced, until quite recently, in Japan. I shall mention this as shortly as possible, since my sympathy for, and understanding of, Japanese manners are slight indeed. Whenever I have been obliged in diplomatic life to indulge in social intercourse with my Japanese colleagues and their wives, I have felt embarrassed by their almost wordless courtesy, and bewildered by my total inability to comprehend what it was all about.

Six

We have always been assured that the Japanese ideal of civility is the samurai, or warrior. He bears in his manner of life some resemblance to the Spartan of the time of Lycurgus, being trained for a life under arms. He was instructed to be frugal in his diet, to eat little more than unhulled rice, to avoid all forms of self-indulgence among which dancing and hot baths were, in the best period, included. The samurai was expected to "live and die with his sword in his hand," to defend his personal honor and that of the Emperor by every means in his power, to endure pain with great fortitude, to be stoical in all his ways, to be almost fanatically patriotic, and if reproved for some dereliction of duty or distressed by the conduct of his superiors, to commit suicide according to a traditional and agonizing formula. The creed of the samurai was known as "*bu-shi-do.*" It implied unquestioning loyalty to the Mikado, truthfulness in word and deed, a contempt for money and all venal occupations, faithfulness to all pledges and promises so that there should be "no second word," and chivalry towards defeated enemies and prisoners of war. This final principle of *bu-shi-do,* or "the way of the warrior," was not, I have been told, given any continuous emphasis in the Second World War.

These virtues were matched by the defects that always attend a narrow theory of human perfection and a harsh discipline by which the individual is subordinated to the type. The Japanese under the influence of this ideal completely lost the sense of humor which so sensitive a culture might otherwise have developed. They came to display a marked tendency towards national self-esteem, accompanied by exceptional secretiveness. Their preoccupation with personal "honor," or "face," became an obsession which often numbed their enjoyment of the vivacious present and rendered them difficult for westerners to understand. Their women, as we are assured by Lafcadio Hearn and others, became models of exquisite femininity, being tolerant, protective, and wonderfully neat. Yet in comparison to the Chinese, their art, even their literature, seems lacking in force; even their gardens were fussy, finicky, little things.

There were other, more mystical obligations, which the Japanese gentleman was expected to inherit and observe. There was an abiding sense of obligation, or "*On*," to the Emperor in the first place, and thereafter to parents, teachers, and superior officers. The repayment of these obligations was also a matter of almost schematic formulas. Under *Gimu* one is bound all one's life by a debt of gratitude, to Japan in the first place, and thereafter to one's ancestors and profession. Under *Giri* a man is supposed to repay exactly within a certain time the benefits he has received. This involves him in a succession of precise duties, towards the State, towards his family, towards his friends. But he also possesses a *Giri* towards his own name, which involves him in sense of personal honor or *Ehre* in the German sense of that term. From this devolves the often inconvenient "duty" of clearing one's own name from insult, or imputation of failure, and of living according to the proprieties. A theory of civility which exaggerates the importance of *Ehre* or "personal honor" (which of course bears no relation at all to personal honesty) is invariably second rate. The Japanese all their lives rotated in circles *of chu, k-o, giri, and jin:*

such regulated virtue, however great may be its practical efficiency, can never become exhilarating. Moreover, whereas *bu-shi-do* was supposed to apply only to the class of feudal warriors, *giri* applied in its pattern of obligation to the whole nation.

Against this grim background of schematic duty and gratitude there existed the delicate courtesy for which the Japanese were so justly famed. Readers of the *Tale of Genji* will recall the exquisite symbolism governing the thoughts and actions of a court lady, Murasaki no Shikibu, in a century when our own ancestors had not progressed beyond the crude table manners of the Anglo-Saxons. At a date when a young Samurai would be pondering whether it would be more seductive to send his love a branch of half open blossom, or only a row of buds, indicating expectant reserve, our own Tostig, earl of the Northumbrians, would let the mutton fat congeal upon his matted beard. It is unfit that we, so recently barbarian, should criticize types of civility more venerable than our own. To us westerners the ritual of Japanese deportment may seem too complicated for understanding. All we should do is to sit back and admire, with respectful uneasiness, their incessant smiles.

Lafcadio Hearn has established the principle that "there must be something lacking, or something very harsh, in a nature to which Japan can make no emotional appeal." Certainly, there must be great strangeness and charm in the cherry blossom, the paper sliding screens, the bat-like giggling of geishas, the reed mats and the lanterns at night. I accept with respect Hearn's analysis of Shinto and its development, since I admire the purity of his mind and prose. Yet my comprehension of him is chilled by the knowledge that he in the end forgot all about his Ionian origin, turned himself into Yakumo Koizimi, and became a subject of the Mikado. I must, however, accept his verdict that, in my approach to Japanese manners, customs and art, "there is something lacking, or something very harsh." And in any case I could never feel attracted to people who take so much time arranging flowers or making tea.

I have written enough in this chapter about the manners of the Far East to show that my ignorance of the subject is unredeemed by any glow of sympathy, any impulse of attraction, any stirring even of curiosity. I have devoted space to the subject for the sole purpose of indicating that I am hostile to all patterns of conduct that are formalized, stereotyped, or rigid.

I now pass to those other types of civility which I think I know; and which I hope I understand.

Chapter 3
Charmides

---❦---

The Greek conception of the superior man—The
Homeric idea—The Court of Alcinous—The Greek
country gentleman—Hesiod and Xenophon—The
Spartan type—The Athenian ideal of Kalos Kagathos—What was thought fitting or unfitting—Conventional deportment—The three requirements of
beauty, intelligence and adaptability—The defect of
the Athenian idea was the misprisal of women—The
Hetairai—The Charmides type—The education of
the Kalos Kagathos—Gymnastics and music—The
aim of symmetry and a sense of fitness—Athenian
manners—Their meals—Decline of manners—The
Just and the Unjust Argument.

One

THE KALOS KAGATHOS, the perfect gentleman of fifth century Athens, is a radiant figure, lit by the sunbeams of the Saronic Gulf.
Always, in relation to the ideas and images of the great

Greek age, there recur the two epithets of "shining" or "glistening" (λαμπρὸς and λιπαρὸς): it was in a lucid climate that the Athenians thought and lived. Their conception of civility was never a drawing room, still less a boudoir, conception. It was mainly concerned with the relation between men and was discussed and analyzed in the open air, either under the shade of olive groves or in the wide porticoes that lined the Agora. It may be true that the ideal of the Kalos Kagathos was in practice never realized to the extent that the Roman, French or English ideals were realized. Yet it still shines for us as a resplendent fiction, as the image of an individual combining personal beauty with great qualities of mind and soul, as something simultaneously nervous and serene.

The other types and prototypes evolved by the Hellenic mind must first be mentioned. There was the heroic, or Homeric, type of perfection. There was the country gentleman type depicted in Hesiod and Xenophon. And there was the tough young man of Sparta, who was perhaps also a fiction, but whose supposed qualities have exercised an unfortunate influence upon those who believe that virility and obedience are the highest human virtues.

Amid all the blood and clangor, through all the ferocity and boasting, of the Homeric poems, we can from time to time detect a slower and more placid note: it is the note of civility. I am not thinking solely of that startling passage in the twenty-fourth book of the *Iliad* when Priam comes to the tent of Achilles, and the warrior is moved to tears by the sight of an aged king groveling at his knees: "and he took the old man by the hand and softly pushed him away." Assuredly the little adverb "ἦκα" sounds strangely amid the din of spear and shield. I am thinking also of more equable instances and especially of the picture of the court of Alcinous amid the happy bays and orchards of Corfu. Nausicaa assuredly is the perfect type of young woman—sensible, alert, graceful and entrancingly gay. How deftly, with what quick recovery, does she deal with a situation of surprising embarrassment! A Jane Austen heroine would not have displayed equal presence of mind if Mr. Knightley had emerged upon the beach at Weymouth, stark naked from the sea. It was not merely that Nausicaa was natural: it was also that she was excessively well-trained.

The manners expected of a Corfiote courtier in that age are well illustrated by the story of Euryalus, the son of Naubolus, "who of all the Phaeacians was the most beautiful to behold." Odysseus, having just been washed ashore in shipwreck, was evidently not at his best, and Euryalus taunted him for being no more than a merchant, mindful only of "the gains of his greed." Odysseus, scowling under his heavy eyebrows, replies that although Euryalus may be beautiful as a god he has not been endowed with the grace (χάρις) of good manners. Thereafter Alcinous obliges Euryalus to apologize, which the young courtier does becomingly, presenting Odysseus with a sword, and receiving in return congratulations for "making amends with courteous speech." A tone of civility softens the whole of the seventh and eighth books of the *Odyssey.*

A simple picture of the country gentleman of his time is given by Hesiod in his *Works and Days.* His remarks on civility are a compound of sound maxim and totemic superstition. Never, he says, jeer at the poverty of another man; be truthful to your friends and "do not let your face put your heart to shame;" always wash your hands carefully before pouring a libation; do not indulge your lusts after a funeral; if you are obliged to urinate in public be careful to do so with decency; always wash and say a short prayer before crossing a river; never trim your nails at mealtimes; do not allow boys of twelve to sit on tombs; never lay the ladle upon the mixing bowl; never wash in water that has been used by a woman; and be restrained in your language, remembering that "even talk is in some ways divine." Such was the deportment considered recommendable for a Boeotian squire, seven hundred years and more before the birth of Christ.

In the *Oeconomicus* of Xenophon there is a much later description of the Greek country gentleman, written some three hundred years after Hesiod's death. Ischomachos, the gentleman farmer, is interested in agriculture as being "the most philanthropic of the arts." He keeps his estate, his home farm, his laborers, his wife and his garden tools in the most perfect order. Yet from time to time he goes up to Athens and listens with pleasure to discussions on the nature of the beautiful and the good. Xenophon possessed a regimental mind, liked everything to be austere and tidy, and despised the Persians because of their effeminate habit of having carpets in their bedrooms. Yet to him no person, not even the worthy Ischomachos, could really be a gentleman unless he were interested in intellectual and aesthetic matters. In his *Memorabilia,* Xenophon explains that the purpose for which he and his friends would leave their farms and pace with Socrates up and down the Stoa of Zeus Eleutherios was:

> Not that we might become popular politicians or successful barristers, but that we might become gentlemen. In order, I mean, that we should learn how to behave rightly to our own families and dependants, how to perfect our relations with our friends, and how to serve our country and our fellow citizens.

Thus even the farmer in Greece was expected to cultivate his mind.

The Spartans, for their part, never evolved even a rudimentary standard of civility. Their aim was the suppression of individual character in order to create a uniform type. For this purpose they invented the prefectorial system in their public schools, the prefects being called by the suitable name of "herd leaders."

"In general," writes Plutarch in his *Lycurgus,* "the Spartans were so disciplined as to lose all desire for a private life; like the bees, they were brought up as organized parts of the common machine, taught to cling round a leader, and in an ecstasy of enthusiasm to sacrifice themselves wholly for the good of the community."

There were some Greeks, of course (and Xenophon was one of them), who pretended to admire these rough Doric ways. Yet to the real Athenian the restrictive methods of the Spartans appeared to cloud the glory of free and private thought. Nor was this frightful sacrifice justified by the result:

"They," said Pericles, "seek to achieve virility by a most laborious discipline. Yet we Athenians, in spite of our liberal way of life, are equally capable of confronting danger."

I shall not, therefore, say anything more about the Spartans.

Two

The Kalos Kagathos, the Athenian ideal of a perfect human being, was expected to combine in his own person a variety of physical, intellectual, aesthetic and moral capacities and gifts. It was essential that these endowments should harmonize with each other, that no disproportion should appear, and that the personality of the individual should be an integrated whole.

In defining the seventeen gifts and virtues required of the Kalos Kagathos, the Greeks used strong and lovely words. The five intellectual virtues were wisdom, reason, common sense, knowledge and a certain gift of creation. The twelve moral virtues were justice, temperance, courage, generosity of soul, ambition, good temper, pride, truthfulness, wit, magnificence (by which was meant "fitting expenditure involving largeness of scale"), a capacity for being ashamed, and a certain degree of affability (καὶ φιλία τὶς). Modesty, pity and consideration for others did not figure with any prominence in their philosophy.

There were other attributes or manners which the Athenian gentleman was expected to possess or cultivate. He must be a free-born citizen, in the sense that he must not be directly descended from barbarians or slaves. This did not imply that the Kalos Kagathos had to be of noble birth. It is true that Aristotle contended that "lack of nobility" (which he defined as "the inheritance of ancient wealth and virtue") was apt, as was personal ugliness, "to sully happiness." Yet Plato argued that it was disgraceful for a man to claim eminence, not on account of his own merits, but on account of those of dead ancestors; and Socrates in the *Theaetetus* applies ridicule to those who boasted of their forebears, some of whom might have been respectable, whereas others were certainly the reverse. Even Aristotle, who was not much given to little jokes, makes mock of the Athenian patrician who shows off abroad. "Our nobles," he writes in the *Politics,* "regard themselves as noble whether they be in their own city or in the cities of others: whereas they regard foreign noblemen as noble only in their own countries, and not when they come to Athens." In the same way, in our own nineteenth century, a Hungarian count appeared less noble in London than he did at Zegedin.

The Athenians, moreover, were not as preoccupied as we are with social position or respectability. Phaedo, for instance, had been captured by pirates as a boy and sold to a brothel keeper in the Piraeus, where he remained for several years until bought out by Cebes. Yet Phaedo was immediately admitted into the Socratic circle and became the eponym of the most solemn of all Platonic dialogues. The Athenian gentleman, although always garrulous and often vain, was never snobbish.

Although the Kalos Kagathos must possess sufficient means of subsistence to be in a position to enjoy leisure, "that most exquisite of delights," he should not engage too much in commerce and should certainly not ply any manual trade. The Greeks had no conception at all of the dignity of labor and the words they used to express vulgarity were the same words as they used for dockworkers, porters and artisans. The gentleman should be adequately good at games, should be able to ride and shoot, but should avoid "the crafty snaring of little birds." "This," Plato remarks, "is no very gentlemanlike pursuit."

Although the gentleman was expected to sing loudly at dinner, it was not considered good form to dance at parties after one had passed a certain age. Yet on the whole dancing was not regarded by the Greeks with the same horror that it inspired in some Roman patricians. Herodotus' story of how Cleisthenes, tyrant of Sicyon, at the last moment cancelled the marriage of Hippocleides on the ground that he, being a prospective bridegroom, had danced at his wedding feast, might lead to misconception. It was not that Hippocleides danced only (a performance that might well have been pardoned), it was that he danced on the table, stood on his head, and waggled his legs in the air. That could not be forgiven. "Oh, son of Tisandros," bellowed Cleisthenes, "you have danced away your marriage." At which Hippocleides, who must indeed have been a brash young man, replied: "I couldn't care less (οὐ φροντὶς Ἱπποκλείδῃ)."

All Greeks had been taught as boys to dance in some liturgical procession, and even elderly men regularly indulged in what they called "gesticulations" corresponding to our own physical jerks. Socrates, himself, in the privacy of his apartment, would dance a solo, believing that it reduced his weight. Xenophon tells us that on one occasion the old man was caught by his pupil Charmides dancing alone before breakfast. How clear, how young, the laughter that must then have echoed through the little house! And Socrates, who never took himself too seriously, must also have been much amused.

There were certain conventional rules of deportment which the Kalos Kagathos was expected to
observe. He should walk with a leisurely grace and
never display haste or fussiness. In his language and
diction he should observe the proprieties. He should
not use demotic expressions, should avoid the juxta-
position of vowels, and should eschew loud laughter, which, as Aristotle rightly remarks, "is a form of
derangement and deceit." His voice should be deep
and sedate rather than shrill or fast. His dress must be
simple and unadorned: Socrates expressed the view
that to ornament a chiton or a himation was "ignoble,
illiberal and fraudulent." The Kalos Kagathos should
know "how to throw his cloak from left to right as a
gentleman should;" he should never, when speaking
in public, permit his arm to extend outside his himation; and, when sitting down, he should be careful not
to display too much of his person, a solecism which,
according to Theophrastus, was the sure sign of a provincial or a foreigner.

Such conventions are not essentially different
from those evolved in other civilized communities.
Yet there were three requirements which render the
Kalos Kagathos distinct from all the other figments of
aristocracy.

Three

In the first place, he was expected to be of handsome appearance. It is difficult for us to understand the immense importance assumed in Greek thought and life by purely aesthetic considerations. "Surely," exclaims Socrates, "the aim and consummation of all education is the love of loveliness." One of the many terms they employed to designate vulgarity was the word "ἀπειροκαλία" signifying an inability to appreciate beauty. Plato placed personal good looks, after health, as second on his list of the desirable things in life. In the *Symposium* of Xenophon, the handsome Critobulos remarks that he would not exchange his beauty, even for the crown of Persia. Aristotle, who took a more jejune view of such matters, agreed that nobody could be happy who was "absolutely ugly;" and Xenophon, who was certainly no aesthete, includes among the qualifications for high office "a physical appearance agreeable to the eye."

Socrates, being himself without comeliness of person, was not satisfied with this convention. Is it really essential, he asks, that the good man must also be beautiful? Is it really true that no man can claim to be *agathos,* unless he be *kalos* as well? He himself had often met men of surpassing beauty who were mean of soul, even as he had known ugly men who were generous and intelligent. Let the epithet *kalos,* therefore, be interpreted as signifying, not physical beauty, but beauty of the soul.

However much Socrates might endeavor thus to sublimate the Athenian passion for physical beauty, his contemporaries persisted in regarding beauty as a divine gift and thus as a virtue in itself. In this they differed much from the modern European. It is inconceivable that any Englishman should boast in public of the symmetry of his own features, nor would Alcibiades, in spite of his mesmeric beauty, have been in London long esteemed.

The second difference was that it was considered essential for the Athenian gentleman to be intelligent, or at least deeply interested in general ideas. When Alcibiades remarked that virtue was the specialty of Athenian gentlemen, Socrates asked: "But what do you mean by gentlemen? Do you mean the intelligent or the unintelligent?" "I mean the intelligent," answered Alcibiades humbly. The Kalos Kagathos, moreover, must be able not only to take part in philosophical discussion, not only to tell the difference between a good and a bad work of art, but he must also play an active part in public life. The man who was devoid of civic sense was regarded as eccentric or *idios*. Conversely the prig, the pedant, or the doriphore were thought unworthy of the name of gentleman. "The supple use of words and phrases," says Socrates in the *Theaetetus,* "and the avoidance of strict accuracy is a general sign of good breeding." Never should a man display his own erudition or triumph over the ignorance, or imprecision, of others.

A third difference that separates the ancient Athenian from the present-day German, American or Hellene, is that it was thought unbecoming for a liberal-minded gentleman readily to take offense. Their dislike of all that was rigid, perfunctory, or stereotyped, led them to regard as ridiculous any ossification of manners or any airs of self-importance. With their comparative disregard of personal status, they did not worry much about "personal honor" in the German sense of that term. In ancient Greece the institution of dueling was unknown; they were not rendered miserable by "loss of face;" nor did any boy, or even adult, imagine that he had been personally outraged if whipped for his transgressions. Thus Alcibiades, the very glass of fashion, having when drunk insulted a respectable citizen, called upon the man next morning and offered to submit to a beating in reparation. Herr Becker's Charicles (who was of a Teutonic cast of mind) would have considered it humiliating thus to be chastised. Certainly the Greeks sought honor, but that was an objective ambition rather than a subjective sensitiveness; a great gulf is fixed between the *philotimia* of the ancients and the touchy *philotimo* which is so irritating a characteristic of the modern Greek, and which must have been imported into Hellas by the Macedonians, Albanians, Turks or other barbarian invaders.

The Kalos Kagathos, therefore, in addition to all other virtues, must be beautiful, intelligent and not too concerned with *Ehre*. How far did the Athenians seek to put this ideal into practice? Socrates, as one might expect, was somewhat contemptuous of the whole business. "As for Hermogenes," he remarks, "who among us is not aware that he is wasting away, all for love of this *'kalokagathia'* whatever that may mean? You notice how glum is his expression, how sedate his demeanor, how refined his language, how demure his diction, how polite his whole bearing? In spite of the fact that all the most important gods are his intimate friends, yet he contrives not to despise humble mortals, such as you and me."

Yet whatever Socrates might say, it is evident that the system of primary and secondary education at Athens (about which in fact we know curiously little) was carefully devised to produce the type of Kalos Kagathos that has been outlined above.

Four

In a community in which paederasty was an accepted, and indeed a valued, institution it was but natural that all manner of rules should have been evolved governing the correct deportment of boys.

This aberration on the part of the ancient Greeks has been attributed to a major defect in their civilization, namely the misprisal of women. Unlike the women of the Homeric period, the women of fifth century Athens were regarded as belonging to some different species; although possibly endowed with reason, they possessed that faculty in an unconvincing way. Girls were scarcely educated at all, were married off at the age of fifteen, were treated in law as perpetual minors, and were regarded by their husbands as necessary evils, useful only as servants and nurses. They were not allowed to leave the house without permission; they were excluded from the theater; they were very seldom able to receive visitors even of their own sex; and they spent their days indoors with the women slaves spinning, chattering and munching beans. They had the reputation, in Athens at least, of being heavy drinkers. It never occurred to an Athenian husband that a wife could ever become an intellectual companion. Xenophon it is true took some pains to educate his child-wife, instructing her "so soon as I found her docile and sufficiently domesticated to carry on a conversation." Yet even Xenophon represents his Ischomachos (the Sir Roger de Coverley of Greek literature) as praising his wife for her subservience: "a word from me, and instantly she obeys." "Is there any person," remarked Socrates to Critobulus in reference to the latter's wife, "with whom you converse less?" But then Socrates' own experience of conjugal felicity was arid indeed.

This disesteem of marriage explains also the curious institution of the Hetairai, who were of varying grades of distinction, from the common prostitute maintained in the city *porneia* (admission to which cost only one obol), through the flute players and the dancing girls, to the *haute cocotterie* represented by such famous women as Aspasia, Lais, Phryne, Lamia or Pythionice. These women, who were a specialty of Corinth, were, as the Japanese geishas, trained specifically for the entertainment of men. They wore prettier clothes than those permitted to the families of the free citizen, were far better educated, and supplied the Athenians with that feminine companionship of which they were deprived in their homes. Yet in spite of the Hetairai, the idols of Athenian society were, not Aspasia or Phryne, but youths such as Charmides, Lysis, Autolycus, Menexenus, or Critias.

Charmides is the type of all these clever adolescents who ran their races, garlanded with the balsam poplar, under the sacred olive trees of the Academy. The trunk of one of these old trees can still be seen by the credulous, crouched beside the dusty road that leads from Athens to Eleusis. Charmides had golden curls of the Achaean variety; he was well born, being the nephew of Glaucon and thus cousin of Plato himself; he was proud of his poverty; he combined modesty with pertness, could make bright remarks, understand everything that was said to him, and blushed as deeply and as frequently as Fanny Price.

We may question whether the high excitement, the tremendous admiration, experienced by and accorded to, these young Kaloi Kagathoi in the Academy gardens or in such wrestling schools as that of Taureas, were in the end good for their characters. It is bad for a boy of fifteen to be made too much of, even by such men as Agathon or Socrates. Plato mentions that the boys of his time had become so conceited that their schoolmasters were frightened of them. Such was the adulation paid to youth, that elderly men would go out of their way to flatter schoolboys. "They indulge in pleasantries," writes Plato, "imitating the youths themselves, so as not to be thought pompous or disagreeable." Nor in fact did all these palaestra lads do credit to their teachers in after life. Critias became one of the Thirty Tyrants and put Autolycus to death: the latter's father, Lycon, joined with Meletus and Anytus in prosecuting Socrates for corruption of the youth: and, as we learn from Xenophon, Charmides went on blushing for the rest of his life, thereby confusing what might have proved a useful public career.

Five

The young Athenian was thus never accorded any continuity of family life or the valuable fusion of maternal solicitude with paternal discipline. Until the age of six he was brought up by the women: after the age of six his education was exclusively male. As a baby he would be swung from the ceiling in a wicker basket shaped like a boot: his earliest memories would be the crooned lullabies of Thracian or Anatolian slave-women. He would be given toys such as carts and little dolls of clay, and would be frightened into obedience by barbaric tales of the two witches Akko and

Alphito who enjoyed sucking the blood of naughty boys. Occasionally his mother would tell him about the gods or recite one of Aesop's fables. On great occasions his father would make an appearance in the women's quarters and amuse the children for an hour; we hear of King Agesilaus entrancing his young family by careering round the courtyard on a hobby horse. At the age of six the Athenian child was taken out of the harem and entrusted to a pedagogue, who often remained his watchdog for ten years. These aged family retainers accompanied the boy to school or gymnasium, acting as duennas or chaperones, carrying the boy's lyre and luncheon, leading him home at dusk, and spending the whole day gossiping in a bunch with other pedagogues leaning upon their tall forked sticks. The pedagogue was a slave, not a tutor; he was often a barbarian and we are told that the pedagogue of the admirable Lysis was a disgruntled old man who spoke with a harsh foreign accent; his function was analogous to that of the trusted lady's maid who accompanied Victorian virgins to dancing classes. Often the pedagogue must have exercised a pernicious influence during those ten creative years.

Education in Athens was entirely private and the teachers were ill paid and often of low origin. The Board of Control, or *paidonomoi,* were in no sense similar to our own Education Authorities and merely saw to it that the schoolrooms were adequately clean, that the sand on the benches was changed regularly, and that a decent standard of morals was preserved. Instruction was divided into three branches, namely gymnastics, music and letters. Boys were taught to read and it was considered essential for a gentleman to know long passages of Homer and Hesiod by heart; Niceratus, the son of Nikias, claimed that he could recite the whole of the *Iliad* and the *Odyssey* without glancing at the text; and Alcibiades thrashed his own schoolmaster on finding that there was no written copy of Homer in the school. At a later stage boys were instructed in mathematics, astronomy and music. Alcibiades set the fashion of condemning the flute as an instrument unworthy of a Kalos Kagathos in that it distorted the features; the more refined lyre and kithara became the vogue. At the gymnasia the boys were made to run races and to wrestle naked, and were taught how to throw javelins and quoits. As minor amusements they would play draughts and knucklebones, and would indulge in that curious game of guessing numbers, the sound of which, under the name of Morra, still echoes in the villages of Greece and Italy. At sixteen they came of age; at eighteen they underwent their military service; and thereafter they spent their time as jurors, advocates, or politicians, attending the lectures of sophists or the discussions in the academy and the colonnades. In the intervals they would train Laconian or Mollossian hunting dogs or would go in for breeding race horses, paying as much as £50 for a good "koppa" stallion.

SCHOOL DISCIPLINE IN GREECE
Herakles breaks a stool over the head of his music master
Linus, while the other pupils manifest delight, by Duris.
(from "Griechische Vasen," by R. Lullies and M. Hirmer)

Gymnastics, or as we should say "compulsory games," were not unreservedly approved of by the poets and philosophers. Euripides condemns excessive indulgence in athletics as "a useless pleasure," and both Plato and Aristotle warn gymnastic instructors not to specialize too much in any single branch of sport. Socrates himself, although he derided the games fetish, felt that it was the duty of a young man to keep his body in fit condition. He sharply snubbed the youth Epigenes for allowing his muscles to become flabby. We may none the less question whether in fifth century Athens the cult of athleticism, in spite of Pindar and the adulation accorded to Olympic champions, was very much more intense than in the England of today. To concentrate on this single element of perfection would have been alien to the Greek idea.

That idea, the lasting conception of a perfect gentleman, was based on the symmetrical development of all human faculties. It was on this theory that their education was founded. Isocrates, for instance, defines the four main purposes of education as follows. First, it should provide boys with a "sense of fitness," thereby enabling them to cope with the ordinary affairs of later life. Secondly, it should train young people to conduct themselves properly in any society, to control their tempers and to treat all strangers, even dull or offensive strangers, with politeness. Thirdly, the boy should learn how to practice self-control and how to dominate his own vices. And fourthly, a boy should leave school with "a soul well-tuned to any circumstances." In truth *aretê* for the Athenians meant, not virtue in our sense, but excellence; and excellence meant balanced achievement.

It was thus the Athenians who first discovered the merits of what we today call "a liberal education." Aristotle in the *Politics* asserts that education should be valued "not because it is necessary or useful, but because it is liberal and beautiful." This ideal of παρρησία, or "the liberated mind," could alone, in the view of the Athenians, produce the virtue of adaptability. In boasting justifiably that Athens was "the school of Hellas," Pericles asserted that the Athenian Kalos Kagathos was an "individual who can show himself capable of the most varied forms of activity and adapt himself to different circumstances with versatility and grace." Here, therefore, are the two key words of Athenian civility—in the first place, versatility, in the second, grace.

Much as the Athenians admired self-control, as "the harmony between the superior and the inferior in nature," they also regarded any individual as incomplete or unfulfilled unless he also possessed "spirit." They called it "*thumos*" even as the Italians called it "virtù." "Every man," writes Plato in *The Laws,* "ought to be both as passionate as possible, and as gentle." It was to achieve this difficult combination that Greek education was designed.

Six

What then were the actual manners that the Kalos Kagathos, as a boy and man, was expected to acquire and observe? Great importance was attached to deportment, or "*eukosmia.*" A boy was taught to walk in the public streets with his eyes fixed on the ground, not glancing either to right or to left; to rise from his seat gracefully and to be careful always to obliterate the marks left by his person on the sand of the school bench; to drape his himation with elegance; to touch salt fish with one finger only, although two fingers might be used if the fish were fresh; never to talk in the presence of his elders; to sit upright at a dinner party and not to loll; to realize that it was a sign of effeminacy to scratch the head with the forefinger; and to keep himself clean.

A free Athenian youth was also expected to move with dignity and above all with grace. The instructors in the gymnasium devoted much time to teaching boys how to walk delicately, and the trainer Hippomachus would boast that he could recognize his own pupils by the beauty of their gait "even from a distance, even if they were carrying home a leg of mutton."

The Greeks were cleaner than our own ancestors. The public baths were regularly attended and, as in Turkey today, slaves were sent on in advance, carrying their master's private towels, oil flask and strigil. The Kaloi Kagathoi were carefully scraped and massaged by the bath attendants and anointed with scented oil. They cleaned their teeth with powdered pumice stone. Plato, in the *Sophist,* speaks of "those impurities such as are disagreeable to mention but which are dealt with by the art of the bathkeeper." He himself always insisted that his pupils should come to the Academy neatly dressed and with washed hair, faces and hands. The Stoics and the old fashioned survivors of the Periclean age affected to despise hot baths, but we know that most Athenians enjoyed both private hot baths with scented water and the delights of the public vapor bath. Nor were their sanitary arrangements as primitive as is sometimes asserted. They had night stools, similar to what in the East are still called "thunder boxes" and a special slave, a "*lasanophoros*" was employed to keep them constantly clean and available. Although adults allowed their hair and their beards to grow, they were careful to keep them trimmed by professional barbers. Shaving only came in with Alexander the Great, although Agathon, being a dandy, possessed a personal razor. It was thought natural for men to dye their hair, even if they chose a bright color such as sepia or gold. It was regarded as improper for young men to cut their hair too short, after the initial shaving of the head on coming of age. Aristophanes makes fun of Cratinus for having his hair trimmed by a razor round the edges "as if he were an adulterer."

The Athenians were austere; not quite as austere as the Spartans of the best period, but certainly not as self-indulgent as the men of Corinth. They had three meals a day, namely breakfast or *akratisma,* consisting of bread dipped in sweet wine, luncheon or *ariston,* at which hot dishes were often served, and at sunset came the *deipnon* or principal meal of the day. Sappho is recorded as having eaten roast nuts for her breakfast and Plato lived almost entirely on figs. But the usual diet of an Athenian was a form of polenta called "maza" consisting of barley meal mixed with garlic and oil. Butter was regarded as a Thracian indulgence. The Athenians were specially fond of fish, were noted for fried *aphues* and were able to serve in many different ways the eels from Lake Copais. The best cooks came from Sicily, and cookery books were plentiful and carefully studied. The *Gastrology* of Archestratos was much favored, but it is the long and boring "*Deipnosophists*" of Athenaeus that has survived. Menus were written in Doric, much as with us today they are written in French.

From time to time somebody (it might be Agathon) would give a dinner party or symposium. Nine guests were usually invited, but it was customary for other uninvited guests, including professional diners-out and parasites, to appear while the meal was in progress. After the *deipnon* was finished slaves would clear the tables, and distribute garlands of myrtle and violet as well as unguents and scents to the guests. The libation would follow, first to Zeus the Deliverer and then to Hygeia. While the libation was being poured the guests would intone a little hymn. A *symposiarchos,* or master of the feast, was then chosen by lot, and the drinking began. The Greeks were not heavy drinkers and it was thought bad manners to get drunk, except during the Dionysia, or to spoil the party owing to "*paroinia*" or the incapacity to drink as a gentleman should. "Nobody," remarked Alcibiades, "ever saw Socrates drunk." In fact their wine was diluted in the proportion of a third of wine to two thirds of water. Unlike the Romans, the Greeks had little knowledge of wine, regarding sixteen years as an old vintage, mixing honey, spices and snow with their Chian or their Sicilian, and adopting even the bad Euboean habit of using resin as a flavor and preservative.

Their table manners were excellent indeed. Unpunctuality was ill-regarded and no host waited for any guest who was late. Two guests generally shared one couch and there was a special technique for arranging the cushions gracefully, the left arm resting on the couch, the right being held free for eating. There were no forks or knives and on finishing a course the guests wiped their fingers on a piece of bread which was then thrown to the Maltese spaniels that were the inmates of every Athenian home. For very hot dishes gloves were used to protect the fingers, or even small shields made of horn.

Such therefore were the manners of the Kalos Kagathos, perhaps the most intelligent and appreciative human being that has ever lived upon this earth. Unfortunately he only lasted in his full perfection for some eighty years. In the *Republic,* Plato has much to say about the degeneration of manners inevitable in any democratic system. The younger generation, he complains, come to regard temperance as somewhat effeminate, they lose the old reverence and sense of shame, they indulge in lascivious pleasures such as playing the flute, they are given to "false and vaunting words," and they will even be seen entering a public house. How different from the boys of the old school, described by the Just Argument in *The Clouds!* Unlike Pheidippides with his hunting crop and his sophisms, the descendants of those who fought at Marathon would, on their way to school, sing old fashioned songs without any modern trills and trimmings; would never rub their limbs with oil or speak in an effeminate voice; would never giggle, laugh loudly, or cross their legs; would not start arguments in the gymnasium; would rise in the presence of their elders; and would run races in the Academy orchards, accompanied by a good young friend, "rejoicing in the hour of spring when the plane tree whispers to the elm."

It was by slow degradations that the Kalos Kagathos lost his dignity and charm.

Chapter 4
Gravitas

The decline of the Kalos Kagathos—The slave
system—The period 98–48 BCE a good example of
Roman civility—The senatorial aristocracy—The
equestrian order—The "poor whites"—Vulgar and
liberal professions—The Roman gentleman and his
qualities—The ideal of *gravitas*—The Roman regard
for women—Terentia and Pomponia—Clodia—
Education of boys—Neglect of religion—The pre-
cariousness of Roman life—Adventurism—Legacy
hunting—Clients—Deportment as recommended
by Cicero—Dress and cleanliness—Manners—
Food—The grossness of Roman society.

One

NEITHER THE PHILOSOPHY nor the deportment of the Athenian gentleman was maintained during the two thousand one hun-
dred and sixty-five years that separate Chaeronea from
Navarino. Already by the fourth century BCE a decline

in the solidity of the Hellenic character had been observed. The sophists, whom Socrates denounced as "the prostitutors of wisdom," charged high fees for their lectures and the old uniformity among free citizens was split by a distinction between those who could afford the higher education and those who could not. Although the sophists must be esteemed as the pioneers of humanism, yet their teaching, in that it concentrated on intellectual analysis rather than upon integrated character, increased the natural tendency of the Greeks to indulge in ingenuity. The loss of liberty, however much it might be mitigated under the Macedonians and the Romans by flattering grants of municipal self-government, deprived them of their magnificent self-respect. As the centuries passed, the pure Hellenic strain became contaminated by the blood of barbarians, even by the blood of their own slaves. They sank to the level of the middlemen of the Roman Empire or to that of the courtiers of Byzantium. Even Alexander had noticed that the Persian nobles possessed a certain impassive dignity that was lacking among his Athenian or Corinthian associates. In the end we reach the sad spectacle of the "greedy little Greeks" of Juvenal or that of Trimalchio the Levantine millionaire. Even Cicero, who possessed for Greek culture a reverence comparable only to that felt by our own Gallomaniacs for the arts of France, regretted that the poise of Demosthenes had not been transmitted to those Greeks who battened on Roman society. "Their too expressive use of the rolling eye and the shrugging shoulder" grated upon his nerves. "I am tired," he wrote to his brother, "of their lack of character, their obsequiousness and their preference for expediency to principles."

Only after a frightful War of Independence, only after successive triumphs over disasters that would have broken weaker patriotism and endurance, has the Hellene of today recovered and established his self-esteem which, in the age of Pericles, had created the legend of the Kalos Kagathos.

Two

Before considering the special form of dignity, or *gravitas,* which was the main Roman contribution to civility, mention must be made of the slave systems upon which these ancient civilizations were based. The effects of slavery were regrettable, if only because it accustomed children to mingle intimately with a caste that was regarded as almost animal, and taught adults habitual indifference to human misery. Its economic effects were vicious, in that it stifled technical progress and created in the cities a large population of unemployed freemen, or "poor whites." It is outside the scope of this study to consider the slave gangs employed in mines or on the great provincial estates or to dwell upon the horror of the cellars, or *ergastula,* in which they were chained at night. Such cruelties bear but a remote relation to civility: it was the ordinary house-slave of Greek or Roman citizens whose presence and status affected their way of life and the nurture of their children. It must be realized that even the noblest examples of ancient civilization, even Aristotle, even Cato, never considered that it might be ethically wrong to buy a fellow human being in the market as one buys a mule or a pig and confine him in a stable or a sty.

The experts disagree about the proportion of slaves to freemen in Greece and Rome. It has been esti-mated that in Athens of the fourth century the free citizens numbered 21,000, resident aliens 10,000, and slaves 400,000. At Corinth there are said to have been 460,000 slaves and at Aegina 470,000. We know that it was regarded as a sign of poverty to be attended by one slave only; that Demosthenes' father, who was not a wealthy man, possessed 50 slaves, and that Nikias leased 1,000 slaves to the Thracian mines. We know that Alexander the Great sold 30,000 Theban citizens into slavery, that Aemilius Paulus similarly disposed of 150,000 Epirotes, and that Marius after his victories sold 60,000 Cimbri and 90,000 Teutons. We know that in the year 200 BCE 10,000 slaves were auctioned in the market of Delos in a single day, and it is esti-mated that the slave population of Rome in the last century of the Republic numbered 650,000. These fig-ures have been questioned by scholars. Professor Cary goes so far as to contend that it is doubtful whether the slave population outnumbered the free citizens to anything like the extent that has been claimed. Most of these slaves were barbarians or prisoners of war. The Greeks regarded it as bad taste for a Hellene to enslave another Hellene; the Romans imposed an absolute prohibition against any Roman being enslaved by a fellow citizen, even for debt. Whatever be the truth about these statistics, the fact remains that in every Greek or Roman home there was a considerable number of house slaves of foreign origin.

In Greece a master could only put a slave to death with the sanction of the courts; a slave who was intolerably ill-treated could take sanctuary in the Theseion. In Rome a slave was regarded in law as a *res* and not as a *persona;* he could be flogged, tortured, suspended for hours with weights tied to his feet, and even crucified, at his master's pleasure. This theory that a slave was a "thing" belonging to his master persisted until the age of Hadrian: the only restraint on an inhuman slave owner was that of public opinion. Thus Pliny refers to Larcius Macedo, himself the son of a freedman, as a man who did not know how to treat slaves properly; and Seneca records that Vedius Pollio, who was supposed to throw his slaves into his stew pond in order to fatten his lampreys, "was pointed at with scorn throughout the whole city and despised and loathed." Yet, in spite of this sanction of public opinion, the children both in Greece and Rome must often have observed their father and even their mother committing repeated acts of the most atrocious cruelty.

The slave dealers, whether those of Delos or the *mangones* who ran the slave market by the Temple of Castor in Rome, would display their wares in the manner of horse copers, allowing prospective purchasers to examine the teeth and muscles of the animals, taking them for little runs on a string to show their paces. Slaves were exhibited for sale in a wooden cage, their feet being smeared with whitewash, and tablets stating price and qualifications hung round their necks. Prices varied from £8 to £240 according to their age or skill; slaves of outstanding capacity or beauty would fetch large sums, and Mark Antony is said to have purchased a pair of handsome twins as a present for Cleopatra for the sum of £800 apiece.

Horace, who wrote frequently and well about the pleasures of the simple life, asserted that ten slaves were the minimum quantity for a respectable citizen to possess and men of fortune would maintain as many as 4,000. These were divided into detachments and, apart from ordinary domestic duties, fulfilled such varied functions as copyists, accountants, librarians, secretaries, painters, architects, topiarists, house physicians, dentists and reader companion. There was a slave called a *silentiarius,* whose business it was to prevent the other slaves making too much noise, and another called a *nomenclator,* who was there to whisper to his master the names of those whom he met on his way down to the Forum.

The Romans, being without a sense of humor, enjoyed laughing at the physically afflicted, and would amuse themselves by keeping dwarfs, hunchbacks, and deformed children in their households. Seneca tells us that some dealers specialized in slaves who were quick at making impertinent jokes or salacious sallies. Even Augustus, who disliked monstrosity of any kind, kept a tame dwarf of the name of Canopus to amuse his niece: and Seneca himself had a jester, or *fatuus,* at whom to laugh.

Abominable as may seem to us this degradation of human beings, there did exist a gentler side to the slave system. A slave was regarded as part of the family and many of them had been born in the house and watched and trained from infancy by their masters. Atticus, for instance, had a young slave, Alexis, whom he treated with paternal affection and Tiro, the slave, and only later the freedman, of Cicero had probably been born on the family property at Arpinum, and was thus a *verna,* or "home product." Tiro was in every way regarded by Cicero, Terentia and the children as a part of the family. If we are to believe Aullus Gellius, he actually helped Cicero with some of his philosophic treatises and he certainly lived with his master on terms of the deepest mutual affection and respect. It was with anxious solicitude that Cicero prescribed for Tiro when the latter fell ill with fever at Patras. In the most ideal circumstances, however, there did persist the sense of caste. Thus when one of Cicero's readers, young Sositheus, "a charming fellow," died in Rome, Cicero excuses himself for his depression with the words: "I am more upset than I should be at the death of a slave." It is as when we say: "One really should not allow oneself to become so attached to an animal." The greatest of Roman humanists could not, under the slave system, be described as ideally humane: Cicero took it for granted that refractory slaves should be punished immediately: their punishment was harsh.

Thus when at Formiae he would entertain his friends in the Corinthian dining room opening on the sea, discussing with them the proper relation between expediency and honor, the calm of their discourse would be pierced by a scream from the servants' quarters, where a slave was being branded with a hot iron upon the face—a mere lad whom Quintus, almost as a joke, had sent his brother as a present from Chichester or Lympne.

Three

At what epoch in the history of Rome can the perfect type of patrician be best identified? Certainly not in the early stages of the Republic, when autumn after autumn the Romans decimated the Aequi or the Volsci, only to find them in the following spring once more howling and gibbering beyond the *vallum* and the stockade. Certainly not during the recurrent wars with the Samnites, the Sabines and the Etruscans, or when the Gauls lit their fires in the Forum. Not even when Hannibal, prowling round and round Italy, camped beneath the Colline Gate. The old Roman virtues were laudable indeed and they combined to build an Empire against enormous odds; but they remained for long the rough virtues of the rustic Latin, nor were the two Catos, for all their stoutness, models of civility. Good manners could not achieve much importance among a people who, in Livy's proud boast, had been "eight hundred years at war."

Shall the opposite course be chosen, and an example taken from the early days of the Empire—let us say Petronius Arbiter, the dandy of the period, the author of the Latin *Bourgeois Gentilhomme,* who surprised them all by proving himself a vigorous proconsul in Bithynia, and who, when elegantly committing suicide, smashed a precious vase so that it should not fall into the tasteless hands of Nero? No, there is too little interesting difference between Caius Petronius and the Exquisites of a later age.

It is best perhaps to take the last fifty years of the Republic, between 98 BCE and 48 BCE, when the old patrician virtues were still admired, and quite often practiced, but when the new learning had come to widen the minds, and soften the manners, of the warrior race. What, at that date, was the Roman conception of the perfectly civilized man?

The old narrow aristocracy of, say, 300 BCE, which was in fact an agrarian military caste, consisting of some 100 families such as the Fabii, the Aemilii, the Marcelli, and so on, scarcely survived the Punic Wars.

Yet in the last century of the Republic the aristocratic tradition still continued in the Senatorial Order of some 500 senators, who strove not unsuccessfully to perpetuate a monopoly of magisterial function. Thus Cicero was the first man for thirty years to be elected consul from the middle class. The aristocratic tradition was maintained by something approaching ancestor worship, and the busts and waxen portrait masks of forebears who held curule office were preserved with almost religious veneration in the home.

The equestrian order, or middle class, was composed mainly of business men, whether merchants or publicans, who amassed great fortunes when money came to circulate rapidly after the Second Punic War. A man such as Rabirius Postumus, whom Cicero defended in 54 BCE, speculated in millions, lending vast sums at high interest to Ptolemy Auletes, the deposed King of Egypt, and the father of Cleopatra. There was a South Sea Bubble atmosphere about the last fifty years of the Republic. Below the two upper orders whom Cicero strove always to unite came the lower class of free citizens, often no more than "poor whites," who lived in tenement buildings, called *insulae,* who had few occupations in view of the universality of slave labor and who subsisted on bribes during election time and on doles of wheat. It is estimated that in 46 BCE some 320,000 of the third order of free citizens received their daily ration.

Each of the three orders was class conscious. Cicero was despised by the optimates as being a *"novus homo,"*

PORTRAIT BUST OF CICERO
(From the Capitol Museum)

and was never quite able to master the pangs of inferiority that had so plagued him when he first arrived from Arpinum. Yet Cicero in his turn cherished contempt for the shopkeeping class and for those who indulged in manual labor. There is an interesting passage in

Chapter XIII of *De Officiis* in which he analyses what professions are in his opinion vulgar and what are not. It is best, he writes, to avoid being a tax collector, an auctioneer or a money lender, since "these occupations arouse enmity." It would be "sordid" for any free citizen to indulge in manual labor, since artisans are paid by the hour and "not for artistic skill." "The wages they receive," writes Cicero, "are proofs of their slavery." Retail shop keeping also, to his mind, is a vulgar profession, in that it tempts to deception. The factory worker is necessarily engaged in a vulgar occupation "since no factory can ever have anything liberal about it." Yet by far the most despicable tradesmen are those who minister to the needs of the flesh, such as poulterers, butchers, cooks, fishmongers, perfumers, dancers, acrobats and variety artists. On the other hand there do exist such things as "liberal professions," nor need any citizen be ashamed of being a doctor, schoolmaster or architect. Big business, in that it has scope and splendor, is not a sordid profession. But for the real gentleman, in Cicero's opinion, there is no calling that "is more delightful, profitable or becoming than the pursuit of agriculture." Cicero was a snobbish man, but Livy assuredly was not. And even Livy could write of Terentius Varro—"He sprang from origins that were not humble merely, but actually sordid. His father was a butcher who sold meat." One of the chance misfortunes that did damage to the old Roman world was that clerical work was also regarded as a servile occupation. The Civil Service and the Imperial Secretariat thus became increasingly stocked with freedmen and foreigners. It was this evil that wrung from Juvenal the piercing cry: "I cannot bear it, I cannot bear it, oh my fellow Romans, that our city should become Greek!" (*non possum ferre, Quirites, Graecam urbem*).

In spite of their rigid caste distinctions, there did exist among the late Republicans and their successors the conception of the natural gentleman, or "ingenuus," who must of course be a free citizen, but need not be of noble family. The men whom Cicero called "*homines belli*" (by which he sometimes meant "the Conservative party" but sometimes merely "decent folk"), the men whom Pliny called "*togati et urbani,*" were certainly differentiated from the newcomers of the type of Trimalchio, who besides being ostentatious, had a deep dislike of intellectuals whom he called "*istos scholasticos.*" "Moreover," adds Petronius, "those who think money so important hate the idea that other people might admire something that they cannot themselves command. Thus they despise men of letters, seeking to make money appear more important than education."

In his *De Officiis* Cicero lays down eight rules for the conduct of the gentlemen, or "*liberalis.*" He should remember always the dignity of human nature and live simply and soberly. He must cultivate "propriety" in his every action and every word, "even in every gesture and attitude." For "propriety" Cicero used the word "*decorum*" as a translation of the Greek term "*to prepon.*" With

dignity it combines the graces of tact and taste. A gentleman again must feel it his duty to play his part in public life. In his relations with his fellows he should remember always "that it is right to respect, defend and
maintain the common bonds of union and fellowship
existing between all members of the human race." This
social conscience, or instinct, Cicero calls "*communi-
tas.*" The gentleman again should cultivate a dignified
attitude towards life, namely the famous Roman *gravitas.* Cato, he remarks, although a very rude man, had a
degree of *gravitas* that was "almost incredible." The gentleman should eschew vulgarity in any form and should
never boast or talk too much about himself. And finally
he should show reverence to all men, even towards the
humble, even towards slaves. "The good man," writes
Cicero, "is one who harms no man but seeks to help
everyone. Unless of course he be provoked by some
injury to himself." Only rarely did Cicero in practice live
up to these high standards. They represented the philosophy of the Stoics, as adapted to Roman conditions
of life by Panaetius of Rhodes.

It is noticeable that Cicero, although himself a
scholar, did not include intellectual activity or aesthetic
perception in his list of qualities. The Romans, even
at their finest hour, were not an imaginative people.
Although quick at absorbing the knowledge of others,
and although excelling in the arts of war, administration, jurisprudence and engineering, they were weak in
the realm of abstract reflection or aesthetic invention.

Even their *gravitas,* as Warde Fowler remarked, "was full of dignity but a little wanting in animation." Compared to the Greeks, the Romans, in their conception of gentility, were clumsy and a little dull. Their fingers, in such matters, tended to become thumbs.

But behind it all there remained the splendid tradition of virility and good faith that was the Roman heritage. For ever rose the lamentation at the loss of ancestral piety and honor (*heu pietas, heu prisca fides!*), and every schoolboy was taught the story of Regulus, who, rather than break a promise, returned to certain torture and death at Carthage, as calmly as if he were journeying to take the waters at Llandrindod Wells.

Four

In one respect only were the Romans more civilized than the Greeks, namely in their higher regard for women. No Greek matron earned such universal regard or influence as did the supercilious, legendary figures, Cornelia and Sempronia. No Greek author would have devoted pages of eulogy to the "portrait of a noble woman" such as the picture given us by Pliny of Arria, the wife of Paetus. The materfamilias was a far more important person than the housekeeping Athenian wife. She was not shut up in a harem, and could be seen with her husband in the atrium; she was allowed to go to dinner parties and to the theater; she could give evidence in the law courts and could to some extent administer her own fortune. Juvenal remarks that men who married heiresses frequently found themselves in humiliating positions.

At the same time even the materfamilias was not expected to be highly educated or to take part in male conversation. According to Juvenal it is annoying for a husband if his wife corrects his grammatical mistakes. "Let not your spouse," says Martial, "be too highly educated." (*Sit non doctissima conjux.*) Cicero did not communicate his intellectual tastes to Terentia, whom he divorced, after thirty years of married life, on the suspicion that she had conspired with the freedman, Philotimus, to make a little money of her own out of the domestic accounts. Pomponia again, sister to Atticus and wife of Quintus Cicero, was typical of the woman who indulges in self-pity at being unable to command her husband's intellectual respect. She made a scene at a picnic because she had not been consulted about the luncheon basket. "I might as well," she exclaimed in front of the guests, "be a stranger in my own home." But Pomponia was worse, far worse, than a merely disagreeable woman. Mark Antony, in one of his capricious quirks, handed over to her the freedman Philologus by whom both her husband and her son had been betrayed to their executioners. With her own hands Pomponia, who was no less vindictive than Fulvia, tortured the man to death, forcing him to swallow grilled steaks cut from his own flesh.

Apart from these dull, silly, or fierce matrons there were of course women of culture and charm. Tullia, the beloved daughter of Cicero, shared her father's literary studies, but she married badly and died young. Caerellia was another blue stocking, who enjoyed conversing with Cicero and his circle upon the defects of Epicurus, or the needs of the Republic. It was a licentious age, and women such as Clodia, profligate and brilliant, could fill their salons in Rome or their weekend parties at Baiae with a host of elegant or gifted lovers. It was Clodia who almost succeeded in getting Caelius convicted of attempted murder; who broke the tender heart of Catullus, thereby achieving two thousand years and more of immortality for herself and her pet bullfinch.

What prospect was there for a boy, brought up in an atmosphere so lax and so exciting, attaining true civility? The whole family centered round the father, whose "*patria potestas,*" which endured until the reign of the Emperor Constantine, gave him, at least in theory, the power of life and death. So late as 63 BCE a Roman patrician executed one of his own adult sons without any protest from the magistrates. Although in Greece a boy ceased to be the property of his father once he came of age and acquired the rights of full citizenship, in Rome he remained for ever in his father's power, unless he happened to become a *flamen dialis* or priest of Jupiter, or unless his father was deprived for some reason of his civic rights. In childhood a boy remained with the women and was taught the rudiments of manners. He was, for instance, not allowed to use the expression "by Hercules!" when in the home; if the temptation to utter these words became irresistible, he must go outside the front door and say them in the street. Rich men would provide their boys with private tutors who generally taught in Greek. Other boys, as Horace tells us, went to a primary school, where they were whipped into acquiring a knowledge of arithmetic and letters. At sixteen or seventeen the boys assumed the *toga virilis,* and thereafter entered upon the study of rhetoric, which, as we are told by Tacitus, was regarded as the essence of education. They would be trained to speak against each other in mock debates and were crammed with little apophthegms or epigrams called "*sententiae.*" Many of them on reaching eighteen were sent to Greece to study philosophy and most Romans from the last age of the Republic and throughout the Empire were bilingual in Greek and Latin. On his return, a young man would do his military service or be apprenticed to some prominent barrister or politician. In this manner he acquired the ways of the great world and also certain oratorical habits which the Romans called "*commoditates orationis.*" Yet the more we examine the Roman system of education, the more clear does it become that it was haphazard and ill-conceived. In the primary and secondary schools the masters were of a low standard and much derided by their pupils. The boys who went to a finishing course at Corinth, Cos or Athens, often returned intellectually corrupted. The whole educational system seems to us to have been devised with feckless opportunism and Warde Fowler was certainly right in stressing the absence of all "scientific method," with the result that the Roman youth, on leaving the university, was devoid "of solidity, both intellectual and moral."

Religion, of course, played but little part during the period we are examining. As a child the young Roman would have assisted daily at family prayers, serving his father as acolyte or *camillus*. Throughout his life he probably retained some respect for Vesta, as the symbol of national vitality, and perhaps even for Jupiter in his role of Optimus Maximus, protecting Rome against all ills and enemies. Yet the word "*religio*" to a lad of 50 BCE could have meant little more than childhood memories of morning libations to the Lares and the family images and an enduring terror of ghosts and portents. The Romans, even of the stern republican age, were incredibly superstitious. Again and again does Livy interrupt his magnificent narrative to talk nonsense about two-headed calves born in Apulia; Cicero was horrified by an ill omen that came to him at Durazzo; Brutus was convinced that he had been visited by the outraged ghost of Caesar; and Sulla, who was certainly no weakling, believed in what he called "the demon of the night" and would keep a little idol of Apollo under his pillow and kiss it repeatedly when the demon threatened to approach. So careless a system of instruction, so unhealthy a domestic life, the absurd theory that it was essential for an intelligent man to be bilingual, the absence of all moral compulsion other than that of a dim Stoic philosophy, all these combined to diminish *gravitas*, and to render the young Roman of the last century of the Republic unbalanced, reckless and superstitious. It is no wonder that their two greatest poets should have sought, the one to bring back the ancient and simple piety that had been lost, the other to denounce with fury the neurosis that *religio* had produced.

The stakes were high and the young Roman gambled wildly, exercising prodigies of virtù. Fortunes swept into their possession in the morning only to be lost again before the afternoon. Even Cicero, who prided himself on the orderliness of his life, indulged in the most audacious extravagances and but a momentary consideration of his finances causes the brain to whirl. Apart from his two large houses in Rome, he possessed no less than eight country properties, each rich with libraries, works of art, terraced gardens, baths and colonnades. He was vain about the beauty of his villas, styling them the "jewels of Italy," *ocellos Italiae,* and he would travel constantly from one to the other, spending the night at one of the several resthouses or *deversoria* that he owned on the main roads. The wild adventurers, who figure so vividly in Cicero's correspondence, were in the end murdered one way or the other. Only the sagacious Atticus avoided catastrophe: only the boy Octavian lived to establish his chill Augustan reign.

Five

A part from the adventurism of this great race of soldiers and jurists, there were two curious customs which differentiated the last period of the Republic from any society that has existed before or since. There was in the first place, the extraordinary convention according to which some rich man of the middle class would acquire posthumous honor by leaving legacies to the more eminent among his contemporaries. The banker Cluvius, for instance, left half his fortune to Cicero and the other half to Caesar. The moneylender Caecilius, who was so hated that the mob attacked his funeral procession, bequeathed £80,000 to Atticus, whom during his lifetime he had barely known. This practice can only have increased their tendency to live on the unexpected. To the young, it must have been a disturbing element.

A second convention, which to us would prove intolerable, was that a man of eminence, or even promise, had to be accompanied in public by a retinue of clients or parasites. In a letter to his brother Quintus, Cicero divides clients into three categories. First there are those who merely call in the morning to perform the *salutatio matutina,* to receive their fee, or *sportula* for so doing, and to collect the news. These parasites were, as depicted in Juvenal's fifth Satire, exposed to much humiliation. Martial complains that the *sportula* offered him by Bassus was only two shillings a day; and we learn from Juvenal that the client, if asked to dinner, was not offered the best dishes or his patron's wine. The second category of clients are those who take the trouble to attend their patron throughout the day, accompanying him back to his house when sunset came. When a boy assumed his *toga virilis* it was expected that all his friends should follow him through the streets, and we know from the *Pro Murena* that these clients could be hired for so much a day. Only amid the woods of Arpinum could Cicero escape the clients who buzzed round him in Rome, at Tusculum, at Formiae, at Pompeii, at Puteoli, at Cumae, even at Astura. For all their seaside villas, the Romans, like the French, were essentially urban and it was in and around the Forum that they wished to live. "It is the town," writes Cicero to his young friend Caelius Rufus, "it is the town, my dear boy, that you must cultivate. That is the light in which to live!" They passed their existence on the edge of nervous collapse. The deportment expected of a Roman citizen was, as I have said, governed by the traditional rule of dignity, or *gravitas*. In his *De Officiis,* Cicero has much to say about the manners expected of a young gentleman. He should show respect for old age, rise in the presence of magistrates, distinguish between a fellow citizen and a foreigner, and adopt a different manner towards aliens, according as to whether they have come to Rome in a private or an official capacity. Unlike the Athenian Kalos Kagathos, the Roman need not worry too much about his personal appearance.

"We ought," says Cicero, "to regard physical beauty as the attribute of women and dignity as the attribute of men." A gentleman, therefore, should never sing in the street, should never dance in public ("unless he be drunk or mad"), should not display his knowledge of the Greek language in the presence of those less educated than himself, and should observe propriety "in standing, in walking, in sitting, in lying down, in the movement of his features, in his gestures, and in the expression of his eyes." He should be careful as to his gait. If he hurries, he will get out of breath, which may distort his features and is in any case evidence of a lack of poise (*constantia*). At the same time the gentleman should be careful not to "saunter listlessly" as if he were but a super in some religious procession. He should avoid the affected manners so often inculcated by the gymnasium instructors; his clothes should be neat but never elaborate; he should be careful not to imitate the locution or gestures of any actor; and he should take sufficient exercise to keep his complexion clear and fresh, "since dignity of appearance is often improved by a good skin." Pliny contended also that regular exercise was good for the imagination.

The prohibition against dancing was not as absolute as Cicero implies.

"Scipio," writes Seneca, "would move his splendid martial frame to music, not of course with the lascivious wriggles that are in fashion today (and our young men even when they walk seem to squirm with the voluptuousness of women), but in the virile style in which men of old were wont to dance at festivals or at sport meetings, risking no loss of dignity, even if their enemies happened to be there."

In the sturdiest days of the Republic, Romans washed their arms and legs daily, but had a steam bath only on market days, namely one day in nine. Cato contended that no boy should be given a daily bath and was pleased by the fact that Scipio's bathroom was small and dank. Ovid, in his greasy little poem *The Art of Love,* advised young men not to rely too much upon cosmetics. "Phaedra," he writes, "loved Hippolytus who was not in the least well-groomed, and Adonis, a woodland boy, became the darling of Venus. It is by simple cleanliness that you should seek to attract; your skin should be tanned by exercise on the Campus; your toga ought to fit well and should be spotless; don't let your shoe-strap become twisted; keep your teeth clean and don't wear shoes too large for you; take care to have your hair trimmed and your shaving done by the best barber available; don't let your nails grow too long and keep them clean; pluck the hairs in your nostrils. . . . More than this is the business of strumpets and catamites."

Ovid, as his successor Gabriele d'Annunzio, was born in the Abruzzi, and should not perhaps be quoted in any book upon civility. It is, moreover, doubtful whether at his date even the most prim young men observed the cold bath plus brisk exercise rule. By then both private and public baths had increased in splendor and the hair of the patricians became caked with oil of saffron and other heavy scents. Until the age of Hadrian, who owing to a scar on his face reintroduced the beard into polite society, the Romans shaved closely and cut their hair fairly short. The barbers, we learn from Horace, were often unequal to their task. As at Athens, it was regarded as effeminate to scratch one's head with the forefinger.

The Roman dandy was satirized by Martial in his portrait of Cotilus, the "*bellus homo.*" He curled his hair, he scented himself with cinnamon and balsam, he was an authority on who was related to whom, he loved gossiping with smart women, and he would hum little snatches from Spanish or Egyptian tunes.

In their discourse with each other the Roman Patricians, as befitted men of curule rank, were sedate and solemn. Yet apart from the accustomed courtesy of educated intercourse, they were inclined to indulge over much in what they called *blanditia,* which implied something more than our word "affability" and included an element of deliberate flattery. Conversely, in their forensic and political speeches, they resorted to a violence of invective (*vituperatio*) such as to our minds would have marred the dignity of justice and sullied the amenity of debate. Yet Cicero would have explained to us that *vituperatio* was nothing more than a conventional rhetorical device which was not taken seriously by any of those who practiced it on the rostra or in the Curia.

We are so accustomed to think of Lucullan luxury, or the orgies of Elagabalus, of Juvenal's line about the undigested peacock, that we fail sometimes to remember that the life of the ordinary Roman citizen, say in 50 BCE, was still simple and austere. Thus Atticus spent only £60. o a month on his kitchen expenses, and Cicero records that if one dined with him one must expect badly-cooked vegetables served on a splendid plate. In the old days the family would gather for meals in the atrium, the father reclining on a couch, the mother seated in a chair beside him, the children ranged at the table on stools, and the house slaves at a separate table at the end. This ancient mode was succeeded by the Greek custom of the triclinium, accommodating nine people round the table. If more guests were invited, further tables were arranged for them. There was no table cloth, but each guest brought his own napkin with him which he used as a bib. They wore evening dress in the Greek style, called a Synthesis. The meats were prepared by a skilled carver and handed to the guests on plates. The guests ate with their fingers, but there were two sorts of spoon, one of which was probably furnished with a prong for extracting shellfish. The old polenta of the days of Cato the elder had been succeeded by all manner of exotic foods. Oysters were imported from Richborough, fattened in the Lucrine lake, and then eaten with a special kind of bread. *Pâté de foie gras* was manufactured from geese stuffed for weeks on figs and dates. Wild boar was regarded as a great delicacy, and turbot and sturgeon were also obtained. For wines they had the amber-colored Falernian and the *vin rosé* of Veii; Caecuban of a good vintage was highly esteemed, and Augustus set the fashion for drinking Setinian from the hills above the Pomptine marshes. It was not considered fitting in any respectable house to get drunk at meals. Cicero would have condemned such a solecism as vulgar, or what he called "*amorphos,*" and those who returned from parties shouting through the streets were to his mind "much lacking in civility" (*multum ab humanitate discrepant*). Yet we need not suppose that the parties given by Clodia or Caelius were in any way frugal or grim.

It was a gross and braggart society when men matured in early boyhood and lived short and violent lives. The contributions made by Rome to world civilization are of eternal value; but they were based, not on gentle arts, but on massive achievements (*quanta rerum moles!*) in war, engineering, administration and jurisprudence. It is difficult to contend that any doctrine of how to live fastidiously descends to us directly from the Roman occupation. Their theory of action lacked the brightness of the Greek mind, or the delicacy of later revelations. It should not be, however, by their huge buccaneer types, not by Mark Antony or Crassus, nor by the crapulence of Plautus and Martial, or the slick garrulity of Ovid, that we should assess their taste. It is more comforting to recall the picture of dear Horace, lingering in his arbor after sunset while the scent of box, myrtle and pennyroyal was still warm around him, listening to the freshets swollen by spring rain splashing through the orchard on their way down to the Digentia. And to cherish always the memory of Virgil (*o anima cortese mantovana!*) and his naturally Christian soul.

Chapter 5

The Goths

The patricians of the Republic were under the Empire succeeded by foreigners and freedmen—With the decay of Roman manners the vices of cruelty and gluttony became prominent—The early Christians not interested in civility—They distrusted scholarship and beauty—They did little to mitigate contemporary cruelty or to furnish an example of tolerance—Their doctrine of temperance became exaggerated into mortification of the flesh—They were more disliked by the common people than they were by the officials—The educated Roman regarded them as obstinate and tiresome, whereas the urban mobs assailed them with hatred and fear—Reasons for their unpopularity—Early legends about the Christians—Their pharisaism and exclusiveness—Their puritanism and derision of contemporary pleasures—St. Augustine as the conciliator of the ancient philosophy with the modern revelation—The coming of the barbarians—Sidonius Apollinaris—The survival of Latin among the wandering scholars and the clerics—Illiteracy in the Dark Ages—No recognizable type of civility produced by the Byzantines—A lyric of Rufinus.

One

FTER THE FALL of the Republic, the Roman
Empire ceased quickly to be Roman. The
Emperors of the Julian-Claudian line—
Tiberius, Caligula, Claudius and Nero—succeeded,
within the fifty years that followed the death of
Augustus, in destroying the old patrician caste and in
raising freedmen and foreigners to supreme positions
in the State. The predominance of the Quirites, even
of the Latins, faded into the past. It did not seem so
strange to the later Romans that men of alien origin
should inherit the powers and perform the sacerdotal
offices which the Julii had exercised almost by hereditary right. Vespasian was a Sabine; Trajan and Hadrian
were born in Andalusia; Septimius Severus was an
African whose native tongue was Punic; Elagabalus
was a Syrian, Claudius Gothicus an Albanian, Galerius a Bulgar, and Maximin a cowherd from Northern
Epirus who spoke with a strong Illyrian accent and
whose real name was Daia. The parents of the mighty
Diocletian had been slaves from Dalmatia serving in
the household of a Roman senator. Seneca, Martial
and Lucan were all of Spanish origin; Apuleius was an
African. As early as CE 96 Juvenal could lament that
it had ceased to be an advantage to be born and bred
in Latium. "Does it mean nothing at all today," he
wrote, "that I was nurtured on the berries of Aquinum
and in my childhood breathed the Aventine air?" And

Persius derided the facility with which a slave could now become a Roman citizen. "Oh men of little truth," he moaned, "do you suppose that you can create a Roman with a twirl of the finger?"

Rapidly the theory of *gravitas* declined; the patrician senator, being carried majestically amid a crowd of clients to the Curia, was succeeded by court favorites of foreign origin; power passed from the great families into the hands of the palace eunuchs. Precarious were the lives of these fleeting parasites: "men," writes Juvenal with his customary concision, "whom the Emperor despised, and on whose faces was imprinted the pallor of the august but terrifying friendship that they enjoyed."

As Oriental manners came to loosen the old republican discipline, two vices, to which the Romans were peculiarly prone, assumed disgusting prominence. The first was gluttony: the second cruelty. No people, not even the *ivrogne tudesque* of the Middle Ages, indulged in overeating as did the Romans of the Empire. The coarseness of their feeding wrapped their faculties in layers of lard. Imagination, which had never been their liveliest gift, became inert: their deportment and their dignity decayed: as generation succeeded generation they ceased to strive for liberty even as their literature and their art became uncreative; such shapes of civility as they had achieved in the days of Cicero—and they were by no means despicable—were buried under mounds of food.

Their cruelty, both to human beings and to animals, became increasingly atrocious. In the days of the Republic a circus audience had been shocked by a massacre of elephants which Pompey staged. From southern Morocco he imported Gaetulian toughs, who had been trained to throw javelins at the animals, aiming at their eyes. The ensuing butchery was incompetent and slow: the blood cascaded down the legs of the elephants, who raised their trunks and trumpeted in pain. The spectators rose in their seats and clamored that the show be broken off. Cicero, commenting on this episode, remarked that the unpleasant spectacle had aroused a curious sense of pity "as if the animals possessed something in common with human beings." In imperial times the nerves of the circus audiences became less sensitive. They much enjoyed watching naked men and women being slowly mauled by beasts.

Less horrible, although almost equally unsympathetic, was the pleasure derived, even by educated Romans, from watching performing animals. Martial again and again refers with admiration to some trainer who had taught lions to hold live hares in their mouths without hurting them. In Egypt baboons were patiently educated to distinguish hieroglyphs. And even the fierce but tender Juvenal was much amused, strolling one afternoon along an outer boulevard, to see a monkey dressed in cuirass and helmet, mounted on a goat, and throwing little darts at the passersby. Elephants were trained to walk on tightropes, or to dance the pyrrhic in a mock lascivious quadrille. It is wrong to oblige animals to imitate the gestures of human beings, or to perform actions unsuited to their nature. Enjoyment of such performances indicates a low standard of civility.

Although the Greeks were devoid of natural compassion, they had the taste not to relish cruelty for cruelty's sake. There is an agreeable story told by Lucian and dating from the middle of the second century. The municipality of Athens proposed to stage a gladiatorial combat in the theater of Herodes Atticus which had just been completed. The project was defeated by the Cynic, Demonax of Cyprus. "Oh men of Athens," he exclaimed, "you must first pull down your altar of pity!" (Τοῦ Ἐλέου τὸν βωμὸν).

The show did not take place.

Two

It would be pleasing to record that it was the advent of Christianity, with its precepts of brotherly love and personal self-denial, which brought refinement to the ancient world. Such a thesis is not tenable. However excellent may have been the influence exercised by the early Christians upon human ethics, their effect upon manners was bad.

The conviction of the imminence of a Second Coming, when they would all be placed on curule chairs to judge their enemies, was so compulsive that they ceased to pay attention to such patterns of behavior as might be woven here on earth. "It was not in this world," writes Gibbon, "that the primitive Christians were desirous of making themselves either agreeable or useful." They were in fact deliberately rude.

It was not the lusts of the flesh only that they denounced: they condemned all pleasures derived through the senses and even the happy pride that comes from intellectual effort. To the ancient philosophers, with the exception of the Cynics, virtue was knowledge, and therefore something implying education and a certain standard of mental equipment. They would have agreed with Socrates that no man could be civilized or wholly virtuous unless he were intelligent and instructed, a necessity that implied opportunities for leisure. Even the most progressive thinkers of the ancient world would have assumed that "excellence" could not be fully attained by the manual worker or the slave.

The early Christians took a different view. They taught that the good life was independent of such worldly advantages as birth, riches or education. They familiarized the world with the idea that good manners were not the exclusive formulas of elegant society, but were the expression of average unselfishness and tact. Yet in thus democratizing civility, they deprived it of some important elements. In overemphasizing the distinction between the soul and the body, between the spiritual and the material, they underestimated intellectual and aesthetic values. Even so great a genius as St. Augustine could warn his disciples against the pleasure derived from the enjoyment of beautiful forms or colors and could question the necessity of "the vain and curious desire for learning." Even so massive a thinker as St. Thomas Aquinas could write: "To strive after knowledge is sin, if it be knowledge other than of God."

Lesser men would insist that beauty, which to the Greeks had been the abiding source of inspiration, was no more than the most subtle of the devil's lures. Tertullian could go so far as to contend that Christ himself cannot have been a handsome man: "*adeo nec humanae honestatis corpus fuit.*" The reaction, inevitable though it was, against the hyper-aestheticism of the pagans was driven too far. It was regarded as commendable that St. Martin should have discarded the shining helmet and the great white cloak of the Imperial Guard, and should ride on a donkey through Touraine pulling down village shrines and smashing with his own hands the little statues of Mercury or Pomona. Iconoclasm in any form is the antithesis of civility.

It is sad also to observe that the attitude of the early Christians towards the two great vices of the age—the vice of cruelty and the vice of gluttony—was too sectarian and esoteric to be influential. It was the pagan Juvenal, and not any contemporary Christian, who denounced the desire for vengeance as the sign of a mean character. It was he who, in his fifteenth satire, could express this truly Christian idea: "When nature," he wrote, "gave to man the gift of tears, she meant him to be gentle and to cultivate the virtue of compassion, which is our finest quality (*haec nostri pars optima sensus*)." Cicero who, although terribly nervous, was on the whole a good man, would scarcely have understood such a sentiment. The two Catos would have regarded it as decadent and lacking in *gravitas*.

Conversely, the Christian Tertullian failed to realize that public cruelty as practiced under the Empire was a slur upon human society. In his jaunty baboo Latin he denounces theatrical performances as liable to tempt men and women to indulge too freely in the pleasures of imagination and to attach too much attention to the charming vicissitudes of life upon this earth. It is the theater, rather than the amphitheater, that arouses his indignation: in his *De Spectaculis* he admittedly looks forward to the day when he would himself be seated in the circus watching the magistrates of the Roman Empire "melting in flames far fiercer than any that they kindled in their rage against the Christians." The precept recommended by the Cynics and the gospel that we must forgive our enemies, was evidently not among those which this vituperative Carthaginian had absorbed.

Nor could it be argued that the early Christians furnished their pagan contemporaries with any shining examples of tolerance or forgivingness. They behaved with the utmost ferocity towards their own sectarians and towards those infidels who later fell within their power. Their persecution of those who disagreed with them was fiercer than any which Julian the Apostate displayed. His repression was mild or *blanda:* their internecine quarrels were violent and rough. They seem to have lost a while the gentleness of their founder and to have forgotten St. Paul's superb rhapsody on charity, or his tremendous sentence: "Above all things, Love, which is the bond of perfectness."

Their theory of sin, their doctrine of temperance, ought also to have had some effect upon the carnality and gluttony of the age. Yet here again extremism intervened to mar their teaching. Austerity was expanded into asceticism, which in its turn degenerated into mortification of the flesh, with its attendant barbarisms and hysteria. The world was called upon to witness and admire the self-mutilation of Origen, the unsocial conduct of the desert Fathers, and the truly ridiculous vigil of Simeon Stylites.

It was thus not the Christians who refined the coarseness of the Empire so much as the later schools of pagan philosophy. It was the Cynic preacher, Demetrius of Sunium, who impressed upon his contemporaries the sadness of self-indulgence and the joy that comes from abnegation. It was Mithraism which first aroused a personal conscience and enabled men to see that sin was a perpetual enemy, and not, as the happy Greeks supposed, merely an accident, a sideslip, a bad shot, a ἁμάρτημα. It was Seneca who taught them that "you must live for others if you wish to live for yourself," and who preached the doctrine of an immanent God. It was Epictetus who was always lecturing about "this paltry body" and the "higher freedom" that came from concentration on the beauties of the soul. The spiritual weariness, the *taedium vitae,* that followed on the loss of the old liberty and religion, was at first filled, not by the sublimity of pure Christian doctrine, but by the later Stoics, the neo-Pythagoreans, the neo-Platonists, the cults of Cybele and Attis, and all manner of Oriental mysteries. It was these pagans who taught that the individual owed a duty, not to the Emperor only, but to all mankind; that it must be in his own interior conscience that he must cultivate the sentiments of affection, trustfulness and tolerance. The Christian doctrine was not at first recognized by the Government as subversive. It was the pagan philosophers who, in preaching individual responsibility, were regarded as the enemies of the established order. It is therefore not surprising that Domitian, who was a most suspicious man, should have sent these sophists bundling back to Prevesa and Chios, to Corinth and to Rhodes.

Three

We were given the impression when at school, and even at the University, that the persecution of the Christians was due to the disquiet they aroused in the minds of the Roman authorities by their egalitarian theories and their belief in social justice. Yet what is so strange is that it was not so much fear, or even uneasiness, that the early Christians aroused, as irritation. Nor did they suffer nearly as much from official repression as from popular dislike. The causes of this unpopularity help to explain why it took so many centuries before the humanizing force of Christianity could change the conduct of mankind.

The official persecution was spasmodic and sporadic rather than general or continuous. It was by the common people, whose status they were destined to enhance, that the early Christians were most hated and feared. It was not the magistrates who dragged the aged Polycarp into the arena; it was the Smyrna mob. "There are none," wrote Tertullian, "more apt to clamor for the death of Christians than the common herd."

Nero, it is true, behaved towards the new sect with sudden savagery. Domitian also indulged in a policy of persecution, as did Decius. But most of the Emperors were tolerant and even friendly. There exists a letter from Trajan to the younger Pliny, at the time Governor of Bithynia, telling him to pay no attention to anonymous denunciations and not to indulge in any witch hunting against the Christians: "*conquirendi non sunt.*" It was the philosopher-king Marcus Aurelius who was one of the few Emperors to display towards them irrational prejudices, objecting to what he called "their obstinate fanaticism." It was he who allowed his friend Junius Rusticus, prefect of Rome, to execute Justin Martyr and his companions; it is probably also that the *pogrom* that took place during his reign at Lyons was due to the impression that it would meet with his approval. Diocletian again, under the influence of Galerius, and much encouraged by the oracle of Apollo at Miletus, made a determined endeavor to extirpate the new religion; but by then the Church had become so widespread and so powerful that the persecution failed.

The attitude of the average Roman official or magistrate throughout the first three centuries was one of slightly contemptuous tolerance; it was in accordance with the general policy of ignoring local sects, provided that their practices were not either subversive or inhumane. At the same time the habits of the Galileans were in some manner peculiarly obnoxious to the educated Roman mind. Tacitus, in referring to them, employs the violent word "*exitiabilis,*" or "deadly," and Suetonius described them as "this depraved sect." The word that figures most frequently in official denunciations is the word "*obstinatio.*" The Roman official regarded it as irrational and tiresome that the early Christians should face death rather than throw a single handful of incense into the brazier that spluttered below the statue of the Emperor. In vain did they reply that they were perfectly ready to pray to their own God for the health and prosperity of the Emperor, but that to burn incense in front of an image would be to commit the sin of "idolatry," which, according to the Pauline dogma, was at that date regarded as a mortal sin. Nor did the heroism with which the early Christians would face death and torture make at all a favorable impression upon the Roman mind. Epictetus himself sneered at this heroism of the Galileans as a form of "madness" or "conditioning." Marcus Aurelius wrote that we should all train ourselves to face death with courage, "but on rational grounds and not in a spirit of utter obstinacy, as do the Christians." It is indeed a common experience that colonial administrators tend to dismiss as hysterical, and therefore unimportant, movements that are created by the fusion of old mysteries with new spiritual passion.

What is more difficult to explain is the hatred aroused by the Christians among the common people. It is evident that they were for long identified with the Jews ("that accursed race" as Seneca called them) who, although powerful in the towns, were universally distrusted and disliked. The early Christians met in secret and in the dark hours before dawn. They were supposed to kidnap and devour Roman babies and to commit incest among themselves. It was rumored that they worshipped a god with the head of a donkey or a pig. One of the strangest quirks of history is that the first of many pictorial representations of the crucifixion is a *graffito* scratched by some private soldier on the wall of his barrack-dormitory on the Palatine. It is a crude sketch of a man with the head of an ass suspended on a cross. Underneath are scribbled the derisive words: "Alexandros worships his god."

Such misconceptions fail to explain the intense personal animosity which the early Christians aroused. After all, the Egyptians worshipped gods with the features of dogs, birds and even cats and crocodiles, yet their practices occasioned mirth rather than rancor. The prejudice against the Galileans was not due to their doctrine or their form of worship so much as to their bad manners. It was their attitude towards the non-elect that irritated people: not their faith.

There was in the first place their exclusiveness; their habit of meeting together in private conclaves; the way they addressed each other as "brother" or "sister" when in no way related. In the second place they adopted a sanctimonious manner, a self-satisfied expression, and indicated in their gait the superiority of their morals. Even thus, in the early days, could the converts to Buchmanism be recognized by the manner in which they would prance along the Tottenham Court Road; even thus would young commissars of satellite republics beam with self-satisfaction when confronted by those to whom the light had not been vouchsafed. In the third place the early Christians committed the gross impoliteness of overtly disapproving of the tastes and amusements of their fellow citizens. Tacitus, in a famous passage, reproves them for their "hatred of the human race;" and they were accused of "marring the felicity of the age." It was not merely that they disapproved of the morals of their fellow subjects, of their homosexuality and other adulteries, of their lax attitude towards the sacrament of marriage, or the importance they attached to food, clothes, perfumes and cleanliness. It was also that they made no endeavor at all to conceal their contempt for the dramatic performances, the sports and race meetings, which constituted the comparatively harmless pleasures, not of the Emperors only, but of the common man. Such overt disdain for the tastes and amusements of one's contemporaries has never made for personal popularity; nor is it attuned to the principles of civility. It was not by any charm of manner that the Christians succeeded, within three centuries, in altering the conscience of this world. It was rather that they perfected the conception of holiness and brought moral enthusiasm to relieve the *taedium vitae* of their age.

It is not until we reach St. Augustine that we find the intellectual ideals of the ancients fused with the new Christian conception of personal piety. Although he also taught that felicity could be achieved only in the life after death, yet he contended that it should be possible to secure partial happiness even on this earth. Although he also believed in spiritual abasement, and held that "a man should be broken by God for his own salvation," yet he insisted always that it was love, or charity, that was the essential clue to perfection. "Love," he wrote, "is the one good that is inexhaustible, even if the whole of mankind be pursuing it at the same time. From this commandment derive the duties of human society." Although, as I have said, he also decried aesthetic pleasures, and "the delight in beautiful or varied forms, in shining or agreeable colors," yet he never taught that holiness necessitated complete severance from the world. "How," he wrote, "could the City of God have a beginning, or be developed, or fulfill its destiny, if the life of the saints were not a social life? (*si non esset socialis vita sanctorum?*)" Even in St. Augustine's incidental precepts we can detect the high importance he attached to standards of civility. Empty laughter was to him anathema; even practical jokes he described as no more defensible than "acts of demons." Here we find the humble disciple and the superb intellectual in balanced union.

And thus, when we read the lives of the early saints and martyrs, when we become wearied by the uniformity of their sufferings and miracles, or distressed by their indifference to all mundane politeness, the tremendous voice of St. Augustine echoes like a bell tolling across Libyan seas, announcing that, as twilight settled on the pagan world, a new light had been kindled which would not be quenched.

A hundred years later the darkness set in. In 475 Romulus Augustulus, the last Emperor to rule in Rome, was deposed by the German Odoacer. Already the Goths and the Franks had occupied Gaul and Theodoric the Visigoth had established his Court at Bordeaux. To him came the Gallo-Roman, Sidonius Apollinaris, who, although Christian, could never rid himself of his passion for the manners and language of the *togati*. Horrible to his eyes were the barbarians who flocked to the palace of Theodoric. There, all around him, were the rude Germans, the Sigambrians, with matted hair, and—far the worst of all—"the blue-eyed Saxons, lords of the sea." Sidonius Apollinaris lived on at Clermont-Ferrand to see Rome crumble, and his own friends, with whom he had been wont to exchange neat epigrams in the old language and metres, allowing their children to be taught the German tongue. With despair he would watch the young princelings of the Visigoths clattering through the streets of Clermont-Ferrand, with heavy gold incrustations on their baldrics and flaming red mantles streaming out behind.

"How can I," he wrote, "compose an ode to Venus when I live among long haired hordes, being obliged to hear German spoken all around me, and having with a wry face to praise the songs of sottish Burgundians who spread rancid butter on their hair?"

> *Inter crinigeras situm catervas*
> *Et Germanica verba sustinentem,*
> *Laudantem tetrico subinde vultu,*
> *Quod Burgundio cantat esculentus,*
> *Infundens acido comam butyro?*

It is not unfitting that we should enter the Dark Ages, with our ears throbbing to the sound of guttural voices and in our nostrils the stench of putrid cheese.

Four

I am aware that it is today considered old fashionable to use the epithet "dark" as applying to the thousand years that stretch between 475 and 1453. It is true that the Roman civilizations of Gaul, Italy and Africa to some extent assimilated their rude invaders and that within two centuries the Germanic dialects had declined. It is true that Rome bequeathed to her conquerors her system of law and therefore something of her value. It is true that the *clerici vagantes,* the scholar gypsies, the "Wandering Scholars" of Helen Waddell's entrancing study, did much to "keep the imagination of Europe alive" and to preserve the old tradition of lyric poetry until it could be renovated and naturalized by the jongleurs and the troubadours. It is true that in the eighth century Charlemagne, King of the Franks, strove to introduce lay education into his dominions and even went so far as to have his daughters taught to read and write. Above all is it true that the Church adopted Latin as its official language and rendered it the medium of communication between the clerks and clerics of every European land.

Yet the fact remains that, at least until the advent of chivalry, the manners of these men were brutish and untaught. The very idea of civility faded from the western mind. The Gothic princelings whose noise and dirtiness had offended the sensibility of Sidonius Apollinaris remained models of refinement for more than five hundred years. It does not seem to me either ignorant or prejudiced to describe as "dark" a millennium from which gentleness and light were excluded.

It was in 445 that the Emperor Palestinian III recognized the Bishop of Rome (who until then had been no more than *primus inter pares*) as head of the visible Church. The powerful organization and discipline that was thereafter constructed and imposed did much to establish ecclesiastical authority and moral rules. But they did little to inculcate into laymen a standard of scholarship or a code of civility. The Church was always inclined to regard lay learning as a mundane lure. Practically all instruction, except in Italy, was in the hands of ecclesiastics: Charlemagne's endeavor to introduce a system of lay education did not survive his death. In theory, the Church taught boys the seven liberal arts, namely grammar, rhetoric, dialectics, arithmetic, geometry, music and astronomy. In practice, this education was confined to those who were ill-attuned to the exercises of war or sport and who sought to conceal their timidity or ineptitude by becoming intellectuals or clerics. The governing classes, even the courtiers, of the time were almost wholly illiterate. The Emperor Otto I did not learn to read until the advance of age rendered physical exercise unenjoyable: such leading German poets as Wolfram von Eschenbach and Ulrich von Lichtenstein were unable to read or write their own, or any other, language. Until the twelfth century, when the rules of chivalry produced an original type of civility, there existed in western Europe practically no culture at all.

It may be said that the lamp of letters, although quenched in Italy, in Gaul, even in North Africa, still flickered on among the dim mosaics of Constantinople; and that any examination of types of civility should include at least one portrait of the ideal gentleman of Byzantium. The difficulty is that, although we know something about the Emperors and Empresses, the generals, the bishops, the saints, the eunuchs and the martyrs of the Eastern Empire, we know practically nothing at all about the ordinary citizens and scholars whose villas and gardens clustered upon the slopes of Galata and Pera, above the Golden Horn. Our knowledge, as Mr. Stephen Runciman has pertinently warned us, is incomplete.

During the years I spent in Constantinople, I devoted time to the study of Byzantine history. I read with interest the works of M. Charles Diehl and Dr. van Millingen: in later years the infectious taste of Robert Byron inspired me with a renewed respect for the architecture of the Byzantines and the sombre significance of their art. From the walls, above which once towered the high palace of Blachernae, I would gaze upon the dull downs of Thrace, even as all those Manuels and Basils had gazed; or from Theodora's own apartments on the beach I would look across the flat Marmora, past Bulwer's island, to where Olympus shimmered above the Bithynian hills. Yet so obtuse was I, that I never came to see that the Byzantines had ever built very differently, or carved and painted very differently, in the course of the eleven hundred years that stretch between May 11, 330 and May 30,1453. Nor did their history become more real to me than would a frieze of repetitive and hierophantic figures making identical gestures of supplication and distress. Yet we are told that from this city, on May 30, 1453, a bright river of taste and enlightenment cascaded suddenly upon the dark western world.

No Roman of the age of Cicero, no Hellene of fifth-century Alexandria, would have recognized even a remote descendant in the bearded, brocaded, Byzantine, who believed so readily in demons and leprechauns and who spoke such curious Greek. Even in the days of Juvenal the toga was worn mainly at funerals; by the fifth century the Byzantines had discarded it entirely. Its place was taken by the pallium and the dalmatic which were richly embroidered. When, as early as 356, the Emperor Constantine II entered Rome, his triumphal robe was so stiff with brocade and jewels that he was obliged to stand motionless as an idol in his car. Silks were introduced from the East and St. John Chrysostom describes the Emperor Arcadius wearing a silk pallium embroidered with golden dragons. When they went to court, the Byzantine nobles put on "robes of honor" even as Persians today. These overcoats were called "caramangia," were kept by the nobles in the cloakroom of the palace, and are supposed to

have been copied from the dresses of the Chinese mandarins. In later centuries the upper classes at Constantinople wore peaked hats edged with fur or enormous
turbans. Shaving was regarded as a western practice
and therefore vulgar. The Palaeologoi introduced the
fashion for men to paint their cheeks and lips vermil-
ion and to dye their hair and beards an auburn shade.
Cicero, or St. Augustine, would have regarded such
habits with distaste.

The ceremonial imposed upon the Emperors was
elaborate indeed. Constantine Porphyrogenitus wrote
a treatise on the subject in which he established, for the
instruction of his successors, the order of precedence
and the route to be followed on all official occasions. If
we are to believe Bishop Luitprand of Cremona, who
went on a diplomatic mission to Nicephorus Phocas
in the tenth century, there was something meretricious
about Byzantine ceremony. In order that foreigners
might be impressed by the glamour and mystery of
the Emperor, the golden lions that flanked his throne
bellowed aloud, the mechanical birds above him burst
into song, and the throne itself was elevated like a lift
by machinery, so that the foreign ambassador, on rising from his kowtow or προσκυνήσις observed that in
the interval the Emperor had risen many feet miracu-
lously into the air.

The Empress possessed her own apartments, into
which the Emperor was not allowed to penetrate,
although she herself could visit his council chamber

whenever she wished. Thus when the Empress Theodora died and Justinian entered her quarters for the
first time, he discovered that the expatriarch Anthimus
had been hiding there for the last twelve years. The
palace was connected by a series of dark blue passages
with the royal box, or Cathisma, in the hippodrome.
Arrayed in their stiff vestments, the imperial couple
could process along these murky corridors, emerging
suddenly into the blaze of the arena and the plaudits
or execrations of 40,000 of their subjects. Heavy is the
curtain of unreality that hangs between our own experience and the ritual of the Byzantine court.

I cannot disagree with Gibbon that the eleven hundred years of Byzantine history give us little more than
"a tedious and uniform tale of weakness and misery."

"The subjects of the Byzantine Empire," he writes,
"who assume and dishonor the names both of Greeks
and Romans, present a dead uniformity of abject vices,
which are neither softened by the weakness of humanity, nor animated by the vigor of memorable crimes."

Yet something must have survived. Across all those
centuries of sacerdotal pomp; through all the clouds of
superstition, sorcery, fanaticism and lust; through the
yells of the contending factions in the hippodrome,
there pierces suddenly an echo of the old anthology, a
voice from a forgotten lyric past. I entirely agree with
Maurice Baring that Rufinus was a clerk in the Foreign
Office, the *skrinion barbarôn,* at Constantinople and
that it was when his colleagues in the department had

all gone off to the races that he dashed out into the local Downing Street and purchased the full basket of a passing vendor:

> I send you, Rhodocleia, this garland which with my own hands I have made from lovely flowers. Lilies are here, and the dewy anemone, and the gentle narcissus and purple violet. Wear this garland and let it teach you to be less conceited. The flowers will fade and so will you.
>
> πέμπω σοί Ῥοδόκλεια τόδε στέφος
> ἄηθεσι καλοῖς.

Although we can find in the liturgical formalism of Byzantium a ceremonial as artificial and as rigid as that of the Li-Chi, those eleven centuries of eastern culture produced luxury rather than civilization, etiquette rather than manners. It may well be that our ignorance of the actions and ideas of the average Byzantine squire, merchant, or scholar induces us to exaggerate the static nature of that civilization and to see in their deportment something uniformly stylized and erect. Yet the fact remains that history does not illumine, and imagination must hesitate to invent, any type of Byzantine civility. In the place of living men and women, possessing authentic, and therefore ever changing, conceptions of conduct, we see effigies only, with palms opened in identical supplication, staring back at us with huge dark eyes.

Chapter 6

Le Fin Amour

Six hundred years of twilight—The coming of chivalry—In France, although not so much in England, the knights constitute an exclusive elite—The cosmopolitanism of the knightly caste—The virtues of chivalry—Liberality—Courtesy—Lavishness—Good faith—Gaiety—Glory—Honor—The service of love—The *fin amour*—The defects of chivalry—Its unreality—It makes no provision for old age—Its illiteracy—It ignores the lower classes—Its general brutality—Yet it did leave a tradition of chivalrous conduct—Its decline—The knight becomes a knight errant or highwayman—How the customs of chivalry affected manners—The page, the squire and the accolade—Cleanliness and table manners—Demeanor—The *menie* of Gaston de Foix.

One

IT WAS IN 475, as I have said, that Odoacer the barbarian deposed Romulus Augustulus, the last Emperor to rule in Rome. However much the Levantines of

Constantinople may have pretended to preserve the humanist tradition of Athens, the continuity and inspiration of the pagan world was shattered, almost for ever. Men clad in skins stewed goats' flesh upon the Rostra, and pigs rootled amid the ruins of Cicero's library or even in that simple pergola where Horace—his sore eyes smeared with blue ointment—would linger in the company of Virgil as the evening fell:

> *O noblesse! o beauté simple et vraie! idées dont le culte signifie raison et sagesse, toi dont le temple est une leçon éternelle de conscience et de sincérité! . . . Si tu savais combien il est devenu difficile de te servir! Toute noblesse a disparu. Les Scythes ont conquis le monde. De pesants Hyperboréens appellent légers ceux qui te servent. Une pambéotie redoutable, une ligue de toutes les sottises, étend sur le monde un couvercle de plomb, sous lequel on étouffe. . . .*

In such despairing terms did Ernest Renan, fourteen hundred years later, address the great goddess whose helmet from her pedestal had flashed fire across the Saronic Gulf, and whose spear was as a beacon, guiding fishermen struggling from Cythnos or Seriphos towards the protecting cliff of Sunium. *Les Scythes ont conquis le monde.* It was six hundred years after the fall of Rome that a new ordering of society, and with it a new and valuable type of civility, began slowly to emerge.

The term "chivalry" has been defined by Warre Cornish as "a body of sentiment and practice, of law and custom, which prevailed among the dominant classes of a great part of Europe between the eleventh and the sixteenth centuries." This new and highly complicated pattern of behavior reached its full perfection between 1250 and 1350, where after it declined. Many of the rules of chivalry were based on conditions that have long since ceased to exist and possess no more than an antiquarian interest: but others, and notably the conception of "chivalrous" or "knightly conduct," are operative today. The ideal of human behavior evolved by the knights of the Middle Ages contained many creative improvements on the standards advocated by the Greeks, the Romans or the early Christians. However wide may have been the gap between their theory and their practice, these warriors and their attendant squires and poets did discover a new range of sensibility and did raise to the status of virtues certain humane feelings and actions which had until then been regarded as unimportant or even unmanly. They invented the theory of what the Americans call "service"; and they gave a lyrical lightness to human pleasure.

It is unnecessary to examine the origins of chivalry, its connection with the feudal system of land tenure, or the institution of such military orders as the Hospitallers, the Teutonic Knights and the Knights Templars. It is evidently incorrect to assume that the knights of the Middle Ages were in any way the descendants of the Roman *equites* or that the dubbing of an esquire bore any relation to the assumption by the young Roman of the *toga virilis*. It is now generally accepted that the order of chivalry developed from the horsemen who from the eighth century onwards played an important part in the levies of the Teutonic tribes. Two facts in the early development of knighthood are, however, of interest in that they affected the conception of civility. Although in the early days there does not seem to have existed any social distinction between the man who fought on horseback and the man who fought on foot, the fact that it was more expensive to be a "*reiter*" or "*ritter*" soon rendered the cavalry a separate class possessing hereditary privileges and prejudices. Gradually the idea became established that only the son of a knight could, except in most unusual circumstances, receive the accolade: and all manner of shibboleths were devised to maintain the exclusiveness and segregation of the elite. In France, this caste system had become almost rigid by the end of the eleventh century. In England it never took full root, being regarded partly as a foreign importation, partly as an invention of the heralds, and partly as in itself ridiculous. Freeman goes so far as to describe the segregation of the knights from the middle and lower classes as "un-English"; nor would a Frenchman of the fifteenth century have approved of King Henry's address to his troops before Agincourt:

> He today that sheds his blood with me
> Shall be my brother; be he ne'er so vile
> This day shall gentle his condition

If class consciousness in England has even today a different tone from that which in France is regarded as inevitable, the difference may to no small extent be due to the circumstance that with us class distinctions never became absolute. The English, with their instinctive sense of proportion, have always recognized the comic aspect of stratification.

The second interesting feature in the development of chivalry was that, according as the knights became in their own countries sundered from other classes of the community, so did they become internationally more corporate. No age, not even the eighteenth century in western Europe, has ever created so cosmopolitan an elite. Chivalry devoted more attention to class than it did to nationality; the paladins, or general staff, of Charlemagne, for instance, were drawn from many different nations, being Welsh, Bavarian, Danish Frisian, Norman and English. Even before the first two crusades had come to weld Christendom into a spiritual unity, orders of chivalry in every country regarded themselves as akin. They possessed the same ideas and conventions; they were accustomed to continuous travel in foreign parts, and they possessed a common language in both Latin and French. Thus Chaucer's simple knight had visited Russia, Egypt, Spain, Armenia and the Baltic States:

> A knight there was and that a worthy man,
> That from the time that he first began
> To ryden out, he loved chivalrye
> Trouthe and honor, freedom and courteisye,
> Full worthy was he in his lord's warre,
> And therefore had he rydden (no man ferre)
> As well in Cristendom as hethenesse
> And ever honored for his worthinesses
> At Alisaundre he was when it was wonne,
> Ful ofte tyme he hadde the bord bigonne
> Aboven anne naciouns in Pruce,
> In Lettow had he reysed and in Ruce,
> No Cristen man so ofte of his degree
> In Gernade at the sege eke hadde he be,
> Of Algezir, and rydden in Belmayre
> At Lyeys was he and at Satalye,
> When they were wonne; and in
>   the Grete See. . . .

The whole travel-adventure of chivalry echoes for us in Milton's tremendous burst of rhetoric:

> And what resounds
> In fable or romance of Uther's son.
> Begirt with British or Armoric knights;
> And all who since, baptized or infidel,
> Jousted in Aspromont and Montalban,
> Damasco, or Morocco," or Trebizond,
> Or whom Biserta sent from Afric shore
> When Charlemain with all his peerage fell
> At Fontarabbia. . . .

Such *wanderlust,* such cosmopolitanism, distinguish the knights of the Middle Ages from any type of civility that mankind had hitherto evolved. There were other contributions that he made to human intercourse which render him no less phenomenal.

Two

The first crusade associated the prowess of the old warrior class with the teaching of the Church. The contact established between the descendants of Germanic marauders or Scandinavian pirates with the high civilization of the Moors and Saracens progressively diminished roughness and increased civility. *The preux chevalier* of the thirteenth century was a far more complex person than the *preux chevalier* of the eleventh century. Godfrey de Bouillon was doubtless heroic in his devotion and humility, but he was certainly more of a barbarian than Saint Louis. The gang leader, dressed in furs and living in a wooden house protected by ditch and palisade, was gradually replaced by the knight or noble, who had brought back from the East, not only the conception of fine castles of brick or stone, but also the velvets of Broussa and the silks of Damascus. The young adventurer who rode out from his rough home in Picardy or Poland upon an emprise inspired by religious idealism, coupled with a lively desire for personal loot and glory, returned after many years, much battered physically, but mentally and even spiritually enriched. It was this rare conjunction between piety and materialism, between atrocious egoism and selfless devotion, which created those exceptional states of mind that rendered possible the elaborate, and indeed fantastic, code of conduct which is known as chivalry.

The page who was destined to become a squire, the squire who was destined to become a knight, were inspired and instructed by secular lyrics and epics as well as by clerical manuals of conducts. On the one hand they knew by heart the great song of Roland, the *Chansons de Geste,* and the many lays and romances sung from castle to castle by the jongleurs and the troubadours. On the other hand they were taught the more peremptory precepts prescribed for them by religious writers. John of Salisbury, for instance, in his work entitled *Policraticus* which dates from 1150, insisted that the duties of a knight were "to defend the Church, to assail infidelity, to venerate the priesthood, to protect the poor from injuries, to pacify the province, and to pour out his blood for his brother."

More popular than the *Policraticus*—which, being written in Latin, was unintelligible to the military caste—were such manuals as Estienne de Fougères' *Livre de Manières,* or Ramon Lull's *Le Libre del orde de cauayleria.* The latter work, although composed in the Catalan dialect, was translated into French and English. It was printed by Caxton and presented to Richard III, "in the hope that the noble order of chivalry be hereafter better used and honored than it has been in late days passed." Ramon Lull's injunction was that the first duty of a knight was to defend the Church and that from this primary imperative should derive such secondary obligations as the protection of women and orphans, the preservation of order, and the extermination of criminals. He added the interesting recommendation that the perfect knight should be rich enough to maintain his place in society; and handsome enough not to provoke ridicule of his person.

A more comprehensive catalogue of the virtues and faculties expected of the perfect knight can be found in a poem by Raoul de Houdenc, written in about 1230, and entitled *Ailes de Prouesse.* In this poem the fourteen requirements are listed under two headings, namely Liberality and Courtesy. The seven virtues or duties comprehended under "Liberality" are courage, or *"prouesse,"* lavishness, charity, loyalty, spontaneity in giving, forgetfulness of benefits conferred, and hospitality. The seven duties comprehended under "Courtesy," are to honor the Church, to be humble, not to boast, to be gay always, to respect women, not to be malicious, and to devote oneself to the service of love.

The inclusions, as well as the omissions, of this catalogue are suggestive. It might be said that the jongleurs, being entirely dependent for their living on the hospitality of knights, placed too strong an emphasis on the virtue of lavishness. Yet other, and more independent writers, such as Chrétien de Troyes, also lauded this particular virtue. Chrétien de Troyes praises King Arthur for the fact that he distributed to his knights, "not cloth and rabbit skins only but also sables and brocades." The true knight must cultivate μεγαλοπρέπει or "magnificence." He must be not only generous merely, but actually extravagant and ostentatious in his hospitality and gifts. The troubadour, Bertran de Born, went so far as to suggest that generosity was a protection against old age, and that lavish gifts, especially those made to strolling minstrels, enabled a knight to prolong his youth:

E joves es quan estragatz dos.

Another distinctive feature of the civility admired during the later Middle Ages was a dislike of malice and a suspicion of those who made promises which they knew themselves unable to perform. "It is a mean thing," wrote Chrétien de Troyes, "to laugh at someone else and to make promises without fulfilling them. A gentleman ought not to undertake anything, or promise anything to another, which he is not able and willing to perform."

Vilenie est d'autrui gaber
Et de prometre sanz doner
Prodom ne se doit antremetre
De nule rien autrui prometre
Que doner ne lui puisse et vuelle.

A third—a most original and precious—quality expected of the perfect knight was that he should be gay. There was no *gravitas,* no puritan glumness, no murky inhibitions, about the age of chivalry. A knight was supposed to enjoy music, poetry and dancing, and to be an adept at "the gay science," "*le gay saber.*" It was considered bad form for a squire to be depressed, nor was he expected to exhibit melancholy, except when unfortunately in love. "*Jouyr loyalement de son estre*" was the essential motto of chivalry: there have been few finer devices in the whole history of civility. In place of the old Viking hilarity, the tough Teutonic guffaw, came the recognition that subtlety can give to lust or pleasure a more exquisite flavor:

> *A la joie appartient*
> *D'aimer moult finement.*

The lad, who as squire, accompanied the knight his father with the other pilgrims from Southwark to Canterbury, was a handsome and well-dressed young man who had distinguished himself already in "chivachye in Flaundres, in Artoys, and in Picardye." He wore an embroidered surcoat and sang songs all the way along the downs. He was incessantly in love, could read and write and even draw, was an excellent dancer and composed love songs. "He was as fresh as is the month of May." He was also modest:

> Courteys he was, lowly and serviceable
> And carf biform his fader at the table.

Among the fourteen virtues catalogued by Raoul de Houdenc there is no specific mention of what we call "sportsmanship" or "chivalrous conduct." This virtue was implicit in what they generally described as "courtesy." Thus Olivier in the *Chanson de Roland* is specially lauded for his moderation: "*Mielz valt me sure que ne fai estultie,*" "it is better to be moderate than excessive." There certainly existed the convention that a knight should treat other knights with civility, whatever their origin or race. When Gaydon placed two swords crosswise on the corpse of a man whom he had just decapitated, Charlemagne is represented as exclaiming: "Oh God! How courteous this duke is!" It is clear from the *Chansons de Geste* that it was regarded as bad form for a knight to assail an unarmed man or to fight two to one. Froissart lays it down as a principle that a captive should be treated with all consideration and that the ransom fixed for his release should not be beyond his known means. It is to be doubted whether such precepts, although applicable to tournaments, were ever respected on the battlefield. Infidel prisoners were generally massacred, and even Christian knights were tortured and thrown into pestilent dungeons until their ransom was paid. Philip d'Alsace, Count of Flanders, who was generally regarded as a pattern of chivalry, used to hide peasants in the fields armed with billhooks with which they pulled stunned knights off their horses. Yet the idea did exist, and was much celebrated in song and fable, that the perfect knight behaved generously to those with whom he fought.

There is no mention either in the Houdenc catalogue of "honor" or "glory." As the conception of feudal service weakened, the young knight would embark upon his travels, not in loyalty to his master, or to defend his fief, but to acquire booty. "He who needs to enrich himself," sang Bertran de Born, "must know how to steal well." In order to sublimate these unavowable motives the conception of *gloire* or "deeds of honor" was invented. It plays a larger part in the lays of the troubadours and in the *Chansons de Geste* than it ever played in actual life. The knights errant became in fact little more than highwaymen, each hunting in his own territory, and waiting at crossroads or on bridges to despoil the passerby. Yet the idea and inspiration of "glory" did certainly exist. A sly minstrel, such as the troubadour Blacas, might evade the obligations of the Crusade with a charming alibi:

> *Je ferai ma Pénitence*
> *Entre mer et Durance*
> *Auprès de mon manoir*

yet a member of the knightly class would have regarded himself as much shamed by any overt dereliction of duty. Froissart certainly believed that "glory" was one of the most serious of knightly motives and that for this reason it was the duty of the historian to record and celebrate chivalrous deeds. The idea of glory for glory's sake never pushed deep roots into the thick soil of the English character. Yet in France such words as "*gloire*" or "*panache*" possess even today a certain sentimental value. The inconvenience was that, as the centuries passed, young Frenchmen tended to confuse, as Julien Sorel confused, "*gloire*" with "*devoir*" and thereby to become "*avantageux.*"

Above all, the age of chivalry invented a conception of the "service of love" such, I am glad to say, as has never existed before or since. This elaborate, this exacting, this almost entirely artificial pattern of behavior, appears to me to have created a wholly false relationship between the sexes and to have been in practice an abominable wastage of time and emotion. Yet we are apt to underestimate the immense part played in the Middle Ages by symbolism and allegory. An age which could indulge ecstatically in the belief that the common daisy of the fields was the loveliest of nature's flowers could induce itself to believe anything. Their idea of the service of love must be considered in some detail.

Three

In the Middle Ages both the Church and the law assigned a low place to women: those addicted to scholasticism would, among other otiose arguments, dispute whether women could be said to possess souls. The Merovingians had not inherited the high domestic virtues attributed by Tacitus to the Germanic tribes: even Charlemagne, while not allowing his daughters to marry, encouraged them to have love affairs with his officers and officials. Concubinage was rife and in England in the thirteenth century there was an officer of the household known as Master of the Court Prostitutes whose salary was derived from the manor of Catteshall in Surrey. It was left to the poets to raise women from their degraded status.

The theory of "courtly love," or "*le fin amour*," was a French invention of the twelfth century and a highly idealized conception of the proper attitude to be adopted by a knight towards his lady. Typical of this romantic attitude was the *Cligès* of Chrétien de Troyes. It is a story of how the Count Alexander visits the court of King Arthur and accompanies him and the queen on a journey from Cornwall to Brittany. On the ship Count Alexander catches sight of the maiden Soredamours: he turns pale and shudders. Queen Guinevere, observing his condition, assumes that he is suffering from seasickness, although he has in fact been stricken by *le fin amour*. For three long months the squire and his lady conceal their passion for each other, only groaning loudly when in bed at night. In the end Queen Guinevere realizing their position, forces them to disclose their mutual passion: Count Alexander is knighted and the lovers are joined blissfully for ever after. This high-minded romance can be contrasted with the story of *Amis et Amiles,* written thirty years after the tale of *Cligès,* which described the love affair between Count Amiles and one of Charlemagne's daughters in terms of crude carnality.

It was the troubadours of Southern France who, flitting with their songs from court to court, from castle to castle, rendered the idealized conception of love, *le fin amour*, the dominant fashion. They exploited the exaltation generated by unrewarded yearning. They taught that such a love enhanced the *prouesse* of the warrior and that it could render even a man of low degree worthy of knighthood. The ladies were themselves not allowed to choose the squires who dedicated themselves to their service; it was in fact considered commendable if the knight had never addressed his lady, even if he had never seen her. A distant love, or *amor de lonh*, was viewed as the most exquisite of all such passions and *the princesse lointaine* became the ideal heroine of many a story and romance.

The page or squire living in a nobleman's castle was expected on reaching the age of puberty to select the object of his worship from among the ladies of the court. He became the vassal or liegeman of his chosen mistress, he often went through some ritual of dedication, and was expected to serve her without question for the rest of his life, even if his devotion were never rewarded or acknowledged, even if she exposed him to cruel tests or ridiculous ordeals. The idea was that a great gulf was fixed between the young man and the object of his worship, and that this gulf could be narrowed only by deeds of prowess and actions of renown. The lover must cultivate *courtoisie*, namely temperance and agreeable manners. It was in the service of his love that a man perfected his own nature. In no circumstances should he ever reproach his mistress for her cruelty; when separated from her he was expected neither to eat or sleep and to cry much at night. When in her presence, he should be struck dumb and tremble all over. Never should he mention to others even the slightest recompense that he might receive. If wearing his lady's favor he vanquished in a tournament he must present to her the armor and the warhorse of his vanquished opponent:

> Mais mon ami est bel et gent
> Quand il vais a tournoiement
> Et il abat un chevalier
> II me présente son destrier.

Thus does the egregious lady sing in the romance of *Flore et Blanchflor.* Nor was any woman expected to display gratitude for this senseless devotion. She must remain aloof, *impitoyable,* unemotional, displaying neither pity nor kindness, neither *merce* nor *chauzimen.* Only by remaining utterly cold and unattainable could she hope to maintain her lover in a constant state of nerves.

In course of time, this atrocious conception of love became part of the conventional conduct of every gentleman. It was assumed that there could be no "courtesy" without love and no love without "courtesy":

> Qu' Amors porte le gonfanon
> De cortoisie et la banière.

It is inhuman to suppose that the ladies celebrated by the troubadours and the jongleurs really displayed the foolish indifference, the utter conceit, which in these songs and romances are attributed to them. We know for a fact that they often, and quite early in the proceedings, surrendered to the passion in their champion's eyes. The idea of "*courtoisie*" cannot possibly have applied to male conduct only, and as the knights became more gentle, so also must their ladies have become less stilted and absurd. Civility is the most infectious of human habits, and it is evident that by the fourteenth century a woman who gave herself the airs of a *princesse lointaine* would have been thought affected: more domestic female manners became the vogue.

Thus Chaucer gives us a picture of a homely sort of woman, wholly different from the individuals portrayed by the poets of Provence:

> She was not nyce, ne outrageous,
> But wys and war and virtuous
> Of faire speeche and faire answere,
> Was never wight misseid of here;
> She bar no rancour to no wight,
> Clear broun she was and ther to bright
> Of face, of body avenaunt.

It is evident also that even at the most horrible period of *le fin amour,* these hard women were not really expected to remain for ever detached from their worshippers. Adultery was regarded as more commendable than marriage and the husband who objected was viewed as a boor. The "Courts of Love" which were instituted under distinguished patronage to adjudicate on points of etiquette arising from the practice of *le fin amour* had no legislative powers; they were in fact no more authoritative than the women's luncheon clubs which today constitute so agreeable a feature of American civilization. But they did preserve the convention that the *prouesse* of a man could be exalted only by illicit love affairs and that no fashionable husband should object to his wife inspiring several different adorers at the same time. One of the most influential of cautionary tales was the story of Raymond de Castel-Rousillon who, having killed young Guillem de Caberstaing, the lover of his wife Soremunda, had his heart roasted and served up to her for supper. When he disclosed to her what she had been eating, Soremunda hurled herself from the window and perished in the fosse below. This lack of complaisance on the part of Raymond de Castel-Rousillon was condemned by contemporary thought. The King of Aragon, when he heard the story, cast Raymond into prison, deprived him of his castles, and buried the bodies of the two lovers with much pomp and in a single grave.

In spite of *le fin amour* and all the exquisite feelings that it was intended to inspire, the pattern of behavior devised by the age of chivalry, however delightful for the ardent or the beautiful, weighed heavily upon the

THE GARDEN OF LOVE

middle-aged. The knight who had outlived the period of jousting and who was no longer, even in his own eyes, adapted for the service of love, must have suffered from atrocious melancholia and long days and nights of sullen boredom. He could not read; he could not write; his horses and his hounds were used by younger men, nor would his falcons come to the fist or respond to his bronchial call. Solitary, inert, stupid, his eyes reddened by the smoke in the great hall, his sole relaxation was to repeat to his sons and their squires the story of that distant dawn when he stormed the Palace of Blachernae: of that burning summer when he assisted at the siege of Tyre. No pity, no mercy even, is extended by the troubadours or the historians to the middle-aged.

Nor does it seem that the women, once they ceased to be the idols and tyrants of the younger knights, enjoyed, when they became elderly, that reverence which today is accorded to an American mother as if by right. There is a passage in one of the *chansons* which describes how a knight, presumably of mature age, when contradicted publicly by his wife, bashed her in the face in the presence of her family and servitors, so that her nose bled profusely and two front teeth were lost.

The defects of chivalry, although not given emphasis in the romances, were grave indeed. They can be judged by incidental references.

However great might be the *prouesse* in tournament and battle of any given knight, however deeply he might bend the knee in service to his chosen lady, he was not expected to pay attention to the humanities. The Emperor Frederick II, for instance, was wont to sneer at King René of Sicily for his addiction to the arts, obliging that monarch to indulge his gift for painting in the privacy of his own closet. Learning was derided as a practice fit only for clerks and bearing no relation at all to knightly duties and accomplishments. Chaucer's squire was exceptional in knowing how to read and write.

The fact, moreover, that the young men of the period actually lived in a climate of symbolism, even of allegory, often induced them to adopt a stylized deportment which was wholly unreal. The medieval mind had no conception of equality, society being organized in strict categories, to ignore or defy which was regarded as actually impious. From his childhood a man would be taught to look upon the poor with contempt and horror. "The peasant," wrote Bertran de Born, "is like a hog; keep his trough empty, lest he become overweening." Behind all the merriment of *le gay saber*, behind the pageantry of tournament, there was a stark background of cruelty and suffering. "Las!" exclaims Eustache Deschamps:

> Las! Que j'ay veu de tribulation,
> De tempests, et de mortalités,
> De haines, de peuples mocion,
> De grans orgeuils et de grans vanitez
> De traisons et de crudelitez!

Yet, in spite of its artificiality, the conception of chivalry remained the standard of human conduct for some four hundred years. It survived the ridicule of Cervantes and the exaggerations of Spenser's allegory. It taught the world the idea of service unselfishly rendered; it inculcated a high standard of generosity, courtesy and faith; it enhanced the position of women; and it forced these young barbarians to realize that love is more lasting than lust, that strength must be accompanied by gentleness, pride by modesty, and that courage can be something more noble than purely personal exaltation. Above all, perhaps, in its insistence on the contrast between *gentilesse* and *vilenie,* in its oft-repeated injunction that a man should be "*debonnaire sans félonie,*" in the recurrence in all the songs of the time of the words "gay" and "courteous," it created a pattern of civility which shines out against the murk of the Dark Ages. A scheme of conduct that could survive so long, that left behind it so many precepts of civility, must have possessed a vigor and a value more serious than its many artificialities may suggest. Of durable importance has been the contribution made by chivalry to modern manners.

Gradually as the centuries passed the armed knight lost his military value and his social position. It was not the increasing employment of gunpowder from 1313 onwards that rendered the mounted warrior an anachronism, since the new explosive was for long regarded as highly dangerous and suitable only for reducing fortresses. It was rather that by the end of the twelfth century the crossbow had been developed as an amour-piercing weapon. In the fourteenth century the English exploited the long bow which obliged the knights to be entirely encased in amour, a necessity which was both cumbrous and expensive. The battles of Poitiers, Crécy and Agincourt proved that cavalry was no match for infantry well equipped and trained; the flower of Austrian chivalry fell before the Swiss peasants at Sempach in 1386.

Concurrently with the decline in the military value of mounted warriors, there came a change in their economic position. The replacement of an exchange economy by a money economy, and the deliberate policy of the French kings during the fourteenth and fifteenth centuries of progressively debasing the coinage, ruined the old baronial families. The dukes and princes, who acquired vast fortunes by the ownership of towns and the dues exacted for transport, found they could dispense with the cumbrous apparatus of feudal service and maintain trained armies of their own. Gone were the days when the young Lusignans or the young Hautevilles could ride away from their manor in Normandy or Poitou and found dynasties in Cyprus or Sicily. The knight errant had become either a local brigand or a professional jouster, traveling from tournament to tournament. The castles fell into disrepair, private wars were no longer countenanced, and the ambitious knight looked for his advancement, not to his own prowess, but to the favor of a court. The kings and heralds maintained the old symbolism, founding decorative orders such as the Bath or the Golden Fleece. Yet the old exclusive caste decayed from poverty or was recruited from lower ranks. The values of chivalry became inflated. Some of the lesser orders could even be purchased for cash. For fifteen gulden a man could buy the order of the Swan, whereas a woman could obtain the same decoration for only five gulden. Rare became the cases in which caitiff miscreant knights were degraded for cowardice or dishonor. The whole spirit of chivalry decayed.

Five

How far did the customs of chivalry influence the actual manners or deportment of the age? The profession of knighthood was an arduous profession, and children were trained early to adapt themselves to its many tasks. A boy was expected, while still in the nursery, to become adept, not at hoop and ball only, but also at using stilts and playing backgammon and chess. At the age of seven a boy was taken away from his parents and sent to serve in the household of some relation, or of some neighboring knight or lord, as pages or "*damoiseaux*" or "*varletons.*" He was there instructed in hunting and hawking, taught to ride and to fence, and obliged to act in varying capacities as a domestic servant. By this method he was supposed to acquire what they called "*curialitas*" and what we should call society manners. In one of the many manuals of the time there is a detailed account of the way in which a page or varlet should accompany his lord to bed. He is first to spread the "foot sheet," then relieve his master of his day gown and put on his dressing gown, then take off his shoes, hose and pants, "throwing the latter over his shoulder." The instructions continue:

> Then comb his hair, and then kneel down and put his kerchief and nightcap around him in seemly fashion. Have the bed, head-sheet and pillow ready, and when he is in bed,

> draw the curtains round about it and see that
> there is enough night light to last the night.
> Drive out the dog and the cat, giving them a
> clout. Take no leave of your lord, but bow low
> towards him and retire.

At the age of fourteen, the page became a squire, accompanying his master to the wars, holding his helmet and his warhorse, and when at home carving the meats and keeping the pages in order. According to the chansons of the time the ideal squire, apart from the inevitable *prouesse* and a marked tendency to fall in love with unapproachable women, should have golden curls, with grey eyes "flashing with changing lights like those of a falcon." His chest and arms should be muscular, but his hands should be white with tapering fingers. His thighs should be as long as possible, and his legs slightly curved or bandied, so as to be well adapted to the saddle. In a great house, the squires were divided into separate categories, such as "Squires of the Body," "Squires of the Table," "Squires of the Wines," or of the Pantry, the handsomest of all being appointed "*Honorius*" or Squire of Honor.

At the age of twenty-one, a squire was supposed to have qualified for knighthood, although it often happened that he would continue in a subordinate status for several years. The ceremony of his initiation, although it varied in different countries and periods, was in its main features uniform. It started with fasting followed by confession. Then came the ceremonial bath, after which the knight was laid on a bed to dry and covered with a black cape and hood. Once properly dried, he would dress himself in a black vest—the symbol of eventual death—and in a white tunic, which was regarded as a symbol of purity. Thus arrayed, he would spend the whole night kneeling before the altar performing what was called "the vigil of arms." The following morning he would be given the accolade—namely first a light blow on the nape of the neck, and thereafter the girding with sword, amour, belt and spurs. When fully armed, he would again kneel before his patron who would deliver three blows on the neck and shoulders with the flat of the sword, followed by the "*soufflet,*" namely a light tap with the gauntlet on the right cheek. Thereafter followed a much-needed banquet, and from then onwards the new knight was qualified to ride off with his own young squire, away to found kingdoms in Sicily or to joust at Montalban.

Yet there must have intervened long periods, especially when the crusades were finished, when the knight could find nothing to do except to practice in the tiltyard for some distant tournament, to gaze at the ladies, and to play chess. The castles were dark, the floors strewn with herbs and rushes, and the latrines generally situated under the dining room. At Erfurt in 1183, when the Emperor Frederick was presiding at a diet, the floor of the hall subsided and many of his councilors were drowned in the cesspool that lay below. In the old Germanic days it had been the custom for the chieftains to gnaw their bones in their own rooms; thereafter the practice arose of having meals in common; with the age of chivalry, women were admitted to take their part in banquets. Although there were no forks, and although knights were often expected to bring their own knives with them, there was even in early days a profusion of plate. The meals were long and heavy. The German knight, Leo von Rozmital, who traveled much, records that the Duke of Burgundy served thirty-one different dishes at a banquet, whereas the King of England served as many as fifty-four. The tables were made of trestles, the boards being covered with tablecloths which the pages and the squires were taught to fold into elaborate shapes.

The knights of the age of chivalry were far cleaner in their persons than were the courtiers of Versailles. Although the Church disapproved of public baths, which were indeed sources of promiscuity, the young squire was supposed to have a regular bath and to scent his body with the perfumes of Arabia brought by the Jews from the Levant. Thus in *The Lay of Garun de Lorrain* the serf Rigaud is decried for "having gone for six months without a bath." Long hair was the sign of noble birth; only men of the lower classes wore their hair short. Until the fifteenth century, it was customary for young men to be clean-shaven, and if they so desired it was permissible for them to weave their tresses into ringlets tied with red and yellow silk. At banquets it was fashionable for the men to wear garlands, or little hats trimmed with peacock feathers, or small diadems of metal and fur. The fashions in dress (since essentially the age of chivalry was rural rather than urban), changed very gradually. It was regarded as improper to wear too short a tunic, and the Chronicle of St. Denis attributes the defeat of the French at Crécy to the fact that they had aroused the wrath of God by wearing coats that were of indecent shortness. The manuals of the time attach importance to gait and deportment. Women were told to keep their eyes on the ground, not to look a man in the face when addressing him, not to swing their arms when walking, and to keep their hands covered. Men were told that it was provincial to raise the hat in greeting and that all that a knight need do when encountering an equal was to push his hat, if he happened to be wearing one, slightly above the brow. A woman, it was thought, should walk with short mincing steps. A man, on the other hand, should take wise slow strides "like a crane." Such was the deportment expected of a knight of chivalry when not pricking, armed *cap-à-pie,* across the plain.

Froissart has left a not unattractive picture of the household life, or "*Menie*" of Gaston de Foix, with whom he lived for three months and whom he much admired in that "he loved that which ought to be loved and hated that which ought to be hated." Gaston said his orisons twice daily and made regular distributions to the poor at his gates. When he left his closet and came into the great hall for supper, he would be preceded by twelve pages carrying torches who would stand around his chair while he ate his meal. The hall would be crowded with knights and squires eating at separate tables; nobody was allowed to address Gaston de Foix or to approach the high table unless invited to do so. While he ate his meal, the torches blazed around him, and the musicians in the gallery played the old songs which Bertran de Born had invented, or which Richard Coeur de Lion had written in his native Poitevin, or which Bernart de Ventadour used to sing to Eleanor of Aquitaine.

Slowly it passed, leaving little more than a flavor of tradition: a faint standard of politeness. "Chevalerie cesse," lamented Eustache Deschamps:

> *Chevalerie cesse*
> *Car les vertus sont de faible merrien*
> *Le labour fault, religion se blesse,*
> *Et vailliance veult estre larronnesse.*

Chapter 7
The Babees Book

Origins of civility in England—Alfred the Great—
The Black Death as a cause of social mobility—The
wool trade—Chaucer—English manuals of civility—
The Boke of Nurture—Cleanliness in fifteenth century England—*The Babees Book*—Deportment for
pages—Lord Mountjoy—Erasmus' *De Civilitate*—
His aim to create a class of polite intellectuals—His
views on bodily functions—On clothes—On table
manners—On social relationships—On gamesmanship—On bed manners—His influence—Five directions in which English manners diverged from those
of the continent—Corporal punishment not regarded
as degrading—Boys sent away from home at age of
eight—Boys taught to execute menial functions—
The country preferred to the town—Physical prowess
regarded as more important than intellectual prowess.

One

I HAVE DEALT HITHERTO with types of civility evolved or perfected among foreign communities. In this chapter I propose to consider the

rudiments of politeness as first imported into my own country. I shall imply that in the soil and climate of England these foreign seeds produced a curiously indigenous plant, which with the passage of centuries became established as "the gentleman conception." It is not my contention that the English gentleman was superior in civility to the varied types of distinction produced on the continent. I do, however, suggest that, of all patterns of behavior, the gentleman pattern is the most adjustable and therefore the most imitable: that as such it may prove a useful transitional link between a stratified and a classless society.

I should much like to begin with Alfred the Great who, it might be contended, was the original model of the English gentleman. He is anything but a mythical figure. It is indeed fitting that the first biography written by an Englishman, in England, about another Englishman, should be Asser's vivid *Life* of the King of Wessex. Alfred was a stupendous warrior, a prudent statesman, an industrious jurist, and a man of such gentleness that he really did merit the title of "protector of the poor." He was a cosmopolitan who had made two long journeys to Rome and who was in correspondence with the courts of Europe. He was also a man of letters. One could depict him in his stockade at Athelney, the rushlights upon his camp table flickering in their cowhorn shades, writing the preface to Werferth's *Dialogues of Gregory,* or translating Orosius and Bede. But Alfred the Great was a rare genius who cannot be presented as typical of any civilization. Nor was he the product of that fine mongrel breed created, after the Conquest, by the fusion of Saxon, Scandinavian, Celtic, Norman and even Roman and Phoenician heredity. It is more sensible, therefore, to begin with the age of Chaucer.

In his masterpiece on *English Social History* Dr. Trevelyan writes as follows: "In Chaucer's time, the English people first clearly appear as a racial and cultural unit. . . . Henceforward England creates her own types and her own customs." What were these types and customs and how did they arise? Not, as we might wish to suppose, owing to the inherent love of liberty implanted in every English breast, but owing to a chain of circumstance. It was wool rather than individualism that first gave us our liberties.

The Black Death of 1348–1349 halved the population of England. The old feudal manor could no longer be administered under former conditions. The lords, having insufficient serfs to cultivate their demesnes, were obliged to lease their fields to yeoman farmers. The latter enriched themselves by the sale of wool and ran their farms by hired labor. Thus, in place of the old feudal system, three new classes emerged. There were the yeoman farmers, the hired agricultural laborers and the city merchants, each of them profiting by the rapidly expanding trade in wool. The former serfs developed into an independent peasantry. They were inspired by the egalitarian ideas preached by Langland and John Ball. In 13 81 the indignation aroused by the low wages offered by the farmers culminated in a revolt organized by Wat Tyler, when the Archbishop of Canterbury was beheaded by a Kentish jacquerie on Tower Hill.

The rise of these three classes produced corresponding institutional changes. The villages ceased to be concentration camps for semi-bondsmen and became self-conscious communities. The yeoman farmers developed into squires: local Justices of the Peace supplanted the old feudal jurisdiction. At the same time the merchants of the great towns, especially after the expulsion of the Jews in 1290, became increasingly efficient and powerful. The City of London possessed its own militia, was money lender to the Government, and controlled the shipping of the realm. Thus, whereas on the continent the political trend was towards centralization and even autocracy, in England the movement was towards local self-government, popular representation, and a balance of power between the upper, middle and lower classes. It is not surprising that this differentiation in social development, this "social mobility," should in spite of the fact that most contemporary manners were imported from the continent, have created a tradition of purely national civility, into which these foreign importations were intricately fused.

Two

Chaucer provides a striking example of this fusion. On the one hand he was a courtier, an official of the Royal Household, a linguist, a diplomatist who went on frequent missions to France and Flanders, to Genoa and Florence. He was the man who translated the *Roman de la Rose* into English; who knew and admired Boccaccio; who probably supped with "Fraunceys Petrark, the laureat poet," in the Euganean Hills; and who urged the English to study the work of "the grete poet of Itaille that highte Dant" Chaucer, as far as I know, is the first English writer to be mentioned in French literature, being celebrated by Eustache Deschamps as "*grant translateur, Geoffroi Chaucier.*" Certainly he was, at least in middle life, immensely influenced by the French tradition, by the great Italians, and by the foreign manners of the courts of Edward III, Richard II and Henry IV, as well as those of Italy and Flanders. Yet few would deny that at the same time Chaucer is the most "English" poet that ever wrote.

There is no need to stress, or even to illustrate, this paradox, since it will be familiar to all. He passed through his French period, even as he passed through his Italian period: at the summit of his powers he was absolutely English. When we think of Chaucer, we do not think of a retired diplomatist mumbling Italian sonnets or French lays to foreign ambassadors in the great hall of

Eltham or of Shene. We think of a stout old gentleman in the Winchester Tower at Windsor, chuckling over some additional lines of his Prologue, chuckling as he paces the floor of his vaulted room, or gazes out across the river, across the empty fields of Eton, to where the line of the Chilterns is faint against the sky.

In spite of the powerful court and foreign influences to which during the whole of his life he was exposed, Chaucer possessed and expressed such peculiarly English qualities as humor, curiosity, a delight in individual eccentricities, observation, a love of nature and a precious capacity for laughing at himself. For him Nature was "the vicaire of the Almighty Lord," and although he would often indulge in the fashions of his time—praising the daisy beyond its worth and indulging in stock eulogies of spring—there are passages that suggest a far more personal, a far more English, sensibility:

> And whyte thinges waxen dimme and donne
> For lak of light, and stares for to appear.

The "Englishness" of Chaucer, even as the "Frenchness" of Racine, are emphasized by the fact that each of these mighty poets has been misunderstood by foreign critics. I admit, for instance, that Chaucer was apt to write too readily about Aristotle and the ancient philosophers, his knowledge of whom was scant indeed. Yet Taine, who was almost as much puzzled by Chaucer as he was by Shakespeare and Tennyson, could say: "*Une érudition troublée vient gâter l'invention pittor-esque.*"

Chaucer's inventive powers were never disturbed by anything but natural laziness, nor was his learning in the very least a bother to him. Of course he liked reading: "On bokes for to rede I me delyte;" of course he showed off sometimes about his knowledge; but he did not pretend to know much more than he did know:

> I sleep never on the Mount of Parnaso
> Ne lerned Marcus Tullius Citbero.

In fact his attitude to literature was an essentially English attitude: it gave him immense personal pleasure, but he never committed the error of supposing for one moment that it was more important than wool:

> The greteste clerks be nought the wisest men.

How wrong was Taine, how right was Longfellow!

> He is the poet of the dawn who wrote
> The Canterbury Tales, and his old age
> Made beautiful with song. And as I read,
> I hear the crowing cock, I hear the note
> Of lark and linnet; and from every page
> Rise odors of ploughed field and flowery mead.

Although, as I have said, the pattern of chivalry never exerted in England the same deep and lasting influence as it imposed upon the Continent, the literary influence of France and Italy continued until the end of the sixteenth century to enliven our imagination and to refine our taste. The lyrics of Ronsard and his contemporaries, which, as George Wyndham has shown, translate so easily into our language, influenced English poets even to the time of Macaulay, who cribbed quite shamelessly from Du Bellay.

Alors Malherbe vint. For many succeeding generations English and French poets sang different tunes. Yet, although for a while our poetry became sundered from continental poetry, it was the Continent that continued to instruct us in deportment.

Three

Of the many manuals and books on etiquette written in the fifteenth and sixteenth centuries in England, one of the earliest is John Russell's *Boke of Nurture* which appears to have been composed about 1430. John Russell was steward or usher to Humphrey, Duke of Gloucester, and his manual is mainly intended for the guidance of servitors and pages in a royal or princely household. It contains detailed instructions on the proper way to lay tablecloths and napkins and how to tie or fold them into elegant shapes. It also contains the order of precedence in which distinguished guests should be seated at meals. The Pope or Emperor (and strange as it may seem the good Duke Humphrey did in fact entertain the Emperor Sigismund at Dover Castle) should naturally be seated on the right hand of the host. The *placement* of other less exalted guests should be as follows: King, Cardinal, Prince, Archbishop, Royal Duke, Bishop, Viscount, Mitred Abbot, the three Chief

Justices, the Mayor of London, Cathedral Prior, Knight Bachelor, Dean, Archdeacon, Master of the Rolls, Puisne Judge, Clerk of the Crown, Mayor of Calais, and finally Merchants, gentlemen and gentlewomen.

Russell says that if a lord desires to sleep after the midday meal he should be allowed to do so, but that his page should be careful not to let him sleep for too long: "For moche sleep is not medcynable in middis of ye day."

The page should see that the *chaise percée,* or "privy house for esement," be kept ready and linen provided. If his lord desire a bath, then the page must make ready a large sponge on which he can rest his head and smaller sponges "whereon to sytte or lene." The page should provide a basin of hot herbs, wash his lord with a soft sponge, and thereafter pour rosewater over him. Finally he must dry his lord carefully and put him to bed in order that he may forget his worries, "his bales there to bete." If it be a medicinal bath that his lord desires, then the page must prepare a cauldron in which the following herbs must be dissolved: pyrethrum, hollyhock, mallow, camomile, hey hove, heyriff, herb benet, bresewort, veronica, and scabious. The bath should be so hot that the lord can scarcely bear even to dip into it. Thus boiled and infused, the lord will emerge from the water cured of every ill.

It would seem that the English, in the fifteenth century, were not given to frequent washing. With them, as with the French of my generation, baths were esteemed for their curative, rather than for their cleansing, properties. We know from the *Paston Letters* that the boys of the family were kept short of clean linen. In the *Liber Niger* of Edward IV's reign it is indicated that the king had a bath on Saturday night only, and then merely washed his feet and hair. Soap, it seems, was used only for the washing of underlinen and in the *Liber Niger* the lavender man is authorized to obtain from the Spicery "sufficient whyte soap tenderly to waysshe the stuffe from the King's propyr person." In the lay of "The Kinge and the Miller," the latter's son, before allowing the king to share his couch, asks the following question:

> 'Nay first,' quoth Richard, 'good fellowe
> >tell me true
> Hast thou no creepers in thy gay hose,
> Ar't thou not troubled with the scabadoo?'

The most popular and instructive of all the early manuals written in English was *The Babees Book* which was composed about the year 1475. It is addressed to the princes, "the Bele Babees," of the royal family and begins with the simple injunction:

> Swete children haue al-wey
> >Your delyte in curteseye.

It provides the English Royal Family of the fifteenth century with detailed instructions as to how they should behave. A scion of the Royal House, and presumably any boy attached to the Court, should observe the following rules of deportment.

When speaking to an older person a boy should look him straight in the face; should not allow his eyes to wander; should answer shortly and sensibly and be careful not to talk too much. When entering the dining hall he must remain standing until told to sit down. He should not scratch his face or rub against a pillar to ease the itching of his back. He must be careful not to handle things which he is not asked to handle. When the king drinks, or a lord drinks, a boy should keep silence and refrain from whispering. He must always be prepared to hand dishes or to hold a torch. He must keep his knife clean, and remember to cut his bread and not to break it. He should not leave his own spoon in the common tureen, or lean his elbows on the table, or dirty the cloth, or hang his head over a dish, or speak with his mouth full, or pick his nose. He must never dip his own piece of meat into the salt cellar, or ask for a second helping. And he must be careful not to use his knife as a peasant might use it: "Kutte nouhte youre mete eke as it were felde men."

The etiquette prescribed in *The Babees Book* is repeated in *Urbanitatis,* another English work on deportment written some fifteen years later. The youth or boy is instructed to greet his lord by falling on one knee, not to blow his nose on the tablecloth, and not to spit or snuffle. The aspirant to courtly manners is reminded that:

> In halle, in chambur, or where you gon
> Nurtur and good manners maketh man.

Yet if we are to judge by the instructions contained in Hewe Rhode's *Book of Nurture,* which was published as late as 1554, these habits of civility had not, even by the reign of Queen Mary, become automatic. The young courtier is told by Rhodes that he must not scratch himself in public, or spit across the dinner table, or clean his teeth with his knife, or stretch his arms in a loud yawn, or emit pectoral regurgitations:

> Belche thou neare no man's face
> With a corrupt fumosytye.

There is one rule of good manners recommended by Hewe Rhodes which has not, I am glad to say, been adopted by future generations. Even in my own day Germans would, on rising from a meal, utter the gross word "*Mahlzeit*" to their neighbors. A more decorous form of the same practice is still preserved in Scandinavian countries. Hewe Rhodes, in his *Book of Nurture,* contended that it was right, on leaving the table, to murmur "gently" to one's neighbors the words: "Much good do it yer." Did Shakespeare or Ben Jonson indulge in so ungainly a notion? I am certain that they did not.

Four

These guides to proper deportment, although ostensibly intended for the improvement of little boys and girls, were also aimed at the atrocious manners of their fathers and mothers. In the French, as well as in the English manuals, of the period great prominence is accorded to such bad habits as scratching, spitting and breaking wind. It was always known that our ancestors suffered more than we do from skin diseases and the attacks of vermin. It seems that they were also afflicted with flatulence and abnormal activity of the salivary glands. The manuals were aimed at checking the most offensive of contemporary indelicacies rather than at creating a high standard of civility or distinction. They were thus negative rather than positive.

For the educated European the first constructive treatise on civility, in the true meaning of the word, was Erasmus' *De Civilitate morum puerilium libellus,* which was published at Antwerp in 1526. This essay was immediately circulated throughout western Europe and translated into several languages. It deserves special consideration.

The deportment recommended in the *De Civilitate* was that which Erasmus had himself taught to his pupil and patron, the "humane, kind and amiable" William Blount, Lord Mountjoy. Succeeding to the peerage while still in the nursery, Lord Mountjoy was sent as a boy to Paris to study under Erasmus. He returned to England to become the playmate and intimate friend of Prince Henry, later King Henry VIII. He was appointed chamberlain to Queen Catherine of Aragon and served his master as intermediary in many of his most delicate transactions. Diplomatist, courtier and scholar, Lord Mountjoy deserves credit for having introduced into England a respect for the humanities and the conception of good manners as something more than the bare avoidance of indelicacy, something more even than the symbol of good breeding. Lord Mountjoy, first of our court humanists, remembered and repeated the lessons which Erasmus had taught.

The *De Civilitate* is unique, in that it was the first—perhaps the last—treatise on civility to be addressed to the intelligent individual, rather than to those who had either inherited, or desired to imitate, the manners of a privileged class. It may seem strange that a scholar of such eminence should have devoted time to instructing young people how to wash and eat. Yet to Erasmus humanism was wider than mere scholarship: it embraced all the refinements and aptitudes which would enable a young man to acquire the art of life. He himself had risen high above the dull Dutch background of his childhood to become a teacher of European celebrity and influence. Would it not be possible so to instruct the intellectuals that they could cope with the men of fashion on their own terms? Erasmus may well have foreseen that the decay of the feudal system would be followed by the creation of a new court caste, admission into which would depend upon heredity rather than on personal merit. In writing and publishing his essay on civility, he may well have desired to prevent such stratification of society by teaching social graces to the new class of intellectuals which, as he hoped, the revival of learning would advance to prominence and power. His aim was to humanize and thereby to "individualize" good manners. He was not writing for any hereditary class, but rather for those who had acquired scholarship by their own talents and industry.

Thus, although his essay is dedicated to Prince Henry of Burgundy, he is careful to assert in his dedication that his rules are not intended for those who have been born into good society but for those who aspire to enter it. He goes so far as to decry "court" manners as being arrogant and exclusive. "It is not pretty," he writes, "to pout with the lips. One can leave that to great nobles when they find themselves in a crowd." Again, whereas courtiers may be permitted to break their bread in their fingers, "you, my boy, should cut it tidily with the knife." He insists above all that learning and the liberal arts are more important than heraldic quarterings.

Erasmus asserts that the purpose of all education is to inculcate piety, "liberal disciplines," the rudiments of social conduct, and such habits as may fit a boy for public responsibility. Good manners may appear to be a trivial department of philosophy but it is in the present condition of society important to teach a boy how to acquire the approval of his fellow men. If a boy be of high lineage he should be instructed above all to acquire modesty and proficiency in the liberal sciences. He should be taught to be modest about his birth but proud of his scholarship.

The *De Civilitate* is divided into seven sections or chapters. The first deals with the functions and discipline of the body. A boy should adopt a modest and serene expression and avoid anything in the nature of superciliousness or scorn. The nose should be kept clear of mucus. When in the presence of a superior, the boy should use a handkerchief; otherwise he may blow his nose by compressing it with two fingers and quickly placing his foot on what falls to the floor. A boy should not laugh too loudly and should be taught that it is uncivilized ("*inurbanus*") to bite the lower lip with the upper teeth or to wet the lips with the tongue. It is uncivilized also to swallow saliva; but when you do spit, be careful to stamp on it immediately. A well-mannered boy should never sit with his legs apart, or scratch himself, or gesticulate, or cough when other people are engaged in conversation, or play with his feet, or clean his teeth with his knife. Erasmus was under the impression that to retain wind was in some manner injurious to health. If therefore a boy when thus afflicted was unable to leave the room, he should cough loudly in order that "*tussi crepitum dissimulet.*"

The second section deals with wearing apparel. Erasmus advises young people to see that their clothes be clean and simple. If your parents present you with a fine new suit you must be careful not to preen yourself and above all not to boast about it to your comrades. The third section deals with conduct in church, a branch of civility that has little contemporary relevance. In his fourth chapter Erasmus discusses table manners. In the first place, unlike the subsequent Puritans, Erasmus contends that the purpose of parties is to cause enjoyment; therefore, if you desire to be polite, you should indicate pleasure rather than distaste: "*in conviviis adsit hilaritas, absit petulantia.*" When attending a dinner party you should not seat yourself in the highest place; if asked to move up nearer your host you should protest modestly, but not too long. Do not fidget in your seat; take off your hat in the presence of superiors or if requested to do so; do not throw your head back when you drink; always wipe the rim of the cup before passing it on; don't dip your bread in the common sauce; don't feed other people's dogs when dining with them; don't chew bones like an animal; don't throw gristle under the table; don't put three fingers into the salt cellar; remember that to speak or drink with the mouth full is both gross and dangerous (*neque hone stum nee tutum*). If you happen to be bored by the company, then it is rude to glower at the table as if concentrating upon your own interior resources. Never stare at a fellow guest, and do not turn sideways and watch while your neighbor is helping himself to a dish. Above all (and in this Erasmus shows himself to be well in advance of his age), do not notice when someone else commits a solecism or eats untidily. "It is part of the highest civility," writes Erasmus, "if, while never erring yourself, you ignore the errors of others."

Little boys, according to this great humanist, should never wait until the end of a meal, but, having once satisfied their hunger, they should remove their own plate to the sideboard, bow politely to the assembled company, and then retire. When at a dinner party a boy ought not to drink more than twice, or at very most three times; when he does so, he should manage the operation in silence "and not make a noise like a horse."

The fifth chapter of the *De Civilitate* deals with social relations. If he meets a superior, a boy should step right off the pavement into the mud of the street and take off his hat. While addressing a superior a boy should look him in the face and not waggle his head sideways which gives an impression of levity. He should not gesticulate, or scratch, or jerk the hair out of his eyes, or pick his nose or ears, or indicate assent or dissent by motions of the head. In conversation a boy should not allow his words to tumble ahead of his thoughts, but should speak slowly and in a correct sequence. He should neither shout nor mumble. The "*ingenu us puer*" or well brought up youth realizes that obscenity is an offence both to tongue and ears. He should never mention matters—such as latrines, or bad smells, or being sick—which might offend his auditors. He should not gossip, tell unkind stories, boast, indulge in self-display, or seek to defeat others in argument. He must never interrupt people when they tell a story. He must not be too inquisitive and must be discreet about his own thoughts and actions.

"It is safe," writes Erasmus, "to admit nothing that might embarrass one if repeated."

Section six of Erasmus' essay is devoted to gamesmanship: it is strangely modern in feeling. A boy's real character, Erasmus writes, is never better disclosed than when he is engaged in some game. It is more noble, he says, to be beaten decently than to win a prize—a sentiment repeated by English sportsmen of the postwar period. When playing games one should be zestful rather than pugnacious; there must be no cheating or dishonesty. This doctrine of true sportsmanship does not figure in other manuals of the period; to the Italians, who set the fashion for manners in the succeeding generation, such unselfishness would have appeared lacking in "virtù."

Erasmus closes his strange essay with a section on bed manners. When dressing or undressing one should be careful not to expose those sections of the body that might cause embarrassment to others. Even when alone, one should remember that angels are always present and that they much dislike the exposure of private parts. Always, when retiring or rising, say a short prayer of thankfulness to God. If sharing a bed with another person—a necessity which in the sixteenth century was customary for all travelers—do not fidget so as to deprive your companion of sleep or the bedclothes. Consider his convenience as well as your own; to be selfish in such matters shows that you are lacking in civility.

The *De Civilitate,* owing to the immense and fully justified repute of its author, became the textbook on contemporary manners. Its influence continued for years; and by 1780, apart from many imitations, 128 editions of the original essay had been published. Erasmus was in fact the first important writer on the subject to assert that good manners were founded, not upon any desire to demonstrate one's own delicacy and distinction, but solely on a desire to show consideration for others. Other codes, other conventions, became fashionable in the centuries that followed. Erasmus had imagined an élite of humanists, drawn from every class, and combining all that was most valid in the old ideals of chivalry with the inspiration and refinements of the new learning. This dream has not yet been fully realized. Kings created courts and courts created an hereditary caste, admission into which had, by the seventeenth century, become increasingly difficult and rare. Yet for generations people continued to read Erasmus and to be reminded by him of the principle that the superior man considers the feelings of others before reflecting upon the impression he is making himself.

Five

The influence of the *De Civilitate* on subsequent English manuals lasted well into the seventeenth century. Thus in the *Schoole of Vertue and Booke of good Nourture* published in 1557 we read the excellent precept:

> Many to honor by lerninge attayne
> That were of byrthe but symple and bace.

Richard Weste in the *Booke of Demeanour* of 1619 repeats Erasmus' recommendations about spitting:

> If spitting chance to moove thee so
> Thou canst it not for beare,
> Remember do it modestly,
> Consider who is there.
> If filthiness or ordure thou
> Upon the floore doe cast.
> Tread out and cleanse it with thy foot,
> Let that be done with haste.

In other respects Weste indicates a slight advance on sixteenth century manners:

> Nor imitate with Socrates
> To wipe thy snivveled nose,
> Upon thy cap, as he would doe,
> Nor yet upon thy clothes.
> But keep it clean with handkerchiffe,
> Provided for the same,
> Not with thy fingers or thy sleeve,
> Therein thou art to blame.

English teachers of deportment in the seventeenth century devoted more space than their continental colleagues to personal cleanliness and bed manners. Thus William Vaughan in his *Directions for Health* published in 1602 urges people on rising to rub themselves down with a coarse linen cloth, to wash their face and eyes with fountain water rather than with well water, and to clean their teeth after every meal. Sir John Harington in 1624 recommends that the comb should be passed through the hair from the forehead to the back no less than forty times. As early as 1557 Andrew Borde, in his *Regyment,* had laid down many excellent rules for healthy sleeping. He recommends his readers "not to sleep in such chambers as myse and rattes and snayles resorteth to;" to wear a scarlet nightcap; not to open the window; to "eschew merydyall sleep," but if you must sleep after the midday meal then do so sitting in a chair or leaning against a cupboard. In bed, one should always sleep on the side, beginning with the left: "to sleep groveling on the stomach and belly is not good; to sleep on the back upright is utterly to be abhorred." In 1602 William Vaughan, while repeating these injunctions, adds that it is best to lie on the right side, to keep the mouth half-open when sleeping, and to have a hole in the top of one's nightcap in order to release such vapors as may accumulate.

If it be true that most of our writers on deportment imitated either Erasmus or the Italian and French specialists, how can it be said that civility in England was always in some manner different from that practiced and inculcated on the continent? There are five main differences.

Although in France and Italy the treatment of children by their parents was cold and even harsh, in England it was positively brutal. Little French boys and girls in the sixteenth and seventeenth centuries were beaten quite as often as little English boys and girls. Henri IV himself did not hesitate to whip his Dauphin and the Princesses of the family were instructed in Latin grammar to the accompaniment of a cane. Yet in the later seventeenth century the idea arose upon the continent that it was degrading for a boy to submit to corporal punishment, since "his personal honor" was involved. In England no such inhibitions arose; to this day the sons of the English aristocracy submit without shame or resentment to frequent whippings administered both by masters and senior boys. The pain, although intense, is transitory: no psychological consequences remain to afflict English boys with torturing doubts about personal honor, such as have led many unhappy German boys to commit suicide for very shame.

In England again a boy was expected to display exaggerated deference to his father and mother, and if he failed to do so he was mercilessly punished. Even when twenty years of age John Paston would address his father as "right reverend and worshipful" and sign his letters "your son and lowly servant." To our more gentle minds the attitude of Agnes Paston towards her sons and daughters was cold-blooded in the extreme. She expected them to marry for money and at the dictation of their father. When Elizabeth Paston refused to be handed over to a widower of fifty years of age she was beaten, or "belashed," once or twice a week for three whole months. In spite of this parental tyranny, John Paston did in the end succeed in marrying the girl of his choice, and in the end Margery Paston was allowed to marry the bailiff. The Pastons were a tough and determined breed: we do not know what happened in less rebellious families. The girls, if disobedient or very ugly, were sent off to nunneries, from which no voice emerged. The boys just left their families and worked out their own fortunes and futures. Yet we know that the meek and lovely Lady Jane Grey was so abominably treated by her parents and uncles that Roger Ascham felt obliged to protest. To survive the nursery stage, the children of the period must have been exceptionally resolute.

The English differed also from their foreign contemporaries in sending their boys away from home when they reached eight years of age. It was the custom for children of good family to be trained as pages or servitors in the house of some great noble or ecclesiastic. Thus Thomas More started as page in the household of Cardinal Morton where he waited at meals. Cardinal Wolsey had in his service many pages of illustrious families, such as Lord Percy, the eldest son of the Earl of Northumberland. John Paston was boarded out as a child in the household of the Duke of Norfolk, being employed in menial capacities and wearing the Norfolk livery. In the larger establishments a tutor was provided for the education of these striplings and for their moral and intellectual discipline. In the monastic and the cathedral schools of the period order was maintained by frequent corporal punishment. Lydgate in his testament records that he was in constant fear of being whipped or "scooryd": and there is Thomas Tusser's familiar indictment:

> From Paul's I went, to Eton sent,
> To learn straightways the Latin phrase
> When fifty-three stripes given to me
> At once I had.
> For fault but small, or none at all.
> It came to pass thus beat I was,
> See, Udall, see!—the mercy of thee
> To mee, poor lad!

Thus conditioned, the more erudite boys would go off to some foreign university, to Paris, Montpelier or Padua: they often returned corrupted.

This heartless treatment of little boys shocked an Italian traveler who visited our country in the reign of Henry VII. "The want of affection," he wrote, "in the English towards their children is a marked feature. Having kept them at home until they reach the age of seven or nine, they then board them out, both boys and girls, to hard service in the houses of other people. Few are born who are exempted from this fate. For everyone, however rich he be, sends away his children into the houses of others, whilst he, in return, receives the children of strangers into his own. On my enquiring the reason for this severity, they said that they did it in order that their children might learn better manners."

To a Frenchman of the period it would not have appeared entirely inexplicable that a boy should be sent to serve in the household of some great noble or some rising statesman. But the English were so eccentric that they allowed their sons to serve in the household even of merchants, serving these bourgeois as if they had been nobles born. Such a fusion of classes seemed to the French to indicate a lack of class consciousness and a deplorably low standard of refinement.

In fact these English habits did contribute to the formation of a national type of civility. To be sent away from home early, as little English boys to this day are sent away to private schools at the age of eight, did certainly foster individualism. To be whipped regularly did assuredly deprive English boys of that sense of "personal honor" which has done such dreadful damage in some continental countries. And to serve even bourgeois families, dressed in their livery and handing dishes to their guests, did without doubt diminish the vanity of caste, provide knowledge of different grades of society, increase understanding of the nature of service and servitors, and stimulate modesty and obedience. This practice has been continued in our public schools by the excellent institution of fagging. The children of rich English families leave school at the age of eighteen with complete awareness of what it means both to obey and to command. Foreign boys only acquire this essential lesson in the cruder and less gradual form of military service.

Even in the fifteenth century the English aristocracy, unlike the continental aristocracy, preferred the country to the town. Whereas to French nobles, relegation to their estates seemed little better than a sentence of exile, to the English nobles of the same date it was a cruel imposition to be obliged to attend the court or to live in London. "The nobles of England," wrote the Italian Poggio in 1437, "think themselves above residing in cities. They live in retirement on their country estates amid woods and pastures."

In spite of Erasmus' recommendations, the "liberal arts" were not cultivated with any great assiduity by the English upper classes. The schools attended by the poorer scholars might insist upon the teaching of Latin and oblige their pupils to talk to each other in that learned tongue even when they were playing skittles in the yard. French also was taught in these establishments "lest the French tongue be wholly lost." The Universities of Cambridge and Oxford soon became rivals of the great continental seats of learning, and the collegiate system introduced at an early date into English universities provided students with most beneficial opportunities for mutual intercourse and personal discipline such as were not given by vague segregation into "nations" as practiced abroad. It was the colleges of Cambridge and Oxford, with their differentiation of type and their useful competitive element, that rendered our universities schools of civility as well as seats of learning.

Among the upper classes scholarship was not regarded as an essential aim. We are often told about how Lady Jane Grey could read Plato in the original Greek, or how wide was Queen Elizabeth's knowledge of foreign languages. But we are not told that even in the reign of King Edward VI there were many peers in Parliament who were unable to read or write. In the preface to Richard Pace's *De Fructu* a country squire is quoted as saying: "It becomes a gentleman to be adept at blowing hunting horns, to be skilful in the chase, and elegantly to train and carry a hawk. The study of letters should be left to the sons of rustics." Erasmus, who was a friend of Pace, would have regarded such an opinion as abhorrent. Yet to this day in England, as in Australia and the United States, the tradition survives that boys who are good at killing animals, or propelling balls, or leaping obstacles, or running very rapidly, are healthier-minded, and therefore more attractive, than boys who devote their attention to art or literature. This seems in many ways an admirable tradition. It renders English intellectuals unassuming, and provides the state and the commercial community with a constant supply of apprentices who lack imagination and are therefore obedient. The disadvantage is that the athlete, after short years of glory, may have to endure an unhappy middle age. Even as the medieval knight, who once his hawking days were over found his afternoons lonely and his evenings dull, so also may those who have rejoiced only in the transient marvel of their physical strength discover in later life that their range has become restricted and their interests few. It is thus recommendable that Olympic champions should acquire the reading habit while still young.

Chapter 8
Florizel

Erasmus' vision of an aristocracy of intellect is unrealized—All elites tend to become hereditary—Aristocracies destroy themselves by their own exclusiveness—England an exception to this rule—Our sixteenth century manners derived from Italy—Many of the more important principles of the Italian manuals are ignored or misinterpreted—Alberti insists on manners as a gift of nature—Sir Thomas Hoby's translation of the *Cortigiano* ignores the emphasis laid by Castiglione on moral qualities and *sprezzatura,* or spontaneity—Sir Philip Sidney as an early model of English civility—The Elizabethans are too impatient to follow his staid example—Shakespeare on manners—His conception of the ideal courtier—His insistence on *sprezzatura* and high spirits as a necessary component of elegance—Florizel as Shakespeare's Charmides.

One

ERASMUS' **VISION OF** an élite composed of polite and classless intellectuals has not, as I have said, yet been realized in any society. The old Chinese system of recruiting administrators by processes of ever-recurrent examinations did not survive the educational reforms of 1905 or the fall of the Manchus seven years later. It had already become stylized, crystallized, and so cumbrous as to be a stoppage rather than a filter. In France, men of letters, artists, musicians and scientists have enjoyed, and still enjoy, a degree of prestige which, to our practical minds, appears exaggerated: but they have never acquired leadership. Thus in the moral dilemma which assailed the French in 1940, the Academicians, for all their glory, failed to provide one joint message such as might have enlightened and encouraged a valiant people bewildered by complex adversity. In England, where rulers rely, not so much upon the brilliance of individuals as on the solidity of the national character, intellectuals are not expected, and do not expect, to exercise any corporate influence at all. It is only our scientists (a fresh breed of men) who suppose that their opinions on subjects outside their own competence are of importance. This illusion will pass.

In some of the smaller universities of the United States, in some of their placid freshwater resorts, something not wholly different from Erasmus' ideal has at least been assayed. Under the supervision of some beaming president, the members of the several faculties labor in the fields of learning without strain or noise. Their political influence, in that a liberal education is regarded as undemocratic, is nonexistent: their cultural influence is slight: yet it is through them, and by them, that is preserved much that is most valuable in the American idea. They toil patiently and without reward, other than the occasional approbation of a few alumni. Their voices are more subdued than are those of their fellow citizens. They are men and women of exceeding modesty: and therefore very few.

In the dawn of humanism, when the gentle Erasmus first taught and wrote, the conception of an aristocracy of intellect, recruited constantly from every layer of society, did not appear to be a fantastic vision. Erasmus failed to realize that intellectuals are by nature self-opinionated and that they can never provide their contemporaries with uniform guidance or advice. He did not see that scholars invariably develop subjective doubts and do not possess the objective assurance which administration requires. Even Plato's philosopher-kings, had they really been philosophers, would not have remained kingly for very long. Moreover, an aristocracy of birth— in that no personal merit is ascribed to those who are included and no personal demerit ascribed to those outside—does not create the same feelings of superiority or inferiority which an aristocracy based upon higher mental powers or education would inevitably arouse. A governing caste does not, in fact, generate the bitter jealousy which would certainly accumulate round rulers selected for their assumed intelligence. Although Erasmus' dream of a classless élite of gifted men may well have been utopian, yet, as an ideal, it is certainly one that should be remembered and admired. It may be that, with our own quick expansion of social mobility, something like his experiment might again become practicable. We should not, of course, give to the experiment any such offensive title as "an aristocracy of intellect." We should call it "equality of opportunity."

It would in any case have to be realized that élites, however established or recruited, tend to become hereditary. Even in communities of the most unsullied communism, there is the danger that powerful organizations, such as the Electricians Union, may seek to transmit advantage to their sons. Privilege, to a certain extent, will always be transmissible, whereas intelligence is not. The children of gifted or powerful parents will always, so long as any form of family life is permitted, enjoy advantages not open to the progeny of louts and callots. Nor is it conceivable that any present or future society will revert to the Spartan system, when mothers were obliged to deposit unpromising babies on mountain tops, there to be eaten by wolves, and to allow the promising infants to be jumbled up together in syssitia, deprived of all parental contact or affection. So long as family life remains an axiom of society, there can never be complete equality of opportunity.

Two

In any case, the dream of Erasmus was very soon submerged under a solid caste system which endured for some four hundred years. The disorder and wastefulness of feudalism in its decline rendered it inevitable that strong central authority should become vested in hereditary monarchies. Kings required the assistance and the protective fluids of courts, and courts begat courtiers. It was thus the courtier ideal, rather than the Erasmus ideal, that from the fifteenth century onwards set the pattern of European civility.

It is unnecessary to dwell upon the great advantages that can be conferred upon a community, during the stage of growth and consolidation, by the existence of a hereditary governing class. Such a class restrains despotism, provides continuity of experience, and furnishes the State with a supply of potentially able, responsible and honest administrators. Yet if a governing class is to be of durable value, it must not degenerate into a stew pond for the culture of large carp with extended bellies and protruding eyes: it must be a lake, fed by clear freshets, with its inlets and outlets unencumbered, and its waters constantly renewed.

The danger of caste systems is that they tend to become static. If the principle of autocracy be centralization, and the principle of democracy be egalitarianism, then the principle of aristocracy may become exclusiveness. This is a sterile principle and one that is invariably subject to the law of diminishing returns.

Hereditary castes—be they nobles, Levites, Incas, Brahmans, Wykehamists, or the priests of Amen-Ra—protect themselves by all manner of barriers and shibboleths against invasion from outside. In extreme cases the wish to maintain purity of blood leads to the highly inconvenient habit of incestuous marriages. In more moderate cases, this urge produces an élite which is increasingly inbred and underpopulated. Thus the Spartan nobles, who in the age of Lycurgus numbered some 9,000 heads of families, had by 418 BCE declined to 6,000, and by 240 BCE to 700. Of the original three hundred patrician families in Rome, only some fifty were still in existence at the time of the fall of the Republic. Even the Venetian oligarchs, who were wise enough to permit occasional recruitment from outside, had by the eighteenth century shrunk to but a fraction of their former numbers. Only in such countries as England, where the governing class was never exclusive, could the patricians survive into an epoch when, although diminished in wealth and power, they still retained a vestigial prestige. Their comparative survival is to be explained by the facts that their pools were never stagnant, their manners only rarely pretentious, their ambitions moderate and their greed concealed. Unlike the nobility of France, Spain and Austria, they never ceased to mix and marry with their social inferiors and to play an active, honorable, and often selfless part in national affairs.

Thus in England the governing class, even in the days of Elizabeth, did not become as exclusive as the courtier classes became upon the continent. The national character was too independent, and social conditions too mobile, to accept the rigid patterns of behavior which afflicted European aristocracies. Admittedly, our manners (when we first began to have manners in the fifteenth century) were the product of foreign importations rather than any autochthonous growth. Yet they always remained "natural," in the sense that they did not crystallize into the wearisome artificiality of "court manners," or become exclusive, false and humiliating in the form of etiquette. In France, the Medicean influence created a code of manners of such elaboration and tenacity that it persisted until the Revolution. In Spain and Austria etiquette became as an iron hand gripping the mind and soul. These misfortunes arose from what, to a very large extent, was a misreading and a misrepresentation of the Italian manuals. In Paris these lessons developed into a complicated esoteric science: in London our natural humor laughed away such popinjay affectations: with us, manners became a spontaneous habit rather than an acquired drill.

Three

The intellectual and aesthetic benefits conferred upon the world by Renaissance Italy can be compared only to those bequeathed by Greece and Rome: her influence on manners was less salutary. Even as Athens became the school of Hellas, so also did Italy in the sixteenth century become the school of Europe. The misfortune was that her pupils, while rapidly assimilating all that was most superficial, were for the most part too crude and too impatient to grasp the sober lessons of humanism that lay beneath.

We are not always aware of the astonishing speed with which, in the lifetime of Shakespeare, the standard of living of all classes in England was transformed. In the year 1568, when Shakespeare was a child of four, we find Thomas Sackville, Lord Buckhurst, writing in despair that in the whole royal palace of Shene there was not sufficient furniture or linen to equip a single guest-room for a visiting cardinal. He himself had to surrender his own basin and ewer since there were no other utensils in that great house. Within the short space of fifty years all had changed. From Italy and the Low Countries there poured into England a torrent of tapestries and cabinets, of velvets and brocades. Although the servants still slept upon straw in the retainers" galleries, huge canopied beds became permanent features in the state rooms; day beds, and even forks, appeared.

It was not merely the excitement of new ideas, the shimmer of new luxuries, that came to England from Italy. It was also that many Englishmen brought back from their travels an imitation or mimic of Italian behavior. Italian professionals had taught them new tricks in fencing, new dancing steps, new wiles wherewith to lure recalcitrant falcons, or how to play the viola-da-gamba. Italian manuals on deportment also taught them much that was affected and little perhaps that was moderate or sane. The reaction, at least in England, against the Italianization of manners is to be ascribed to the excesses of the pupils rather than to any false doctrine on the part of the teachers. The latter were often men of high intelligence and probity. It was merely that their precepts were frequently misunderstood.

Thus the superb Leon Battista Alberti, when not engaged on the study and practice of architecture, would compose little dialogues, such as the *Deiciarchia,* in which the moral principles underlying good manners are examined. Real nobility, writes Alberti in Socratic mood, is not nobility of birth, or even of bearing, but nobility of soul: no man who possesses this great quality would ever vaunt his own achievements or disparage those of others. Above all, insists Alberti, civility must be natural, authentic, and not imitated or assumed. A man of the world should not acquire courtesy from the instruction of some teacher of deportment; it should come to him as a natural gift, *un dono innato della natura.* The superior man should realize that affected manners are invariably bad manners; he should allow nothing in his deportment to suggest either artificiality or design: *che nulla ivi paia fatto con escogitato artificio.* Had the traveling Englishman absorbed these precepts he would not on his return have pretended to be Bolognese.

Even more important than the incidental remarks of Alberti, was the massive manual on manners published under the title *Il Cortigiano* by Count Baldassare Castiglione in 1528. Castiglione was born near Mantua in

1478. His father was a captain of mercenaries, but his mother was related to the Gonzaga family and became the intimate friend of Isabella d'Este. As a young man, Castiglione served under the Duke of Urbino, whose court he regarded as the model of what a court should be. He went on embassies to Henry VII of England, to Louis XII of France, and to Pope Leo X. In his later age, he represented the Pope as nuncio in Madrid, and Charles V recorded that he was "one of the greatest gentlemen in the world" (*uno de los mejores caballeros del mundo*). He died at Toledo in 1529, but his body was brought back to Mantua, where it now rests in the church of the Madonna delle Grazie, under a red marble monument designed by Giulio Romano. It is in the castle of Urbino that take place the fluent discussions between courtiers, prelates and fine ladies that create the wide tapestry of the *Cortigiano*.

In 1561 this famous manual was translated into English by Sir Thomas Hoby, ambassador and man of letters. He called it, in his slapdash Elizabethan way, *The Courtyer of Count Baldesar Castilio.* The book was widely acclaimed and further editions appeared in 1565, 1577, 1588 and 1603. Thomas Sackville, Lord Buckhurst, addressed to Hoby a sonnet of well-merited commendation:

> A rarer work, and richer far in worth,
> Castilio's hand presenteth here to thee:
> No proud nor golden court doth he set forth,
> But what in court a courtier ought to be . . .

Whose passing skill, lo, Hoby's pen displays
To Britain folk a work of worthy praise.

Roger Ascham recommended it to the younger generation. "To join learning," he wrote, "with comely
exercises, Conte Baldesar Castiglione, in his book
Cortegiane, doth trimly teach." Even when Sir Thomas
Hoby had for two hundred years been resting in his
rich tomb at Bisham, Samuel Johnson (himself no glit-
tering example of civility) could praise the *Courtyer* as
"the best book that ever was written upon good breeding." It is no exaggeration therefore to contend that the
Cortigiano was the most influential manual on deportment and courtly education ever published.

Four

In his spirited translation of the *Cortigiano,* Sir
Thomas Hoby provides the reader with a trim
appendix or "summary of recommendations." The
order adopted by Hoby is not that which Castiglione
would himself have chosen, since it manifestly does
not catalogue the list of qualities and attainments in
their correct degree of importance. Yet, since it was
in all probability Hoby's jumbled summary that exercised most influence on English manners in the Elizabethan age, it is well, before examining the more serious precepts of Castiglione, to quote Hoby's summary,
more or less in his own words.

A courtier, writes Hoby, should be man of good family and fine appearance. He should have an amiable expression, should not be effeminate, boastful, gossipy, or malicious. He should not brawl, babble, flatter or tell lies. His manners should not be studied, but should display a certain "recklessness;" he should avoid all affectations or "curiosityes." He should have a noble diction, be able to speak Italian, French and Spanish, keep good company, and know how to write his own language simply, without inserting elaborate phrases or foreign expressions. He should play cards for fun and not mind when he loses; he should be able to play chess well, but not too well. His apparel should be clean rather than gaudy and he should prefer to bright colors the more subfusc hues. He should be polite, especially to his superiors. He should not be presumptuous, or jealous, or spiteful, but honest, of a good conscience, manly, just, temperate and wise. He should "be more than indifferently well in Greek and Latin," but he should not show off or "perswade himself he knows the thing that he knoweth not." He should only talk about the probable, since to tell stories about portents or marvels will diminish his reputation for veracity. He should be able to draw and paint, to sing correctly, to play the viol and the lute, and to dance well, although "without too nimble footings or too busie trickes." He should be a "merrie talker" but with due regard to the occasion and the company present. He should not indulge in practical jokes or "use sluttish or ruffian like pranckes with any man." He should not make jokes that embarrass other people or tease those who dislike being teased, "for he ought not to mocke poor seelie souls, or men of authoritie."

The courtier moreover must be adept at martial feats "which are his chief profession." He should therefore be an athlete and able to distinguish himself in fencing, tennis, hunting, hawking, riding, managing horses, tilting, swimming and other sports. He should not play games with his social inferiors unless he is quite certain of winning. In the lists, he should appear well-caparisoned: in war he should execute deeds of velour, taking care that these deeds should be performed within sight "of the most noble personages in the camp and (if it be possible) before his Prince's eyes." Otherwise he should not run unnecessary risks "in enterprises of great danger but small estimation." A courtier should be careful not to serve bad princes or to commit wicked actions in pursuance of their commands. He should never exceed his instructions, unless he be positive that the profit of such action is worth the risk. In his relations with his prince, his manners should be those of a servant towards his master. He should not intrude upon the prince's privacy or enter his apartments when not invited. He should not seek to gain esteem by chatting intimately to his prince in public. He should not be ambitious for office and should not be insistent on favors for himself. He should even refuse proffered favors but "after such a comelye sort that the Prince offrynge hym them may have cause to offre them with a more instance." His attitude towards women should not be sensual but ruled by reason. In talking to women he should be "gentle, sober, meeke, lowlie, modest, serviceable, comelie, merrie, not biting or sclaundering with jestes, nippes, frumpes, or railinges, the honesty of any." And he should remember always that the aim of the true courtier is to become "instructor or teacher of his Prince or Lorde, inclyninge him to virtuous practices."

When we compare Sir Thomas Hoby's translation with Castiglione's original, we observe important differences of proportion and emphasis. Hoby is really thinking of court advancement, and stresses those of Castiglione's recommendations as appear to him most profitable and most shrewd. Castiglione was thinking rather of the civilized humanist, or educated gentleman, and his approach is more metaphysical than Hoby's excited jumble might suggest.

Castiglione had at the back of his mind the twelve great virtues which Aristotle defined as essential to the perfect man. He assumes above all that the good courtier will possess the two virtues of Magnanimity and μεγαλοπρέπεια, which is generally translated "magnificence," but which also signifies "grandeur controlled by taste." It is greatness of mind and nobility of soul that differentiate good manners from such things as deportment and etiquette, which can be taught "by any dancing master." Moreover, the function of courtier might be humiliating, were it not for the end, or *telos,* that it serves. A courtier should train himself to become a man of such character, ability and standing as to be able to direct his prince along the paths of liberality and justice and to keep him always within "*la austera strada delta virtu.*" Were it not for such high ideals and purposes the position of a courtier might appear parasitic.

APRIL BY FRANCESCO DEL COSSA
(Fresco in Schifanoia Palace, Ferrara)

There are seven other points emphasized by Castiglione which are not accorded sufficient importance in Hoby's summary. Thus the courtier should be of good family, since "only the nobly born possess a real sense of responsibility." That is a provocative phrase. The Italian again is far more violent on the subject of male effeminacy than Hoby's catalogue suggests. No courtier, says Castiglione, should be womanly either in his gestures or his diction. Such androgynies, in his opinion, "should be banished as harlots, not only from the courts of princes, but even from the society of gentlemen." Hoby, again, in translating Castiglione's "*sprezzatura*" as "recklessnesse" may well have given an incorrect impression even to the Elizabethan reader. Castiglione's argument is that civility cannot be really perfect unless accompanied by "grace" (*la grazia*), a virtue which cannot be learnt, but which can be imitated. False or mimic grace is an ugly thing and therefore *sprezzatura,* or as we should say "spontaneity" or "easygoingness," becomes "the fountain from which all grace springs." It is only by possessing spontaneity, or *sprezzatura,* that a gentleman can "conceal all artificiality and appear to do everything without design and as it were absent-mindedly" (*usar in ogni cosa una certa sprezzatura, che nasconda l'arte, et demonstri, ciò che si fa e dice, venire fatto senza fatica a quasi senza pensarvi*). I doubt whether Hoby's contemporaries realized from his use of the word "recklessnesse" how great was the importance attached by

Castiglione to good manners being natural rather than imitated or designed.

In the same way, Castiglione's hatred of all affectation is blurred by Hoby's use of the word "curiosityes." The gentleman, in Castiglione's view, should never seek to imitate others, whether they be of different nationality, or merely of greater charm and address than he is himself. It is difficult for a courtier to be really modest and natural: "*ma la mansuetudine è molto maravigliosa in un gentiluomo.*" The Italian, as we might expect, accords more importance to scholarship than can be gathered from Hoby's list. Apart from the accomplishments mentioned, the good courtier should be a scholar, and "should not despise letters, as the French do." Moreover, he should, without pompousness, possess a certain sense of personal dignity and should "not dance the moresca in the public square." Even when dancing at court he should maintain a certain austerity of manner tempered with an "*aerosa dolcezza di movimenti.*" The ideal woman, moreover, should be not merely temperate and virtuous, not merely literary and musical, but she should know how to entertain properly and should not play games "or bang a drum in the orchestra."

Such therefore were the precepts of civility considered recommendable by the Italian humanists. How were they interpreted and applied in Europe and in England?

Five

It is difficult to explain the fascination exercised upon his contemporaries by Sir Philip Sidney. As a poet and a critic he was more important than is admitted by some literary historians. His *Arcadia,* which he himself rated no higher than glass and feathers, is certainly a dull romance, although it is pleasant to recall Aubrey's snapshot of him riding over Salisbury Plain and stopping every now and then to scribble into his notebook some new image or conceit. Yet the *Arcadia* was the most popular work of the whole Elizabethan epoch, and cured our literature of the euphuistic malady. The *Apologie for Poetrie* is among the best, as it was certainly among the earliest, of critical essays. And *Astrophel and Stella* contains many of the most beautiful of English sonnets. Yet not one of these works was published during Sir Philip Sidney's lifetime. Their excellence does not explain why the citizens of London packed the windows, and even the roofs, of Fleet Street to watch his coffin trundle by.

Even at the age of twenty-three Philip Sidney had acquired a European reputation. International scholars, such as Du Plessis Mornay, Du Bartas and Lipsius could refer to him as "the flower of our age," or "this extraordinary planet." Campion could write of "this young man, so wonderfully admired and beloved of his countrymen." Languet, "the shepherd best swift Ister knows," worshipped him as a young Apollo. William of Orange and the Count Palatine competed with each other to obtain him as a son-in-law. He even charmed the grim Don John of Austria. It was widely believed that he had been offered and refused the throne of Poland. It was to him that Spenser addressed the charming verses, dedicatory of *The Shepheards Calender:*

> Goe, little booke! thy selfe present
> As child whose parent is unkent,
> To him that is the president
> Of Noblesse and of chevalree.

To some extent the adolescent renown of Philip Sidney was due to the fact that he was the nephew of Lord Leicester and regarded as heir-apparent. Few uncles, it is true, have ever been so admiring or so devoted. When Philip Sidney lay on his deathbed in the Gruithuissens house at Arnhem, Leicester wrote home: "This young man was my greatest comfort, next Her Majesty, of all the world. If I could only buy his life with all I have, next to my shirt, I would give it."

Charm, as we know, is incommunicable. We must take it for granted that this auburn-headed, solemn, rather epicene youth possessed transcendent attraction. Royden speaks of "a sweet attractive grace." Fulke Greville writes of him as a boy "possessing a lovely and familiar gravity as carried grace and reverence." He lacked gaiety, and may well have seemed to some courtiers to convey an irritating impression of intellectual and moral superiority. Yet he was most widely beloved.

By the time he was twenty-six, it must have become clear that his political career would not be successful. He may have shared the disfavor into which Lord Leicester fell; he may too openly have revealed his disgust at the ugly Alençon flirtation; he may have urged with tactless piety the merits of his father's Irish administration and have implied that so excellent a servant of the Crown did not deserve niggardly treatment. Or it may just have been that Queen Elizabeth took a personal dislike to this austere young Protestant, who was too proud to mimic infatuation, too reserved to smirk. Fulke Greville writes revealingly of "sparks of extraordinary greatness which for lack of clear vent lay concealed and in a manner smothered up." It may well have been, as Miss Mona Wilson suggests, that Philip Sidney was "too fastidious, too candid and too fragile" to imitate, still less to compete with, the braggart manners of the Elizabethan court. He failed to justify the hopes old Languet had so ecstatically expressed.

His renown, although thus unfulfilled, was deep and wide. It reached its climax when with foolish chivalry he threw away his life in an ill-planned ambuscade at Zutphen. Men of good family were at that date not expected to be killed in battle: that was an adventure reserved for other ranks. The Queen herself was angered by such self-sacrifice, regarding it as inconsiderate. But the Queen, and it is much to her discredit, had always taken a sour view of Philip Sidney.

His fame, we may conjecture, was due essentially to the fact that he became the first accepted example of English civility. In that impatient and self-glorious age, the English, much as they disliked foreign manners, were oppressed by the sneers of foreigners at their backwardness, their ignorance, and their barbarity. Here was a youth of world celebrity, who could cope in humanism with the best of European scholars; who, although he had lived in Italy, and had been painted by Paolo Veronese himself, could remain essentially English, Protestant, calm, unvaunting, unaffected. He had become, as his father wrote to his younger brother, "a rare ornament of his age, the very formular that all well disposed young gentlemen of our Court do form also their manners and life by." In him his English contemporaries recognized the perfect fusion between scholarship and elegance. In him, as Miss Mona Wilson writes, England could recognize "Castiglione's courtier adjusted to a world at once more medieval and more modern than Italy." Yet the Elizabethans, much as they admired Philip Sidney as a paragon of civility, were too excited to retain for long the shape of his decorum.

Six

It is without undue patriotic prejudice or affection that I assert that Elizabethan England acquired a peculiar radiance not seen in Europe since the lost glamour of fifth-century Greece. During that amazing interlude England, alone of western countries, was spared the distraction, the hatred and the cruelty of religious war. Entranced by the fresh miracle of national pride and order, confident that opportunity was both limitless and available to all, rejoicing with no puritan inhibitions in the splendor of youth and health, they felt a great excitement tingling in every English vein. I am aware of the shadows, but the sun was hot and strong. It was an age, if I may again quote Dr. Trevelyan, "endowed with a charm and lightness of heart, a free aspiring mind and spirit, not to be found elsewhere in the harsh Jesuit-Calvinist Europe of that day." Fortunate indeed that all this passion and gaiety should have been witnessed and interpreted by the greatest poet that the world has ever known.

Shakespeare was no social revolutionary: he accepted the established hierarchy, not only without question, but with positive pleasure. He had a natural respect for "instruction, manners, mysteries, and trades, degrees, observances." He was always contrasting the horrors of civil disturbance, of rebellion, of disputed successions, with the "order" and "sense of degree" established in England under Queen Elizabeth's shrewd rule. He had but little sympathy with the middle class, being all too inclined to use the members of that valuable community as comic material. His dislike of the proletariate, "the fool multitude," "the blunt monster with uncounted heads," was unconcealed. Only rarely, as when he portrays John Bates and Michael Williams in the bivouac on the eve of Agincourt, does he make any sympathetic attempt to understand the mentality of the uneducated. To him "Alexander Idem an esquire of Kent," in that he is satisfied with his station, is a more comforting character than Jack Cade, whose communism is caricatured as thoughtlessly as is Gonzalo's brave new world. I do not believe that Shakespeare's social views were determined solely by a desire to placate patrons: it seems to me that he quite naturally preferred the upper to the middle or the lower class. Shakespeare's direct references to manners are infrequent, but it is not difficult to recognize the type of civility which he most admired. His ideal gentleman was a person totally different from the polished conversationalist of Urbino; even as he bore no resemblance at all to the watchful courtiers who, before fifty years had passed, were to loll and dawdle in the galleries of Marly or Versailles. Osric, the typical courtier, is for him no more than "this lapwing" or "this waterfly." He had but slight respect for the outward show of ceremony, which seemed no more than "brittle glory." "And what art thou?" he exclaims:

> And what art thou, thou idol ceremony?
> What kind of god art thou?

He would have agreed with Bacon that, although some etiquette is essential, to attach importance to such matters "is not only tedious but doth diminish the faith and credit of him that speaks." Shakespeare himself, although in a somewhat menial capacity, often attended state functions. He was one of the King's company who, much to the fury of Mr. W. H., was selected in August 1604 to carry the canopy, or "cloth of honor," above the Spanish Ambassadors as they walked from the river steps to the conference Chamber in Somerset House:

> Were 't aught to me I bore the canopy,
> With my extern the outward honoring . . . ?
> No!—let me be obsequious in thy heart.

Shakespeare never supposed that court manners need entail any personal degradation. His frequent use of the image of the fawning spaniel or greyhound indicates with what contempt he regarded all servility. A courtier should be "a lord to a lord; a man to a man." And thus the elegant youths who saunter in attendance on his kings and princes, although they will address their masters as "my liege" or "your highness," never adopt towards them any tone of subservience but maintain always their personal dignity on easy terms.

Affectation of manners was a thing which Shakespeare invariably ridiculed and despised. Contemptible in his eyes were "these fashion-mongers, these pardonami's, who stand so much on the new form." He believed in *sprezzatura,* and could laugh at Malvolio for "practicing behavior to his shadow this half hour." Fashion was but a fleeting thing. "Dear Kate," says Henry V, "you and I cannot be confined within the weak list of a country's fashion. We are the makers of manners, Kate." Especially did Shakespeare despise those who imitated foreign deportment and who returned from the grand tour, "talking of Alps and Appenines, the Pyrenaean and the river Po." To him it was degrading that any Elizabethan youth should listen to:

> Report of fashions in proud Italy
> Whose manners still our tardy apish nation
> Limps after in base imitation.

Harry Hotspur sharply snubs the popinjay who recommends *parmaceti* as a cure for bruises, even as Portia derides the English lord "who bought his doublet in Italy, his round hose in France, his bonnet in Germany and his behavior everywhere." Richard III snarls suddenly: "I cannot duck with French nods and apish courtesy." To Shakespeare, foreign manners were invariably absurd.

His own ideal of civility was a mixture of daring, kindliness and high spirits. It is evident to the attentive reader that Shakespeare was not really as interested in Henry V as he was in Harry Hotspur, Othello and the bastard Philip Faulconbridge. Shakespeare's interpretation of *sprezzatura* was nearer indeed to Hoby's "recklessness" than anything that the sober Castiglione had conceived. He liked his heroes to be simple to the point of incompetence. He loved the bastard, who eschewed all tricks and compromise ("that smooth faced gentleman, tickling commodity"), and who confessed that "I lose my way among the thorns and dangers of this world." Or Harry Hotspur, whom his doting wife upbraided as "you mad-headed ape," who despised "mincing poetry," "velvet guards and Sunday citizens," and all those who indulged in plausible arguments, "this skimble-skamble stuff." Such were the idols of this great and sensitive intellectual. Pretension in any form, the pretension of Holofernes or that of Don Armado, was to him ridiculous and dull.

Kindliness also was a necessary ingredient in Shakespeare's ideal of civility. "Nature" to him "was sick of men's unkindnesses." In his philosophy lack of kindliness begat a multitude of sins, not cruelty alone, but treason, ingratitude and betrayal of trust. Manners, on the other hand, were associated with "pity and grace."

How could we conceive of Shakespeare's vision of perfect civility without adding thereto high spirits, the sort of gaiety that "makes old hearts fresh"? With how many of Shakespeare's heroes and heroines do we feel that "there was a star danced, and under that I was born." It may strike us as strange that Shakespeare could have been so careless of his reputation as to lend his name, at the very summit of his powers, to that absurd potboiler, *The Winter's Tale.* Yet when he treats of Florizel and Perdita—the loveliest pair "that twixt heaven and earth stood there begetting wonder"—the spring of his genius leaps up into a sudden fountain, flashing with love, and loveliness and gaiety. Florizel assuredly was the pattern of what Shakespeare believed a gentle youth should be. Florizel was Shakespeare's Charmides. Although a Prince of Bohemia, he was far more beautiful and merry than any Czech, or Slovak, that I have ever known. He was "the fairest youth that ever made eye swerve;" he made "a July day short as December;" he was the very symbol of the spring flowers with which his Perdita longed to deck their couch. "Be merry, gentle," he says to her, "strangle such thoughts as these." Reckless is Florizel in his joy, wishing to proclaim his love "to the earth and heaven and all;" prepared, as Shakespeare would assuredly have wished, to sacrifice the whole world for faithfulness and love:

> Not for Bohemia, nor the pomp that may
> Be thereat gleaned; for all the sun sees, or
> The close earth wombs, or the profound seas hide
> In unknown fathoms, will I break my oath
> To this my fair beloved. . . .

Was not Prince Florizel, in his reckless rapture, a happier example of civility than were the Duc de Saint-Simon, or the Duc de Luynes?

Chapter 9
L'honnête Homme

The age of Louis XIV—The Hôtel Rambouillet—
The court creates a code of manners different from
that of the rest of the world—This due largely to the
King's policy of segregation—Power separated from
grandeur—The ritual of court ceremonial—The
discipline which the King imposed—Why did the
courtiers tolerate their degradation?—Their actual
manners—Cleanliness and eating manners—The
importance attached to the unimportant—Rank
and precedence—Thus the aristocratic conception of *honnêteté* is during the seventeenth century
wholly different from the bourgeois conception—
Teachers of deportment such as Faret, Callières and
Méré—Contemporary criticism of the artificiality of
the court—Bossuet and La Bruyère—The revival of
Montaigne's doctrine of humanism—The aristocratic
and bourgeois interpretation of *honnêté* are fused
during the age of reason into the concept of "natural
politeness"—But even this retains something of the
original components of exclusiveness, ostentation,
artificiality, arrogance and cruelty.

One

WHEN WE THINK of Versailles in the full sunshine of Louis XIV, there rises in our minds the vision of a long white facade; of a terrace, so vast under the wide sky that men and women seem as beetles creeping; of clipped alleys leading down to grottoes, where, from the mouths of tritons, the water splashes continuously upon the backs of dolphins, river virgins and fat frogs. We see long galleries and high saloons, with trim trees of bay and myrtle in silver tubs, with guards grouped at entrances, with footmen in white wigs and liveries of blue. When a mirrored doorway opens, it swings a reflection of painted ceilings, of great plaques of porphyry and marble, of bronze glinting, of the soft summer sky outside. At night time we picture candles guttering in the sconces, we see brocaded groups seated around gaming tables, we hear the faint sound of stringed instruments playing one of Lulli's dreamy tunes. And we imagine that, when the King has retired splendidly to bed, the courtiers will escape to their own cramped apartments and there discuss the morning's sermon by Bossuet, the latest fable by La Fontaine, the theories of Nicole, Arnauld and Pascal, the injunctions of Jean de Balzac, the impending comedy of Molière, or the haunting rhythm of Racine's careful line. Our vision is colored by the illusions of the Fêtes Galantes:

Votre âme est un paysage choisi
Que vont charmant masques et bergamasques,
Jouant du luth et dansant et quasi
Tristes sous leur déguisements fantasques.

The Grand Siècle was not as yet the age of reason: it was indeed one of the most irrational epochs that the world has known. The dream bore slight relation to reality. It was in some ways a period of crude ostentation, of intricate inanity, of complicated grandeur. Yet it was a period that produced, not merely splendid masterpieces of art and literature, but also the first tentative sketch of what was to be the peculiarly French ideal of civility: *l'honnête homme.*

When in 1661 Louis XIV became his own prime minister, French society had not fully recovered from the shattering effects of the wars of religion and the Fronde. There was much that was still medieval about their manners and the relation between the sexes was still affected by the memory of Henri IV, *le vert galant,* with his brisk and dirty carnality. It was not the King or the court who first brought refinement to French manners: it was that truly remarkable woman, "the incomparable Arthénice," Catherine de Vivonne, Marquise de Rambouillet. At a time when Louis XIV was but a boy, shrinking under the hard and darting eyes of Mazarin, Mme. de Rambouillet, in her boudoir of blue velvet and silver, was imprinting on French manners the feminine pattern of elegance from which they have never quite recovered. She it was who established the art of conversation as the essential grace of polite society; she it was who insisted on *bienséance* or correct deportment; she it was who gave to men of letters that social prestige which, in France, they have ever since enjoyed. As Mlle, de Scudéry recorded, "she was of all women the one who best understood the meaning of politeness." The relation between the sexes was sublimated under her dictatorship into an elaborate pattern of *galanterie;* she taught her circle to treat women with adulatory reverence and to attach extreme importance to the purity of their discourse. Evening after evening the intellectuals of the age would gather in the blue salon of the Hotel Rambouillet and there discuss the latest experiments in art and letters, the new inventions of science, the beautiful precisions of grammar, and the virtues of the ancient Romans. It was not Mme. de Rambouillet who set the fashion for stilted language and absurd pretensions that were caricatured by Molière in the *Précieuses Ridicules:* it was her less gifted imitators such as Mme. de Saint Martin or Mme. de Sablé. In the history of French civility she remains a pioneer of wise and serious originality.

The Hotel Rambouillet was essentially Parisian, the prototype of a long and sparkling sequence of intellectual *salons.* When in 1672 Louis XIV established himself at Versailles and obliged his courtiers to cluster round him, creating what Dr. Norbert Elias has amusingly called his *Monopolmechanismus,* a regrettable dichotomy occurred between court manners and the manners of the rest of France. It became a principle of *bienséance* that a courtier, in his Demeanour, in the tone of his voice, in his every word and gesture, should emphasize the esoteric status of his caste. To existing class distinctions, to the inevitable disparity between the capital and the provinces, there was added this additional segregation between court society and the rest of the population. Moreover the King, in his constant dread of any revival of the Fronde spirit, kept his nobles constantly around him, isolating them from all outside interests, occupations, or contacts. A noble who remained too long on his own estates was regarded with disfavor: "I do not see him" the King would remark grimly, which meant in the language of those days: "He is in disgrace." The damage done by the gulf set between the country and its natural elite was deep and lasting. It was one of the main causes of the Revolution and, more incidentally, it confused the meaning, and delayed the acceptance, of the conception of the *honnête homme.* Before I examine the divergence between the aristocratic and the bourgeois interpretation of those words, before I suggest how this disparity was in the end almost reconciled, it will be necessary to describe how, in the Court of Louis XIV, a courtier was expected to behave.

Two

The great monarch, whose majesty held the seventeenth century spellbound, was not an intellectual. He was ill-educated, hated books, disliked any discussion of serious subjects, and only cared for glory, architecture, deportment, exotic birds, bright-colored flowers, and besieging almost undefended towns. His religion, as his sister-in-law recorded, was "that of a nursery maid." Yet he was a most formidable man and one whose virtuosity in the practice of kingship, as he understood it, amounted to genius. One cannot dismiss as accidental or mythical a sovereign who, by the power of his personality, by the very legend that he created, kept his highly intelligent subjects in awed subjection for more than fifty years.

From Mazarin Louis XIV had learnt the lesson of divide and rule. One of his devices for division was the distinction that he made between "power" and "grandeur." Power he entrusted to ministers of bourgeois origin—such as Colbert, Louvois or Pomponne—who owed their status entirely to his favor. To his courtiers he accorded "grandeur," namely all manner of decorative functions or orders and the honor of serving in the elaborate ritual of his court. To his ministers he gave daily personal access: the courtiers even when they were ambassadors returning from their posts or marshals triumphant after some campaign, were but rarely admitted to private audience. All that they could do was to accost the King as he walked slowly along the gallery towards the chapel, murmuring their petitions while their fellow courtiers listened with glee or malice. "I shall see to it," the King would reply in a low voice as he passed majestically on.

The ritual that he imposed is to us almost inconceivable. Precisely at 8:00 A.M. the valet on duty would draw aside the curtains of the great bed and exclaim in a loud voice (since he was a heavy sleeper): "Sire, it is time." The valet would then throw open the door leading to the adjoining room and there would enter the royal doctor and the bedroom attendants. The King, sitting on the side of his bed, would then be divested of his shirt and rubbed with orange water and spirits of wine. "They often," records St. Simon, "change his shirt, as he is subject to night sweats." Every other day the barber would come and shave the King.

"When," the protocol runs, "the King rises from his bed the High Chamberlain, or the First Gentleman of the Chamber, drapes the dressing gown round His Majesty, while the chief valet supports him. When the King has been handed his shirt, the first valet of the chamber assists him to adjust the right sleeve, while the first valet of the garderobe assists him to adjust his left sleeve."

The door into the Oeil-de-Boeuf would then be opened and those privileged to enjoy the *grande entrée* would file in, group outside the balustrade, and bow deeply. The High Chamberlain would then deliver a basin of holy water and a prayer book; the King would kneel for a few minutes beside his bed and say his prayers. Then followed the *seconde entrée* consisting of the royal secretaries and readers together with a few special favorites such as Marshal de Boufflers or Marshal de Villars. Thereafter came what was called "*les entrées de la chambre*" when the senior officials and the more eminent courtiers were admitted. "The King dressed himself," records St. Simon, "with skill and grace."

Once attired, Louis XIV would disappear for a while into his adjoining study, where he often examined the designs and drawings submitted to him by Mansart or Le Nôtre. Mass followed, preceded by the slow procession along the gallery to the chapel between rows of devout and questing courtiers. Then came a Council of Ministers to which no courtier was admitted; all they could see of the proceedings was the entry and exit of ministers and secretaries carrying black velvet briefcases under their arms. There followed the *petit couvert,* the King eating a long and lonely meal, while the princes, the cardinals and the high officers of state stood in complete silence behind his chair. Thereafter he would change his clothes and his wig and enter a little phaeton drawn by four ponies driven by himself. On his return from his drive would come the *débotté,* when, with the assistance of the Head Officer of the Wardrobe, the Duc de la Roche-foucauld, he would change his shoes. He then retired to Mme. de Maintenon's apartment where he signed

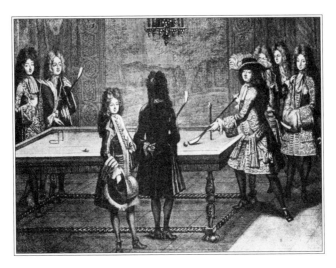

LOUIS XIV PLAYS BILLIARDS

despatches and conducted business with his secretaries. Often thereafter there came a play, a concert, a ball, a lottery, or a ballet. At ten at night supper was served at several tables in the different state rooms and the courtiers were permitted thereafter to play games of skill and chance such as billiards or lansquenet. The day concluded with the ceremony of the royal bedtime. Again the courtiers grouped respectfully behind the balustrade while the high officers of the household undressed their master. It was regarded as a special privilege to be allowed to hold the royal candlestick and a diplomatic incident was once created when the King accorded this rare honor to the English Ambassador, the Earl of Portland. Strange must have been the shadows thrown by this candle up into the painted ceiling, strange the shapes of plumes and periwigs clustering to dress a man in his nightgown; strange the muttered reverences as the courtiers withdrew.

The dignity of Louis XIV s Demeanour was more than regal, more than majestic: it was hierophantic. From the memoirs of St. Simon we catch glimpses of the mesmeric effect that he produced. On one occasion the King, when about to step into his phaeton, turned his head to address a courtier who stood behind him. "This," St. Simon remarks, "was exceptional." In general his progress was as rigid and undeviating as that of an electric hare. On another occasion, when the King lost his temper in public, the courtiers were so astonished that there followed "a hush so absolute that one could have heard an ant walking." "The awe," writes St. Simon again, "which his presence inspired imposed silence and a sense of fear." He possessed a more than royal memory for faces and would recognize each of the three hundred courtiers who hung about the palace, and would notice and remember absentees. What struck people so forcibly were the gradations of look or gesture by which favor or disfavor were conveyed. "Never," writes St. Simon, "has there existed a man so naturally well-mannered, or one whose politeness was so perfectly graduated to convey subtle distinctions in regard to rank, or age, or merit. The gradations of his courtesy were precisely registered in the way that he accepted or returned salutations. Above all, his manners towards women were incomparable:

never did he pass even the meanest skirt without raising his hat, even for housemaids, whom he knew to be
housemaids, as so often happened at Marly. On meeting a woman, he doffed his hat completely. When he
met a man of title he would half raise his hat, and he
would vary the extent to which he raised it, sometimes
going no higher than his ear, sometimes higher than
that. To lesser people he merely raised his hand to his
hat. His bows, always differentiated, but always slight,
possessed unequalled majesty and grace. At supper, he
would half rise from his seat when a woman joined the
company: but never for a man, not even for a Prince of
the blood."

His punctuality was exacting: his unceasing watch-
fulness spread terror: his dignity seemed superhuman.
He hated to see anything inelegantly performed, and
would convey to the clumsy a message to the effect
that, if they could not dance or play billiards better,
they had better abandon the attempt.

How came it that these men and women, who were
not all devoid of intelligence or self-respect, could tolerate the exhausting discipline, the long hours of waiting, the utter boredom and fatuity, the constant servitude and humiliation which etiquette imposed? How
came it that a woman of Mme. de Sévigné's independent mind could say that to be four hours in the King's
presence constituted her "sovereign delight"? How
came it that the desire "to be seen" by His Majesty, to
be classed among those who "know the Court," could

induce men and women to abandon their homes and children and spend weeks of atrocious discomfort in the attics of Versailles? How came it that La Bruyère could write quite seriously as follows:

> When you reflect how the happiness of a courtier depends upon the King's expression, how all his life he devotes his days to the ecstasy of seeing and being seen by, His Majesty, then you will begin to understand how God can become the whole glory and the whole happiness of the Saints.

We are assured that the reason why these adult men and women submitted year after year to such degradation was that the King's favor was for them the sole source of distinction, honors, decorations, appointments and even income. These ambitions appear to us too vain to be explicable. Was it not rather that the life became as compelling as a drug habit, as exciting as a lottery, as habitual as regimental or parliamentary routine? Was it not rather that they were dazed by the splendor that shone from those high windows, and fluttered like moths around a radiance which scorched their characters and seared their minds?

Three

Nor were their manners, whatever M. Taine may say, so very elegant. In spite of the purity of their diction and the grace of their movements, they relished practical jokes and indulged in salacious allusions. Even Mme. de Sévigné enjoyed reporting to her daughter the last dirty story from the court. The women often drank too much: the Duchesse de Chartres and the Duchesse de Berry were both confirmed alcoholics. They never washed, regarding water as bad for the skin and liable to induce toothache and catarrh; the most they would do was occasionally to stroke themselves with cotton wool dipped in spirits of wine. Their sanitary arrangements were, and for two centuries remained, of the most primitive nature. Although in the basement at Versailles there were latrines, which went by the name of "*chambres courteoises,*" these were so filthy that they were used only by the Swiss guards. Unless a nightstool were readily available, the courtiers would relieve themselves under the staircases or even in the galleries and saloons. The Duchesse d'Orléans, writing in 1702, records that she could not leave her apartment without encountering a courtier "*en train de pisser*" in the corridor. She also complains that at Fontainebleau there were no facilities at all and that she was obliged to use the open courtyard for her needs. The French have never

acquired a sense of shame in regard to the more grotesque functions of the body equal to that which our
own puritan ancestors obtruded into our conceptions.
They would spend hours seated on their *chaises percées*
and the Duc de Vendôme would regularly receive
ambassadors in that position. As late as 1768 we find
that model of refinement, Mme. du Deffand, writing
to thank Mme. de Choiseul for the present of a chamber pot: "*Le pot de chambre était en representation hier
toute la soirée et fit l'admiration de tout le monde.*" To
this day the French regard our reticence in such matters as evidence of ineradicable hypocrisy.

Their manners when eating were not attractive. It
is true that by the end of the century they had abandoned the habit of dipping their bread in the sauce-
boat, or throwing unwanted morsels underneath the
table. It is significant, however, that Louis XIV was so
irritated by the clean feeding habits of Mme. de Thi-
anges, the sister of Mme. de Montespan, "who always
used her fork," that he told his valet to put hairs into
her plate. After every meal the men would gargle
with scented water, spitting it out into their finger-
bowls. St. Simon speaks of "that moment of confusion after a meal when everyone is busy washing out
their mouths." I have myself, at the Cercle de l'Union
in Paris, witnessed elderly senators using their *rince-
bouche* with clamor but no shame.

The feeding habits of the courtiers were no doubt
more refined than those current even in the best

houses of the metropolis. M. Franklin, in his study of court manners, has discovered and reproduced an illuminating conversation recorded as having taken place as late as 1786 between the poet Delille and the Abbé Cosson, professor of literature at the Collège Mazarin. I summarize it as follows: Professor Cosson tells Delille that a few nights before he had been dining at Versailles. "I bet," Delille says, "that you did everything wrong." "Not in the least," answers Cosson, "I behaved exactly as everybody else." "Well, what did you do with your napkin?" "Well, I tucked it into my collar." "Not at all, courtiers spread their napkins over their knees." "Then what about the soup?" "Well, spoon and fork, of course." "Courtiers don't use forks when they have soup. And your bread?" "Well, I cut it into small pieces." "Courtiers don't cut their bread, they break it. Then what about coffee?" "Well, it was very hot, so like everybody else, I poured it into my saucer." "Courtiers don't pour their coffee into their saucers." "Well, that's odd, but I seem to have done everything the wrong way." "Yes," replies Delille, "you did, my dear Professor."

From the manuals of court etiquette published during the seventeenth century we derive further evidence of the different codes practiced respectively in Paris or at Versailles. Thus Nicolas Féret, in a manual published in 1633, lays down the following principles for a young man newly arrived at court. He must remember never to knock at a door, but to scratch at it with the nail of his little finger; the more professional courtiers allowed this nail to grow specially long for this purpose. When waiting in an anteroom, one should not take a chair, since they were reserved for very distinguished people, but seat oneself upon one of the chests ranged against the wall: it is in fact from this practice that comes the expression *"piquer de coffer."* Children of good family should never refer to their fathers except by their titles: St. Simon tells us how the courtiers roared with laughter when a German princess was so ignorant as to refer to "Monseigneur mon papa." A courtier never crosses his arms or knees; he never gesticulates; he never uses words such as *"testenon"* or *"jarni;"* he never pokes the fire or stands with his back to it; he never examines books lying on the table; and when some great person asks the time, he must wait for other more distinguished people to supply the answer.

Louis XIV would not allow his courtiers to discuss politics or diplomatic affairs; they were not themselves deeply interested in general ideas or intellectual discussions; their conversation therefore centered upon court gossip, clothes, hunting, genealogies, family connections, and above all problems of etiquette and precedence. St. Simon may have been a difficult, tetchy little man; but he was certainly not stupid. Yet page after page of his memoirs are packed with reflections which to me appear inane:

> She had married the Comte de Quintin, who
> was a Goyon of the same branch as M. de
> Matignon, who was the son of the Marquis
> de Moussaye by a daughter of Marshal Bouil-
> lon, who was a sister of the Duchesse de Tré-
> moille, of Mmes de Roucy and Duras, and of
> the Duc de Bouillon and Marshal Turenne.

One can hear him chattering such rubbish in his shrill little voice while they lolled hour after hour in the foetid anterooms of Versailles. "One could not say," wrote the Duchesse d'Orléans, "that at court there is any place for conversation. People are too afraid." Boredom brooded over Versailles like a heavy fog. "I am bored to death," wrote Mme. de Maintenon, "we gamble, we yawn, we have nothing to do, we are jealous of each other, we tear each other to pieces." "What a torture," she wrote later about Louis XIV, "to be obliged to amuse a man who is unamusable." Inevitably in such circumstances questions of precedence assumed an importance devoid of all reality. Had they observed the look that the King gave Mme. de Torcy, wife of the Foreign Secretary, when she had the audacity to seat herself upon a tabouret reserved for a duchess? Who would be accorded the apartment vacated in the Chateau by the death of the Duc de Chevreuse? Would the Electress of Hanover, if she comes to court, be asked to sit in a chair with arms, or only on a stool? Who was on the list of those to be invited next month to Marly? And was it true that the Chancellor on his last visit had been given the honor of the "*pour*"? The latter distinction was the most absurd of all; even St. Simon admits that it was foolish to attach such vast importance to so small a matter. For what did it amount to? Namely whether the intendant or billeting officer at Marly wrote the words "*pour M. le Duc de St. Simon*" in white chalk upon his bedroom door: or whether he did not.

How, in this welter of sham values, could the conception of the *honnête homme* develop or survive?

Four

I have already stated that the interpretation given to the term *honnête homme* by the courtiers at Versailles was, at least in the seventeenth century, different from that accorded to it by the bourgeoisie, or by the nation as a whole. The ordinary Frenchman used the term to signify a combination of qualities not dissimilar to those implied in our own use of the word "gentleman." To the courtier, the term meant very little more than "a man of the world," or more technically a person who "*se faisait voir du roi*" and who "*savait la cour.*" The distinction between these two interpretations is relevant to our understanding of the special, and in many ways valuable, type of civility which, during the eighteenth century, France was able to evolve. It was a type which exercised great influence upon the continent of Europe: in England, our rural habits and our distaste for conversation rendered us comparatively immune.

To the ordinary Frenchman, the term *honnête homme,* or the word *honnêteté,* signified a certain standard of education, coupled with such solid virtues as honor, dignity, and good faith. The words were used as an estimate of character rather than as a definition of status. To the courtiers, however, the expressions had no ethical or cultural associations whatsoever: they meant nothing more than a man of good family who had the entree at Marly or Versailles.

The manuals of the period, which were designed to instruct the sons of noble families how to get on at court, render it abundantly evident that *honnêteté* was regarded by the aristocracy, not as a standard of conduct, but as a technique of success. Thus J. de Callières' adaptation of the *Cortigiano* to French conditions, conveys no suggestion of the easy and high-minded brilliance of the court of Urbino, no hint of *sprezzatura,* and is avowedly written for young careerists who wish to be taught how best to please. The desire to please has in fact always constituted a fungus, destructive of the bright flower of French civility. According to Callières, the *honnête homme* is one of "the most perfected achievements of art and nature." There are certain principles of deportment which qualify a youth for this high title. He should learn how to make the best of himself and how to impress others: he should not be too virtuous or too malicious: culture is of no importance and scholarship ill befits a gentleman and can be left to the *noblesse de robe.* He need know only just enough to avoid the more glaring solecisms "such as asserting that Nuremberg is in Italy or that the Doge of Venice is Count Bucentaur." He should cultivate the society of women who are always the best teachers of *bienséance*. He should take pains to listen to the more expert conversationalists of his day, since the art of conversation "has often made people *honnêtes gens* without the aid of letters." Above all he should remember that he must always agree with important people and never contradict.

Another teacher of the period was the insufferable Chevalier de Méré, who regarded himself as an arbiter of elegance, and who between 1635 and 1668 addressed letters to many distinguished women of the court instructing them on the finer shades of civility and worldly management. Méré also contended that the most important lesson that a young man could learn was how to please. For this purpose he must cultivate "urbanity," which Méré defines as the gift of being able simultaneously to flatter and amuse. Charm, doubtless, is a boon from the gods and cannot be transmitted either by precept or example: but a young man should train himself into paths of moderation in order that, even if he be unable to give pleasure, he can at least avoid causing offense. He should thus not be too obviously ambitious, or clever, or gorgeous, or even compassionate. To feel pity for the defects or misfortunes of others is apt to disturb equanimity. His manners should be kept under perfect control and he should realize that *bienséance* is little more than a correct relation between one's own actions and exterior circumstances. If you wish to become an *honnête homme* you must master all the rules of *bienséance* and know when and how to apply them. You need not worry too much about metaphysical or moral subtleties but remember always that "what is appropriate is good, what is inappropriate is bad." In his own career as a courtier, the Chevalier de Méré was, I am glad to say, none too successful: the most interesting thing he did in life was to force Pascal to read Montaigne, when they were rumbling along in a coach together, between the poplars that line the road to Poitiers.

These and other manuals have been analyzed in Professor Magendie's detailed but ill-composed volumes on the theory of *honnêteté.* The doctrines of Méré and his fellows were regarded as gospel by the young nobles of the court and were perpetuated by the "deportment teachers," the *maîtres d'agrément,* of the eighteenth century. As the manners of the Trianon, of Marly, and of Versailles became increasingly stylized and standardized, books on etiquette were published which strike us today as no less restrictive and ridiculous than the I-Li or the Chou-Li. Antoine de Courtin in his *Civilité* gives a list of compliments and gambits for self-depreciation that should be exchanged on paying visits. Bary's *L'Esprit de la Cour* (1662) contains as many as a hundred sample conversations of the most precious inanity. Yet it is from the incidental references of the period, rather than from the actual manuals on manners, that we can deduce how wide a gulf opened between the French courtier's conception of *honnêteté* and our own undefined but quite positive generalizations as to what constituted a gentleman.

Thus Anne-Marie-Louise d'Orléans, known to her contemporaries as "La Grande Mademoiselle," in describing the then King of Portugal as "by nature malicious and cruel," as "a drunkard and a debauchee," as a man who derived "a singular pleasure from killing people," could add that he was an *honnête homme* none the less. Scarron paints a portrait of a man of fine character, noble presence, and every accomplishment, who all the same "lacked something." What was it that he lacked? "*Étaitil honnête homme? Ha! Non!*" We find Loret boasting of having been asked to a smart dinner party "just as if I had been *quelque honnête homme.*" And St. Simon, writing in 1699 upon the death of Racine, uses the revealing phrase: "Meeting him in society, one would never have supposed that he was a poet; he struck one as a complete *honnête home.*"

Honnêteté, therefore, in the courtier conception, had nothing to do with morals or even with religion, which were private affairs. The *honnête homme* was a man of noble birth who was qualified to become a good courtier, owing to his capacity to please, his social adroitness, his mastery of *bienséance,* his gallantry towards women, his grace, his taste, his gaiety and his conversational powers. At its best, this type of civility did imply a special competence in the art of living, which assuredly is no mean thing. At its worst, it reduced men and women to the level of pantins, of puppets, or jumping jacks who, without a trace of *sprezzatura,* bowed and grimaced.

There were deep faults in this ideal of civility. In the first place it was exclusive, not merely of the rest of the French nation, but also of all foreigners. The French nobles of the seventeenth century were convinced that they alone were civilized and that there was nothing on this earth that they could learn from any other nation. They were a trifle jealous of the Italians, and were not too contemptuous of the English, mainly because Charles II was himself an example of French manners and because both St. Evremond and Gramont spoke well of London. But the Germans and Dutch were to them ridiculous, the Spaniards abominable, and the rest nonexistent. In the second place their conception of *honnêteté* did not include the important components of honorable conduct or personal modesty, and omitted all idea of kindness. These faults of exclusiveness, arrogance and cruelty have infected the successive elites of French society ever since. The third fault of the seventeenth century courtiers was that they despised learning, considering that the study of books was the business of the *noblesse de robe* rather than that of the *noblesse d'epée.* In the eighteenth century, with the advent of the philosophers and the age of reason, this fault was eliminated. Thenceforward the *honnête homme,* however grand he might be in birth and swagger, was expected also to possess a cultivated mind.

Five

It is not of course to be supposed that the artificiality and false values of court life escaped the criticism of contemporary observers. "What is court life?" thundered Bossuet from the pulpit. "To subordinate every one of one's desires to the sole motive of making a career: to conceal what delights us and to endure what offends us, solely in order to be agreeable to those whom we wish to please. . . . He who does not thus mortify himself is accused of not knowing the court, *il ne sait pas la cour.*"

La Bruyère's evidence is less objective, since he was a dyspeptic man, whose views on life were harsh. He had been inconsiderately treated in the household of the Grand Condé, who forced him to dance and play the guitar in public, and he loathed his pupil, young Henri de Bourbon, who was in fact podgy, yellow-faced, homosexual, indisciplined and mean. His criticisms, which were cast in the shape of Theophrastian "Characters" and were published in 1688, were important since they achieved wide popularity and did much to expose, and thus to mitigate, the faults of the whole system. La Bruyère attacked the manners of the court with acuity and venom. "The most flattering of all reproaches," he wrote, "that one can make to a man is to accuse him of not knowing the court." A young man, he contended, who spent a few months at court returned having lost something of his natural uncouthness and most of his natural honesty. The ideal courtier, he contended, possesses neither candor, kindness, generosity, dignity, nor strength of character. The life at court was no more than "a serious and melancholy gambling game," to succeed in which one's "impudence must be both authentic and naive." "Who," he asks, "is more of a slave than an assiduous courtier, unless it be an even more assiduous courtier?"

La Bruyère taught his contemporaries that the essence of politeness is not etiquette, or even *bienséance,* but a gift of rendering others at ease and satisfied with themselves. The true *honnête homme* always considers the self-esteem of others and never seeks to humiliate them by being too amusing, boastful, glorious or pedantic. Politeness to La Bruyère was a matter of the heart. "Incivility," he writes, "is not merely a single vice; it is the compound of several vices—of stupid vanity, of ignorance of one's duties to others, of not wanting to take trouble, of jealousy, of contempt for other people, of absent-mindedness, of lack of intelligence."

Such criticisms of existing conventions, such indications of a more humane conception, gradually loosened the taut assumptions which Louis XIV, with his extraordinary hypnotic gifts, had succeeded in imposing. In spite of Pascal's warnings about the dangers of self-centeredness, in spite of his accusation that Montaigne was "careless on the subject of salvation," the men and women of the late seventeenth century returned avidly to the *Essais* which, almost a century ago, the little humanist had written, in his ivory tower above the valley of the Dordogne. Montaigne taught them that personality was a complicated but sacred thing, not to be restricted or endangered by conventions. "We must try," Montaigne had written, "to cultivate our own authenticity. Such wisdom as I learnt is based on truth, reality and freedom of expression." To him the concern with precedence was not more than a "foolish pretension;" he regarded ceremony as unworthy of human dignity and was himself careful to observe in his own household only the most meager formulas of politeness. In his château at Montaigne he would, when neighbors called, "keep silent, absent-minded and self-absorbed;" when they had gone, he would shuffle across the courtyard to his separate tower, the steps of which are still worn by his impatient little feet, and shut himself up alone in his study, alone with the great Stoic mottoes inscribed upon the rafters, alone with his books and papers, alone, above all, with the delicious privacy of himself.

To his contemporaries and to those successors who were wearied of the narrow emptiness of the court, Montaigne explained that men and women, whatever might be their birth, were primarily individuals, and not mere names scrawled in white chalk upon the bedroom doors at Marly. He taught them that every individual possessed a given personality or "*maîtresse forme*," which it was his or her duty to examine, to cultivate and to exploit. He taught them that truthfulness and sincerity, rather than a superficial regard for the conventions, were the real tests of decency. "I should rather," he wrote, "commit adultery than tell a lie." He taught them to be tolerant in everything and not to accept as eternal verities the prejudices or aphorisms of commonplace people. Upon the rafters of his study were carved the mottoes: "I determine nothing, I do not pretend to understand things; I suspend judgment; I examine." "Rejoice," runs another motto, "in the things that are present; all else is beyond thee." And in sharp letters incised upon the beam ran the great precept of humanism: "*Homo sum: humanum nihil a me alienum puto.*"

It was Montaigne also who had insisted that a man who had once learnt the true art of living would not be able to endure the narrow exclusiveness of an esoteric society, but would get out into the world, forget all about class or caste distinctions, and find that there were great lessons to be learnt from men of differing status and of differing nationalities. "The well-bred man," he wrote, "must be an all-round man. I regard all humanity as my compatriots." In the end he returns to his central doctrine, and concluding the last volumes of his essays with the immortal injunction: "It is an absolute perfection, and as it were divine, to know how, in all sincerity, to get the very most out of one's own individuality: *de scavoyr jouyr loiallement de son estre.*"

In spite, as I have said, of the great Pascal, the insidious insistent voice of Montaigne penetrated to the conscience of the seventeenth century and served, as Professor Boase has taught us, to connect the humanism of the Renaissance, which had almost been forgotten, with the age of reason that was to come. The concept of the *honnête homme* owing duties to universal conscience rather than to clique *bienséance* was repeated and expanded by St. Evremond and La Rochefoucauld. "We should strive," wrote the latter, "to discover what is natural to ourselves and not to depart from the area of personal authenticity." That, assuredly was a restatement of the Montaigne doctrine. To a courtier, on whom it was already beginning to dawn that he was no more than a cog in the *Monopolmechanismus,* it came as a revelation of a better self-respect.

Gradually, therefore, the narrow court concept of the *honnête homme* as an example of drawing room behavior widened into the bourgeois belief in a duty towards one's neighbor as part of the duty towards one's self: civility broadened into civilization. Voltaire, when dedicating *Zaire* to Sir Everard Fawkener ("*à M. Fakener, Marchand anglais*"), speaks of the cosmopolitanism of letters and uses the old old term in a new eighteenth century way. "All those," he writes, "who care for the arts are fellow citizens. *Les honnêtes gens qui pensent* share the same principles and constitute a single republic." In this passage the term is used, not to designate those who knew the court, but as we might write: "All men of intelligence, whatever their nationality." It was Voltaire again who, while claiming that the French were "the most sociable and polite of all nations," contended that their manners were "no arbitrary rule of behavior, or what we might call "civility," but a law of nature, which the French have cultivated perhaps more than any other race."

The concept of the *honnête homme* developed therefore during the eighteenth and nineteenth centuries into a valid type of civility. He was expected to be a man of probity, culture, intelligence and taste; he was expected to perfect the art of living, even of good living, but without excess; he was expected in his social relationships to be, not courteous only, but also stimulating; he was expected to polish his own pattern of behavior till it became both distinguished and urbane. Yet the truly excellent type of civility represented by the *honnête homme* retains to this day a few vestiges of courtly faults. Modesty is not prominent among the recommended virtues. Even as the young courtier was taught to "*se faire voir du roi,*" so also is the young normalien of today encouraged to "*se faire valoir,*" or, as we might say, to show off. The environment of the *honnête homme* is urban rather than rural; he shines more brightly in a drawing room than on the downs. The old exclusiveness may have ceased to be a caste exclusiveness, but it is still nationalistic, in the sense that most Frenchmen, even today, regard foreigners—their languages, their arts, their letters— as of comparative unimportance. I should not say that the competitive covetousness of Marly or Versailles had left no traces of jealousy in their souls. The high price that they set on brilliant conversation renders their society alarming to the inarticulate. Nor do they feel it necessary to be kind.

Chapter 10

The English Gentleman

King Arthur—Spenser's romanticism and Shakespeare's gift of enjoyment—Reasons why the gentleman idea differed from the French conception of
the *honnête homme*—Decline in court influence—
Primogeniture—The middle class—Importance of
country pursuits—Agriculture—Sport—Cricket—
Deportment of a gentleman—Richard Brathwaite—
Sir Tobie Matthew—Snobbishness about trade—
The drunken squire and besotted parson—Cobbett's
criticism of the English landowning class—Defoe
on the cult of stupidity—Dr. Johnson and civility—
Lord Chesterfield not an example of English civility—Whig Society—The Devonshire House circle—
Their glory and defects.

One

I T WOULD BE agreeable if we could trace the origins of the English gentleman back to the sixth
century and take as our first example Arthur, son

of Uther Pendragon, who ruled at Caerleon on Usk. It was he who killed the giant of St. Michael's Mount, who conquered Ireland and Iceland, who married the Roman lady Guanhamara, who defied the Emperor, who was mortally wounded by Modred on the banks of the Camel, and who was borne away to Avalon on a mystic barge. It was he, we are assured, who formed the Round Table from his knights, Bediver, Gwalchmei, Walwain, Kay and others as examples to the world of purity, politeness and courage. It must be confessed, however, that King Arthur was little more than the vestige of some forgotten Celtic legend and that, even when reanimated by Geoffrey of Monmouth, Malory, Chretien de Troyes, Lady Charlotte Guest and Tennyson—he remains, not English, but Welsh.

I have already suggested that the age of chivalry and the Renaissance produced in England types that were markedly different from the current continental mode. Edmund Spenser, although "called from faery land to struggle through dark ways," did certainly transmit to his contemporaries the shimmer of medieval fantasies and ideals which in Spain, in Italy, and in France had long since become outmoded. The evanescent mists of Spenser's poetry hung in the brisk Elizabethan air:

> *Qual è colui che somniando vede,*
> *E dopo il sogno la passione impressa*
> *Rimane, e l'altro alla mente non riede;*
> *Cotal son io; che quasi tutta cessa*
> *Mia visione, ed ancor mi distilla*

Nel cor lo dolce che nacque da essa.
Così la neve al sol si disigilla
Così al vento nelle foglie lievi
Si perdea la sentenza di Sibilla.

The graciousness of mild Spenser is reflected in Philip Sidney's verse and prose. In Shakespeare it becomes virile, handsome, active, liberated, gay. The color of his characters is every decade rendered fresh and new; the thoughts and feelings of successive generations are molded, often quite unconsciously, by their Shakespearean experience. Undoubtedly the gentleman idea is to this day lit for us by many memories of our greatest poet, even as the thoughts of Germans and Frenchmen are still conditioned by Goethe and Racine. Such theories, although relevant, are speculative. It is wiser to examine the evolution of the gentleman idea in the more concrete terms of historical development and insular conditions.

The divergence between the English type of civility and the French conception of the *honnête homme* can be ascribed to precise causes. There was the transference of authority from Crown to Parliament; the social mobility afforded by the custom of primogeniture and the self-confidence of a respected middle class; a congenital preference for rural over urban life; insularity; realism, with its attendant gift of proportion; and that sense of individual responsibility that comes so readily to men who live in climates that are equable but grey.

Our feudal nobility had all but destroyed itself by the Wars of the Roses: the Tudors sought to complete this process. The great families of the past were deliberately impoverished by sumptuary laws and the depreciation of the currency. A fresh class of hereditary administrators was created: the old conception of feudal service was succeeded by a new and lasting conception of service to the state.

Although, until 1649, the English *noblesse de robe,* in that their status was dependent upon royal favor, were more or less subservient to absolutism, they tended in succeeding generations to form themselves into an oligarchy which after the Glorious Revolution, became the source of power. In France, until the final collapse, the court remained the sun round which the system revolved; in England it ceased to be the focus of ambition or even the mint of elegance. After the death of Charles II, who as Defoe remarked had "a world of wit and not one grain of ill-nature," the glamour of court life was but intermittently revived. In 1698 the palace of Whitehall was almost totally destroyed by fire; William III was Dutch in any case, suffered much from asthma and could not tolerate the London mists; Queen Anne was an almost constant invalid; the first three Georges were but crude examples of civility. The court ceased to be the nucleus of London society and became a national exhibit of domestic, and even bourgeois, virtue. Those who were attracted by the flamboyance of the Regency, or the luxury of the Marlborough House circle, were not fully representative of the political or social values of the time. Thus while French youths of rank and ambition still dawdled in the galleries of Versailles or Fontainebleau, their English counterparts would gather in the lobbies at Westminster, in the anterooms of rising statesmen, or at the country seats of the Whig and Tory magnates. The courtier was a far less imposing figure than the man of the world.

The custom of primogeniture rendered it necessary for the younger sons of all but the wealthiest landowners to earn their living. The great territorial magnates might be able to send all their boys to a public school and thereafter to find a pocket borough for them or a sinecure. But during the reign of Queen Anne the country gentry were hard hit by the land tax imposed as a result of the Whig wars and the sons of the squire were frequently obliged to attend the local school, where they would mix on equal terms with the sons of farmers and tradesmen. Instead of wasting their years in penurious gentility, these young men went out into the world to seek their fortunes, or at least to earn their livelihoods, as sailors, soldiers, dons, civil servants, lawyers, diplomatists, clergymen, and even merchant adventurers. This mobility prevented the English aristocracy from becoming static, inbred or dull.

The expansion of trade had meanwhile created a large and powerful commercial community. Instead of remaining in their counting houses, these mercantile magnates sought invariably to acquire territorial status. "Merchants," wrote Adam Smith, "are commonly ambitious of becoming country gentlemen." It was not difficult in England for a member of one class to rise or marry into the class above him. Although in theory a man could only claim to be a "gentleman" if he were an *armiger* possessing a coat of arms duly registered with the College of Heralds, in practice it was easy to acquire or evade such registration. "As for gentlemen," wrote Sir Thomas Smith in 1583, "they be made good cheap in England." The English, moreover, being a mercantile people, were always inclined to attach as much importance to wealth as they did to breeding. "Gentilitie," wrote Lord Burghley, "is nothing but ancient riches." As the centuries passed, it was the extent, rather than the antiquity, of a man's fortune that made him welcome in society.

The English, again, have never been an urban, still less a municipal, people. Being intelligent rather than intellectual, inarticulate rather than garrulous, they have always preferred the country to the town. As early as 1489 Poggio Bracciolini had asserted in his *De Nobilitate* that the English were unworthy of aristocracy owing to their debased affections for rural pursuits. Even the merchants, he complains, once they had acquired their fortunes, immediately purchased rural estates and were absorbed into the landed gentry. Although in France, the courtier was always regarded as the social superior of the squire, in England gentility came to be associated with the possession of land. Sir

Walter Elliot, who is depicted in *Persuasion* as a typical Tory landowner snob, when referring to a curate of excellent manners but remote territorial connections, uses the revealing phrase: "You misled me by the term *Gentleman.* I thought you were speaking of some man of property." The ownership of an estate, rather than the brilliance of a court appointment, thus became the aim of all ambitious men. It was a salutary incentive, in that plough land and woodland possess their own humanism, rendering calm the temperament of man; and his mind, slow and gentle.

The love of country pursuits exercised a leveling influence on English society. The ancient nobility had taken but slight interest in agriculture. "Feudal barons," remarks Lord Ernie, "are rarely represented as fumbling in the recesses of their armor for samples of corn." Yet by the eighteenth century our great landowners had become the pioneers of scientific farming. There were men like Jethro Tull, Lord Townshend known as "turnip Townshend," Robert Bakewell, and above all Coke of Norfolk, whose sheep shearing exhibitions at Holkham became national events. They mixed with farmers and yeomen on comparatively equal terms.

The practice of field and other sports also rendered our rural society more democratic. In 1769, for instance, the Duke of Dorset captained a cricket eleven composed of the Knole servants and gardeners Pattenden, Minchin, Fish, Bartram and Shearey. These matches took place on the Vine cricket ground at Sevenoaks and were celebrated in contemporary verse:

> His Grace the Duke of Dorset came
> The next enrolled in skilful fame
> Equall'd by few; he plays with Glee
> Nor peevish seeks for Victory.
> His Grace for bowling cannot yield
> To none but Lumpey in the field,
> And far unlike the modern way
> Of blocking every ball at play,
> He firmly stands with Bat upright
> And strikes with his athletic might,
> Sends forth the ball across the Mead
> And scores six notches for the deed.

These encounters, and they were frequent, between Lumpey and His Grace, produced a tone different from the injunction of Castiglione that a man of good family should not play games with his inferiors unless he were quite certain to win.

Such were some at least of the causes and conditions which went to create the English type of civility. The qualities of gentleness, modesty, tolerance and humor distinguished it from other types.

Two

Although during the seventeenth and eighteenth centuries the actual deportment of a man of the world was still derived from Italian manuals and

French examples, the conduct of an English gentleman was based upon an original, an indigenous, attitude towards life. Great importance was attached to "freedom" of manners, which, during the zenith of Whig aristocracy, may have led to arrogant insouciance, but which forms a continuous fibre in the pattern of English civility, a recurrent thread of *sprezzatura*. "Behavior," wrote Francis Bacon early in the seventeenth century, "is the garment of a mind and ought to have the conditions of a garment. For first, it ought to be made in fashion; secondly, it should not be too curious or costly; thirdly, it ought to be so framed as best to set forth any virtue of the mind and supply and hide any deformity; and lastly, and above all, it ought not to be strait, so as to confine the mind and interfere with its freedom in business and action."

It is interesting to note how early the qualities and capacities expected of an English gentleman diverged from those recommended for the courtier abroad. At the date when the Chevalier de Méré was composing his precepts of *bienséance,* or when Callières was instructing young Frenchmen how to render themselves agreeable at Marly, Richard Brathwaite had already published his *English Gentleman and English Gentlewoman,* which appeared in 1630.

Born in Westmorland and educated at Oriel, Brathwaite practiced at the Bar and took the King's side in the Civil War. He thereafter retired to Catterick, where he served for years as Justice of the Peace and where he died much honored at the age of eighty-five. His son, Sir Strafford Brathwaite, was murdered by Barbary pirates off the coast of Algeria. Brathwaite had varied experience of urban and rural life, wrote many pastorals and madrigals, and was a master of tense and vigorous prose. His principles of civility are of considerable interest.

Brathwaite's English gentleman differs from the *honnête homme* in five significant respects. In the first place, Brathwaite insists that good manners are something more than mere external politeness, but must reflect the moral nature of man. "Virtue," he writes, "is rather expressed by goodness of person than greatness of place." "Gentility," he writes again, "is not known by what we wear but by what we are." In the second place, he insists that the true gentleman, while possessing the virtues of piety and self-discipline, must also cultivate modesty. "In very deede," he writes, "there is no ornament which adds more lustre to a gentleman than to be humbly-minded, being as low in conceit as he is high in place. The gentleman scorns pride as a derogation of Gentry." The gentlewoman also should value humility as "the princesse of virtues, the conqueress of vices, the mirror of virgins, and the crown of chieftains." In the third place, unlike his French contemporaries, Brathwaite sets great value on the virtue of compassion. "It is," he writes, "the badge of gentry to show compassion towards misery." In the fourth place, he insists that the gentleman and the gentlewoman should not spend their days in town or at the court, but should devote most of their time to their estates and their country neighbors. The gentleman should learn to admire the beauties of nature, since "there is no delight of mountain, vale, coppice, or of river whereof he makes not a useful and contemplative pleasure." The gentlewoman should also live on the family estates: "Her constant reside is in the country, where hospitality proclaims her inbred affection for works of piety. The open fields she makes her gallery." All this takes us far away from Marly or Versailles.

Finally Brathwaite makes the highly original statement that no man can claim to be a gentleman unless he has something to do. Idleness must be condemned "as the very mothe of man's time." Since the days of Adam it has been the duty of man to work for his living. Sloth, he contends, "maketh of men women, of women beasts, and of beasts monsters." A gentleman should see to it that he never provides an example of indolence, "since he sins doubly who sins exemplarily." A man must examine his own aptitudes (what Montaigne would have called his *maîtresse forme*) and decide whether he be better suited for public or for private activity. "There is a necessity of vocation," he writes, "enjoyned of all, of what ranke or degree soever. . . . A peculiar vocation is deputed to everyone in this pilgrimage of human frailty." Brathwaite would not have classed the lounging life of a French courtier under the heading of "vocation." To him inactivity was an ungentleman like defect.

The rules of deportment which he advocates are also different from those of the continental manuals. He is strongly opposed to the "cringe or ducke" of court etiquette, holding that "legges were held for useful supporters, but no complimentall postures." A gentlewoman should be careful to walk soberly and to avoid circular movements, or "tinkling with the feet," or "a jeeting and strutting pace." "We were not," he remarks, "borne to glory in our feet, the bases, of mortality, but to walk as children of light in holiness and integritie." A young man should never adopt "a neglectful or scornefull countenance, contemptuously throwne on an inferior." He should not strive to shine in conversation but should remember that the tongue "is a small member but very glibbery." He should realize that "gorgeous attire is the attire of sinne;" should remember always that clothes are the symbol of man's first fall ("Adam was his own taylor"); and, instead of copying foreign fashions, he should follow the examples of "the Russian, the Muscovian, and Ionian, nay even the barbarous Indian," who all retain their national dress unaffected by foreign styles. Similarly the English gentlewoman should avoid the "phantastique habits of forraine fashions;" she should observe that in continental courts there is much to condemn and little to imitate; she should avoid all artificial or conventional manners, striving "not to entertaine ought that may estrange her from herself," and preserving always "the incomparable liberty of her mind before the mutable formality of a deluded age."

Richard Brathwaite's attitude towards sport and games was not exuberant. He derided the practice of hawking as no more than "a desire to follow feathers in the ayre." He fears that a man may become "besotted" by the love of sport and contends that a surfeit of hunting and shooting may weaken the mind. "How soon," he remarks, "were the Israelites cloyed with quailes!" A gentleman may go to the theater, provided that he does not make a habit of it; he may drink wine moderately but should never forget that taverns are "devil's booths;" he may even gamble, provided that the stakes are not so high as to provoke "base and unworthy feare." Fencing and dancing are recreations suited to a gentleman, although he must be careful never to make a display of his prowess or adopt "those mimicke trickes which our apish professants use." Chess is a respectable game, but if a man become too proficient he should recall "that we have heard of an ape which played chess in Portingall." If he cares for cards he should choose those card games which exercise the mind:

> The Maw requires a quicke conceit and present pregnancy: The Cleeke because of variety requires a retentive memorie: the Cribbage a recollected fancy: the Pinache quick and unenforced dexterity.

In practice the English gentleman of the seventeenth century was formed, not so much by precepts such as those of Richard Brathwaite, as by the tolerance born of insular security, an equable climate, and a gentle soil. "No man," wrote Brathwaite's contemporary, Sir Tobie Matthew, "is more remote than an Englishman from the diggedness of long-standing and indelible revenge." Sir Tobie had spent most of his life in Italy, in Spain and in the Low Countries. As a Catholic, he was exposed in his own island to many disabilities and some persecution. He died in exile at Ghent. Yet in spite of his misfortunes he could write that the English possessed as it were a monopoly "of a certain thinge called Good Nature."

By the seventeenth century, therefore, the gentleman was supposed to be considerate to others, to avoid foreign or courtly fashions, to spend most of his time on his estates, to be employed upon some useful function, and to possess, in addition to humility, tolerance, forgiveness and compassion. These are precious components of true civility. What were the defects?

Three

It is many centuries since the title of gentleman was given only to people of good birth. Until late into the eighteenth century, however, the idea persisted that no man could claim to be a gentleman if he were engaged in commerce. "Trade," wrote John Locke, "is wholly inconsistent with a gentleman's calling." This exclusiveness did not long survive the establishment of an influential and highly cultivated middle class. We already find Addison in the *Spectator* deriding these sprigs of nobility "who would rather be starved like gentlemen than thrive in a trade or profession that is beneath their quality." Richard Steele sturdily contended that it was just as gentlemanlike to be a scholar or a merchant as it was to be a man about town. It became unintelligent to regard as inferior such admirable characters as Josiah Wedgwood or Matthew Boulton. The latter, who was known as "princely Boulton," was founder of the Lunar Club, where he entertained highly eminent people including Benjamin Franklin, Erasmus Darwin, Joseph Priestley and that entrancing character R. L. Edgeworth. A rightful distinction did, however, persist between the long-established city merchant, or the cultured manufacturer, and the speculators or the adventurers. Against the young men who went out to India to collect rapid fortunes, and to return to England as nabobs, Burke delivered one of the most justified of his invectives:

> Animated with all the avarice of age and all the impetuosity of youth they roll in one after the other; wave after wave; and there is nothing before the eyes of the natives but an endless, hopeless prospect of new flights of birds of prey and passage.

Yet throughout the eighteenth and the first two-thirds of the nineteenth centuries a prejudice did persist against those who, while not living on their estates or practicing one of the liberal professions, assisted the community by making or trafficking in commodities. This form of snobbishness was unsuited to a commercial nation.

A second defect in the English system was that the country gentry were not entirely composed of the rosy sportsmen of our Christmas Supplements. Many of them were bad landowners and most of them were illiterate and drunken. Even the Church was apt to become rurally degraded and the besotted parson was a not unusual figure in the community:

> The reverend wig, in sideway order placed,
> The reverend band by rubric stains disgraced,
> The leering eye in wayward circles rolled,
> Mark him the pastor of a jovial fold,
> Whose various texts excite a loud applause,
> Favoring the bottle and the good old cause.

Crabbe may have suffered from excess of moral indignation, but his portraits were not inaccurate. The gentleman ideal, both in the pulpit and on the hunting field, was frequently debased.

It is well to check our eulogy of the beneficent landowner and the jolly squire by recalling William Cobbett's indictments. It may be true that Cobbett wrote with exaggerated bitterness, but he does remind us that England was not peopled wholly by a prosperous peasantry doffing hats to Sir Roger de Coverley and his grandchildren. "There is," writes Cobbett, "in the men calling themselves English country gentlemen something superlatively base. They are, I sincerely believe, the most cruel, the most unfeeling, the most brutally insolent. I know; I can prove; I can safely take my oath that they are the most base of all creatures that God ever suffered to take human shape."

Cobbett was not thinking only of enclosures and evictions; he was thinking of the game laws of 1671 which still persisted little modified in his own day. Thus whereas Sir Roger de Coverley who, after all, was a little mad, would fiercely punish a boy found with a dead rabbit, he would himself net as many as forty coveys of partridges in a single season.

In the third place, the English country gentleman was contemptuous of education. As early as 1728, Daniel Defoe, in what was the last of his invectives, condemned the patrician who despised intelligence. "To me," he wrote, "an untaught, unpolished, gentleman is one of the most deplorable objects in this world." In England the landed gentry were the richest in the world; unlike their French contemporaries they were not dependent on royal favor or obliged to dance attendance at the Court. Yet these advantages remain unused, "because of a voluntary and affected stupidity and ignorance, which they adhere to as obstinately as the Muscovites." They are unable even to realize the difference between a liberal education and "the mere old woman literature of a nurse or a tutor." If they examined themselves, or compared themselves with others, the gentlemen of England would soon recognize how empty they are within and how poor they seem in relation to the educated. Why is it, asks Defoe, that our aristocracy should be so illiterate and unaesthetic? "No Russian stupidity," he asserts, "was ever more gross in its nature or half so pernicious in its consequences." They allow others to fight their wars and conduct their politics. As a result, the government of the realm falls into the hands of "knaves, politicians, mercenaries and screwed up engines." "Their business," he concludes, "is to hunt the stag and the fox with their own hounds and among their own woods. Their fame is on the field of pleasure, not on the field of battle."

It must be confessed that the English gentleman, especially if he be devoted to field and other sports, is apt to attribute slight importance to mental felicity or learning. I happen to enjoy the system, having suffered much on the continent from people who pretend to be intellectuals when they are not. Yet it is undeniable that a type of civility that excludes or misprises the humanities compares ill with the ideal of the perfectly endowed and developed human being which the Greeks and the best teachers of the Renaissance held as examples for emulation.

But it is time that we left the country and considered the town, exchanging kind Sir Roger for Buttons or the Cocoa Tree.

Four

Immediately we find ourselves in the rich, smoky, strepitous city in which Dr. Johnson delighted. "No, Sir," he thundered, "when a man is tired of London, he is tired of life." "His love of London," Boswell tells us, "was so strong that he would have thought himself an exile in any other place, particularly if residing in the country." "A blade of grass," Johnson grumbled to Mrs. Thrale, who was on the point of acquiring rural sensibilities, "is always a blade of grass. Men and women are *my* subjects of enquiry." He asserted that those who were content to live in the country were fit only for the country. "A man," he remarked, "cannot know modes of life as well in Minorca as in London. But he can study mathematics as well in Minorca."

I shall not, for these and other reasons, exhibit this great and good man as an example of English civility. He was kind to his cat, "Hodge," and bought him oysters; he was kind to his strange assortment of dependents; he was wonderfully kind to children, servants and beggars. But he was not kind to his equals or his superiors. No other man could have reduced Charles James Fox to silence or frightened Gibbon into whispering his sneers. He was intolerant of foreigners and presumptuous in the expression of his dislikes. "The French," he asserted, "are a gross, ill-bred, untaught people: a lady there will spit on the floor and rub it in with her foot. . . . A Frenchman must be always talking, whether he knows anything of the matter or not: an Englishman is content to say nothing when he has nothing to say."

To Dr. Johnson conversation was more than a social amenity, more even than an agreeable intercourse: it was "a trial of intellectual vigor and skill." He would defend an impossible argument and browbeat his interlocutor, whereas he became sulky if himself talked down. His ideal conversation was a discussion in which he triumphed over the company by the weight of his erudition, the splendor of his memory, and the amazing range of his vocabulary and discourse. "No, Sir," he once replied to Boswell's enquiry, "we had talk enough but no conversation: there was nothing discussed."

What is so strange about this uncouth but lovable man is that he really did admire the elegance of which he was himself incapable. "Any man of any education," he remarked, "would rather be called a rascal than accused of deficiency in the graces." With his respect for established institutions he was frankly fond of the aristocracy. His friend Topham Beauclerk who was a man about town, was a constant glory to him. He contended even that the aristocracy were more moral and temperate than the middle and agricultural classes; it was merely that their vices acquired greater prominence. "Few lords," he said, "will cheat." He appreciated dignity and distinction in an aristocrat, provided that it was not accompanied by a contemptuous tone. Speaking of

Lord Chesterfield towards the end of his life Johnson observed: "His manner was exquisitely elegant and he had more knowledge than I expected." What he lacked was consideration. "Lord Orrery was not dignified: Lord Chesterfield was, but he was insolent." And thus Lord Chesterfield is dismissed with the remark that he had at first seemed a lord among wits only to be discovered as a wit among lords. As for the *Letters to his Son,* they taught little more than "the morals of a whore and the manners of a dancing master."

We can well understand why Johnson, "a retired and uncourtly scholar," should have been incensed at the disdainful manner of Lord Chesterfield and by the fact that, whereas he the lexicographer was kept waiting in the anteroom, the playwright Colley Cibber should be admitted by the private stair. Yet the letters which Lord Chesterfield over all those years addressed to his son cannot be dismissed as readily as that. For many men and women of his generation they constituted the very textbook of civility; they must at least be considered.

Lord Chesterfield was not seeking to instill into young Philip Stanhope the principles of ethics and religion or even the foundations of a liberal education. He left such instruction to the several tutors by whom the lout was led through Europe. His aim was to assist Philip in acquiring "the air, the address, the graces and the manners of a man of fashion." Since these embellishments were perfected at the court of France, it is to French manners, rather than to English manners, that he directs his son's attention. Philip must cultivate '*les Manières, la Tournure, et les Graces d'un Galant Homme et d'un Homme de Cour.*"

Modesty, for instance, is not to his mind a social virtue. The English, he writes, are often apt to be shy but "a gentleman who is used to the world comes into company with a graceful and proper assurance. This is called usage of the world and good breeding: a most necessary and important knowledge in the inter-course of life."

"The perfection of good breeding," he writes again, "is to be civil with ease and in a gentleman-like manner. For this you should observe the French people; who excel in it, and whose politeness seems as easy and nat-ural as any other part of their conversation. Whereas the English are often awkward in their civilities, and, when they mean to be civil, are too much ashamed to get it out."

He goes on to ridicule those "English boobies," who are so self-conscious that they are constantly afraid of being laughed at. To our minds, on the contrary, no Englishman can be a perfect gentleman unless, like the Duke of Wellington, he be often shy; nor is the fear of ridicule separable from a sense of humor. To teach dif-ferently is to teach something French.

Lord Chesterfield desired his son to emulate what he called "*les manières nobles,*" by which he meant "an almost irresistible address, a superior gracefulness in all you say and do." At the date that he received this particular letter, Philip Stanhope was eight years old. He developed into a clumsy, untidy young man of slovenly habit. He stammered all his life. He must have been a deep disappointment to Lord Chesterfield.

Such moral and educational precepts as were included in the *Letters* were based upon the worldly principle of "do not be found out." It is well, says Lord Chesterfield, "to know about religion and morals and to preserve the appearance of both." It will do young Philip no lasting harm to consort with men of learning, even with writers and artists. But he must be careful not to become identified with any clique: "for if you do you will only be considered as one of the literati by profession, which is not the way either to shine or rise in the world."

The weekly reports from Philip's tutors did not suggest to the anxious father that his son was progressing very rapidly towards perfection of deportment. He urges him to avoid "odd motions, strange postures and ungenteel carriage. Awkwardness of carriage is very alienating." He must be careful about his pronunciation and vocabulary; he must avoid the frequent use of the adverb "vastly" and must not pronounce "obliged" as "obleiged" or "earth" as "yearth." Always he must remember that the most important thing in life is what the French call "*bienséance,*" the Romans *decorum* and the Greeks *to prepon*. In everything, moderation is preferable to excess.

Boswell, who met Philip Stanhope in later life, says that he was a kind but clumsy, sloppy man; Fanny Burney said he had "as little good breeding as any man I met with." Which suggests that it is a mistake to instruct our sons by precept rather than by example.

Five

When we pass beyond the Johnson period, when we leave the coffeehouses of the bohemians, or even the drawing rooms of Mrs. Montague and Mrs. Stillingfleet, we reach the upper altitudes where "the polite imagination" found its happiest level and where all men and women were possessed of "sense and taste." It was in this rarified atmosphere that the correct relation was established between poet and patron, such as that between Harley and Swift, or Dorset and the writers whom he would entertain in the Poets Parlour at Knole. There were men like Burlington, the arbiter of architectural elegance, the friend and support of William Kent. There were men like Shaftesbury, who held the doctrine that good taste, in that it implied a harmony between morals and aesthetics, had a positive ethical validity. As the century drew to its end there came the period of the refined and opulent Whig magnates, with their grisaille colonnades, their parks, their pictures, their love affairs, their flutes and their collections of coins, marbles, hard stones, and hangers-on.

The old conception of *sprezzatura* became enlarged into a seemingly indolent indifference, a good-humored insouciance. Charles James Fox, with his amazing vitality of taste and action, his passion for poetry, his fierce politics, his exuberant oratory, his love of the country, his passionate zest for gambling, and his devotion to his friends, became the idol of them all. His attitude towards life was both more lazy and more erratic than that of doddery Sir Roger. When he died, to all appearances a magnificent failure, he told them how glad he was that he had always "lived happy."

It was in the sixty years that preceded the Reform Bills of 1830 that English society, and with it what might be called the aristocratic concept of a gentleman, reached its zenith. To their minds a gentleman must possess a splendid naturalness; a perfect self-assurance, a gift for all the arts of life. He must be frank and outspoken, capable of manly sentiment, even of sensibility, polished and precise. He must understand the country, attend to his estates and gain pleasure from rural pursuits. He must be able to drink copiously without distortion of feature or enunciation and gamble wildly without manifest disquiet, He must be a man of culture, understand the arts, be able to quote the classics correctly, know all about Vitruvius and Bramante, have a complete mastery of the French language, and be expert about food and wine. He must be good-tempered to the point of laxity; his rages, when they occur, should be sublime. He must love beautiful things and scenery and pay his court to lovely women. He must be fond of animals and be able easily to converse with jockeys, trainers, boxers and fencing masters. Unless deeply in love, he must never permit himself to disclose ill-health or melancholy. His smile, his voice, his every movement, should be expressive of slow grace. He must, while paying all respect to the institution of Monarchy, regard the garishness of the Regent, his satellites and mistresses, with amused displeasure. Never must he imitate the artifices of the dandies or appear in public too elegantly arrayed. His intonation, in the manner of Devonshire House, must be slow, gentle, drawling. He must say "Lunnon" for London, "yaller" for yellow, "balcony" for balcony, "Room" for Rome, "goold" for gold, and "cowcumber" for cucumber. He must remember that he forms part of a mutual admiration society and must admire and even gush. Above all, he must be agreeable in easy perfection, seeking, while remaining perfectly self-centered, to give to others the minimum of pain.

These models of civility may have been arrogant, exclusive, self-indulgent and indifferent to the joys and sorrows of those outside the magic ring. They did not flower for more than sixty years, being replaced by new patterns of behavior evolved from the industrial revolution, evangelicanism and moral earnestness. But while they lasted they did, as Lord David Cecil has said, approach to "the Renaissance ideal of the whole man, whose aspiration is to make the most of every advantage, intellectual and sensual, that life has to offer."

"Perhaps," writes George Trevelyan, "no set of men and women since the world began enjoyed so many different sides of life, with so much zest, as the English upper class of this period."

It is shocking that a tiny minority should extract such splendor from existence, when hunger and injustice seethed beyond the golden gates. For all their warm-heartedness, the social conscience of the Devonshire House circle was as primitive as that of gazelles. Yet as types of distilled civility the Whig aristocrats of 1770–1830 have never been surpassed or equaled. I rejoice that, before respectability came to dim the skies of England, they were there, like fallow deer, to sparkle in the sun.

Chapter 11
Gemütlichkeit

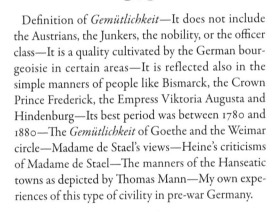

Definition of *Gemütlichkeit*—It does not include the Austrians, the Junkers, the nobility, or the officer class—It is a quality cultivated by the German bourgeoisie in certain areas—It is reflected also in the simple manners of people like Bismarck, the Crown Prince Frederick, the Empress Viktoria Augusta and Hindenburg—Its best period was between 1780 and 1880—The *Gemütlichkeit* of Goethe and the Weimar circle—Madame de Stael's views—Heine's criticisms of Madame de Stael—The manners of the Hanseatic towns as depicted by Thomas Mann—My own experiences of this type of civility in pre-war Germany.

One

I NOW LEAVE THE smiles and whispers, the pastel colors, of Chatsworth and Chiswick for the chocolate brown and spinage green of nineteenth century Germany. I shall examine a type of civility which, for all its value, has been derided or ignored—namely the pattern of behavior suggested by the word *Gemüt-lichkeit*. I must define the meaning of this word and explain which of the many Germanies I am considering and what is the period I intend to cover.

The adjective *gemütlich* and the substantive *Gemüt-lichkeit* imply both an atmosphere and a mood. The atmosphere is one of heavy gentility, porcelain stoves, draped portières, Turkey carpets, and sofas and armchairs of plush. In the *Empfangszimmer* the ladies gather round a table. They do not talk very much, but consume large quantities of coffee and cream cakes. The men retire to the *Herrenzimmer,* where they drink beer. The smell of dead cigars clings to the curtains and through it pierces the thin little smell of anthracite. The double windows are sealed against the snow outside.

The mood of the company is in accord with these surroundings. It is a kindly, amicable, comfortable, somewhat lethargic mood. The English words that best define both the atmosphere and the frame of mind are the words "intimate and cozy." Those who dislike the mood might call it dense and placid: those who dislike the atmosphere might condemn it as "smug and fug." Yet as a code of behavior *Gemüt-lichkeit* is benevolent and protective; it mitigates the German tendency to become suspicious, envious or enraged; it operates as a poultice, comforting them in the frequent moments when they experience spiritual loneliness and self-distrust.

There are two conventional phrases which indicate that in German social relationships *Gemütlichkeit* serves as the restorer and dove of peace. When a note of acrimony enters into a discussion, the hostess, beaming placidly, will exclaim: "*Nur immer gemütlichl!,*" or as we might say in English: "Temper! Temper!" Conversely, when a man is provoked beyond human endurance he may shout "*Da hört die Gemütlichkeit auf!*" meaning thereby that there are occasions when we are justified in displaying rage.

Not all the Germanies have practiced this device of sedative benevolence. The gaiety, the easygoing charm, the *Schlamperei,* of the Austrians are fresher and more buoyant. It may be true that no more exclusive, or snobbish society has ever existed than the aristocracy of the Austro-Hungarian Empire. They might, with their *Erste Gesellschaft* etiquette, their Jockey Club, and their *Gräfliches Taschenbuch,* have become the bores of Europe, had it not been for their rich gifts of laughter, incompetence, and eccentricity. When one thinks of them, one does not think of draped curtains thick with the stench of cold cigars, but of cool corridors decorated with the little horns of roebuck, of saloons in which the parquet squeaks and the small chandeliers tinkle, of chairs and tables of white wood scalloped with silver, of the clear clean fantasies of the Maria Theresa style. To them *Gemütlichkeit* means no more than laughing kindliness: in its German manifestations it seems to them provincial and complacent. I shall not therefore be talking about the Austrians, but shall leave *Schlaraffenland* to its felicity, its tragedies and its unconquerable charm.

Nor shall I be discussing the Junkers of Pomerania and East Prussia, with their old Teutonic ideals and conventions. I shall leave them their sleighs and wolf hounds, their beaver caps, and their tight little shooting coats lined with sheepskin with the soft leather outside. They also, in their old age, may become initiated into the solace of *Gemütlichkeit;* but it is not a quality in which they have been born and bred.

It is necessary, also, in discussing this valuable type of civility to exclude the German officer class. It is difficult for us, who are congenitally unmilitary, to appreciate the prestige enjoyed in nineteenth century Germany by even the most junior Lieutenant in even the most dowdy regiment. Every civilian yearned to be a Reserve Officer so that he could occasionally wear uniform and be at least mistaken for a soldier. I have seen young men whom I knew to be bank clerks shave their heads closely as September approached so that it might be thought they were off to autumn maneuvers. Nor was it easy to become a German officer. Whatever might be one's origins, one could become a *von,* one could be accorded the order of the Red Eagle or the Crown, or be made a Privy Councilor. But, if one's father had been engaged in trade, it required much influence and energy to become a Reserve Lieutenant. Bismarck was a Cuirassier, Bülow a Hussar, and each of them would wear their uniforms on what to us would seem unnecessary occasions. But Bethmann-Hollweg, who had never been through a military training, had to be created an Honorary Dragoon; and Dernburg, the powerful Minister of the Colonies, had to pass a test on the barrack square before he could be promoted from the rank of Feldwebel. Among the military castes, the quality of *Gemütlichkeit* was not encouraged: they had an etiquette of their own. It was stiff, compulsive, jerky, and bound up with a "code of honor" which was arduous to learn and often highly inconvenient to practice.

The interesting fact, therefore, about the type of civility associated with *Gemütlichkeit* is that, unlike most other types, it was not imposed or imitated from above, but grew up naturally from below. The Princes, the Dukes and the great nobles took their manners from abroad and spent much time and money learning how to copy the French, English and even Polish aristocracy. This was unfortunate since, as Mme. de Stael acutely noticed, once a German imitates foreign attitudes he loses his identity. The officer class, as I have said, adopted a highly specialized deportment of its own. It was from the rich soil of the commercial and professional classes that *Gemütlichkeit* was born.

It would be a mistake, however, to define it as a purely bourgeois institution. Its nobler components—kindliness, sociability, duty and the domestic virtues—constituted the very stuff from which the best German characters were formed. The Emperor William I and his son, the Crown Prince Frederick, were examples to all Europe of dignified simplicity. Bismarck himself, however formidable in action, became in moments of relaxation a model of beer drinking, pipe-smoking, geniality. His private life was so simple that Prince Bülow, on his first visit to Friedrichsruh, was profoundly shocked by "the inartistic character of the whole establishment." The Empress Augusta Viktoria, wife of William II, was lauded and admired for insisting that the German women should think always of three things—"*Kinder, Kirche und Küche.*" And Marshal Hindenburg retained to the end of his life a massive homeliness that inspired affectionate veneration.

The period during which *Gemütlichkeit* achieved its full value and influence was that between 1780 and 1880. Until near the end of the eighteenth century it remained clumsy and crude; after William II had infected his countrymen with his own dramatic glamour, life became far too exciting and restless. Yet *Gemütlichkeit* still flowered happily in the lagoons of German life, surviving as an agreeable habit in provincial towns and bourgeois families until, in 1933, the Nazi hysteria came to shatter all that was sedative and most honorable in the German soul.

I agree with Thomas Mann that *Gemütlichkeit* is a quality that is so endemic in the German *Bürgertum* that it cannot be eliminated either by Nazi hysteria or by Marxist dialectic. Serenus Zeitblom—modest, decent, if a trifle absurd in his pedantry and precision—will always remain a dominant character in German society. I am confident that he will survive.

Two

I suppose that, when discussing anything German, one ought to begin with Luther. Heine has called him "the most German German in the whole of German history"—an opinion with which Thomas Mann concurs. Yet although I quite see that Luther was the begetter of the German language and of the tougher sides of the German character, I cannot recognize in him even the most rudimentary seeds of *Gemütlichkeit*. He was expressive both of the idealistic and the realistic sides of the German temperament. "His thoughts," as Heine said so cleverly, "had hands as well as wings." But he remains a man of "god-like brutality" and cannot therefore be dragged from the Wartburg to figure on this page.

I shall start therefore with Goethe, whose influence on his countrymen has been deep, lasting, and wonderfully beneficent. So far as I know, Goethe did not attach to the word *Gemütlichkeit* the associations of coziness that it subsequently acquired. To him it meant little more than "warm" or "heartfelt," as when he writes that they had received him with warm friendliness at Jena or that he sends a friend his heartfelt condolences. Nor was Goethe always and invariably an example of refined or cheerful manners. When a student at Leipzig he was derided for his Franconian accent, his clumsy deportment, and his provincial clothes, which had in fact been cut for him by his father's valet. Even in later life, when the influences of Weimar and world renown had rendered him Olympian, there were moments when he would thunder or sulk; but on the whole he cultivated the more natural forms of courtesy, preferring always the simple to the elaborate, the calm intercourse of ordinary educated people to overt displays of brilliance or erudition.

Even in my own memory, when I was in Weimar before 1914, the little town was the haven and nurse of *Gemütlichkeit* at its very best. In Goethe's day it was no more than a small county capital of some 6,000 inhabitants. The Ducal Court, unlike those of other German Princes, was thoroughly German and unpretentious. The Duchess Anna Amalia, mother of the reigning Duke Karl August, was a remarkable woman who decided that it would be more dignified to render the tiny principality of some 733 square miles a center of natural culture rather than an imitation of Schönbrunn. It was she who brought Wieland to Weimar and thus founded the intellectual circle which gave to the place the justified title of "Athens by the Ilm." It was she who educated her son Karl August to share her intellectual tastes, her progressive politics, and her moral simplicity. It was assuredly a great achievement to attract to this modest court such men of genius

as Wieland, Schiller, Herder and Goethe. It was an
even greater achievement to retain them there for
all their lives. Goethe himself had intended to spend
a few weeks only as the guest of the young Duke; he
remained in Weimar, as the intimate friend and coun-
selor of Karl August, for fifty-seven years.

It all began when he was given the Gartenhaus, the
cottage on the low hillside above the water meadows.
The rooms were tiny, the furniture hard and sparse, the
living frugal. It was close enough to the town for him
to hear the palace clock chiming; it was far enough in
the country for him to sleep on summer nights on a
camp bed under the apple tree, gazing up at the stars:

> *"Euch bedaur" ich, unglückselge Sterne,*
> *Die ihr schön seid und so herrlich scheinet,*
> *Denn ihr liebt nicht, kanntet nie die Liebe.*

By 1782 his ministerial duties required his presence
in the town. Although the Goethehaus in Weimar is
spacious in its way, housing his vast collection of plas-
ter casts, coins, engravings, minerals, skeletons and fos-
sils, his own two rooms remained of Stoic simplicity.
He disliked all period furniture or collectors' pieces,
contending that they distracted the creative mind. On
one occasion he showed Eckermann a green elbow-
chair which he had just bought at an auction. "However," he added, "I shall use it little, or not at all, since
all kinds of commodiousness are contrary to my nature.
In my room you observe no sofa: it is always in my old

wooden chair that I like to sit. . . . Unless we are accustomed to them from early youth, splendid apartments and fine furniture are for people who neither possess, nor can possess, the capacity for serious thought."

His own study therefore was but ill-furnished and his small bedroom contained no more than a hard bed, a minute washbasin, and the high chair in which he died. There were no curtains or carpets in either of these two rooms. Above the door of his study there was a board inscribed with these very *gemütlich* words:

> East and West
> Home is best.

Goethe was a man who liked order and economy in his household arrangements. Every evening he would summon his servants to his room and go through their expenditure during the day and their estimated expenditure for the morrow. When someone expressed surprise that the greatest living poet should occupy himself with such domestic drudgery he remarked: "When I have finished with the prose of life I approach its poetry with enhanced zest." Although for court functions he dressed elaborately, having lace ruffles at his throat and wrists, and the Order of the Falcon on his breast, he generally preferred the white flannel dressing gown and slippers in which he would receive even royal visitors. He liked his food, had a heavy appetite, and enjoyed giving to his guests such rare luxuries as plovers' eggs and caviare. He preferred Bordeaux or Mosel wine to beer, although he contended that Schiller made

a vast mistake in supposing that alcohol was an aid to
the creative imagination. As a host he was magnificent
and lavish. He would carve at dinner with unexampled
dexterity. Wilhelm Grimm, after dining with Goethe,
recorded that: "*Es war ungemein splendid,*" which is an
odd sentence to have been used by the brother of the
world's greatest philologist. Yet the whole way of life at
the Goethehaus, as in the Gartenhaus, was domestic,
simple, frugal, bourgeois, and in fact *gemütlich.*

Goethe was well aware that his countrymen required
a period of seclusion in order to digest their own culture. "The Germans," he remarked, "are of yesterday. A
few more centuries must elapse before it can be said of
them "it is long since they were barbarians."" It was
with this in mind that he lauded *Kleinstädterei,* meaning thereby, not provincial manners exactly, but the
system by which culture was able to develop in small
isolated communities. He always contended that the
creation of a single German Reich with a national capital would destroy the peculiar quality of regional civilization. He hated violence, remarking that: "All
polemic action is repugnant to my nature, and I can
take but little pleasure in it." He hated nationalism,
which he described as "strongest and most excessive
where there is the lowest degree of culture." Although
he fully feared the bureaucratic tendencies of his fellow countrymen, he was sufficiently German to loathe
inefficiency. "I hate bungling," he remarked, "as I hate
sin." Above all, and it is in this that he can be cited as a

model of *Gemütlichkeit,* he hated conceit. "With nar-row-minded persons," he said to Eckermann, "and those in a condition of mental darkness we find con-ceit. With men of intellectual lucidity and high endowment we never find it. In the latter cases there is generally a feeling of joyful strength; and since this strength is a reality, their feeling is not conceit, but something else."

His Olympian nature enabled him to set simplic-ity at the summit of the virtues. "The world," he said, "would not exist were it not so simple." He admired aristocratic bearing, remarking to Eckermann after a visit from young Carl von Spiegel, that "birth and intellect give to their owners a stamp that no incog-nito can hide." What he insisted upon was authentic-ity of manner and natural distinction: "The English," he said to Eckermann, "are at ease in society, as if they were lords everywhere and the world belonged to them. They are dangerous young people, but this very quality of being dangerous is their virtue. The secret of the English does not lie in their intelligence, mor-als, erudition or even their birth and riches. It lies in their courage to be what nature made them for. There is nothing vitiated or spoilt about them, nothing half-way or crooked. Such as they are, they are perfectly ful-filled human beings. That they may also sometimes be complete idiots I allow readily; but to be a really com-plete idiot is in itself something of an achievement and has its place in the scale of nature."

There are several passages in Goethe's writings where the *gemütlich* peeps through the Apollonian—such homely flashes, for instance, as the picture of a woman dropping off to sleep on a sofa with her knitting in her hands:

> *Das Gestrickte mit den Nadeln ruhte*
> *Zwischen den gefaltnen zarten Händen.*

It is soothing to remember that in the great days of Weimar the most formidable German since Luther could think and act in commonplace ways.

Three

Upon this homely community, upon this quiet circle of modest, although immensely gifted men, there descended, on December 23, 1803, the tornado of Madame de Stael. Goethe immediately sought refuge in bed, but she remained on in Weimar, like a cat watching a mouse hole, until he was obliged to recover. She had been warned by Crabb Robinson that she might find German philosophy transcendental and abstruse and that the range of Goethe's learning was so vast that it might affect her with awe. Baring her magnificent arm, she raised it like a Sibyl on high, exclaiming: "Sir! I understand everything that deserves to be understood! What I do not understand is nothing!"

It was in this mood of sibylline self-assurance that she forced an entry into the Goethehaus. Their interviews, and there were several of them, were not a success. Madame de Stael found Goethe stiff, inarticulate and reserved. He objected to her habit of asking questions without waiting for the answers. He was accustomed to speak with a certain measured reflection. It dismayed him, as he confessed in his Journal, that Madame de Stael should hurl questions at him and expect him to return them rapidly "as if they had been shuttlecocks." He was embarrassed by her lack of reticence and discretion. He complained that she insisted on enquiring into feelings "which a man generally reserves for private intercourse between himself and his God." It was not in any sense an agreeable visitation. At last she left Weimar and they returned happily to more *gemüt-lich* ways. "I feel," wrote Schiller to Goethe, "as if I had recovered from a severe illness." "*Le séjour,*" recorded Madame de Stael, "*des petites villes m'a toujours paru très ennuyeux.*" Yet for all her impatience, Madame de Stael was too intelligent a woman not to recognize and to analyze the quality of *Gemütlichkeit.* Her reflections on the more modest and temperate virtues of the Germans constitute perhaps the most interesting passages in the two volumes of her *De l'Allemagne.*

She noted that "the stoves, the beer, the tobacco-smoke create for the ordinary German a thick warm atmosphere from which he hates to emerge." She observed that, whereas in France people were interested in human beings, in Germany they were far more interested in books. "A passion for literature," she commented, "is accompanied by rather vulgar social habits." She objected to the way they gave each other enormously long, and seemingly meaningless, titles such as "Herr Oberpostdirektor," in every sentence that they uttered. She objected to their elaborate formulas of courtesy "which are intended to be polite, but which cause ill-ease both to themselves and others." She disliked the manner in which, at meals, they pressed one to taste of every course and to drink all sorts of wine; in good society nobody is urged to eat or drink anything that they do not happen to want. She admits that it is impossible for any man or woman to be graceful unless he or she has been brought up in Paris and had frequent access to the salon of the Rue du Bac. One should not, she explains, expect the Germans to be elegant, one should be simply grateful to them for their cordiality, their homeliness, their true kindness of heart; one should forgive them their odd jerky bows.

She observed, and regretted, their extreme touchiness. She felt that they did not realize that "language should be a liberal art" and that no man of the world should take offence when teased. "The desire to please," she noted acutely, "is something wholly different from the wish to be loved." The trouble about the Germans was that they all wished to be loved and were wounded when this desire was not fulfilled.

Madame de Stael was not a woman to admire *Gemütlichkeit,* which she would have repudiated as "sugary" or "*doucereuse.*" She found the German women pretty, modest, less shy than English ladies, but so sentimental as to blur anything that might be distinctive or stimulating in their intelligence. "Very rarely," she wrote, "does one find in a German woman that speed of thought that animates human intercourse and gives an impulse to ideas."

Particularly did she deplore that the Germans did not enjoy the delights of conversation. "It is only in France," she wrote correctly, "that the art of conversation is treated as a talent." A Frenchman could always find something to say even if he had nothing to think about: a German, on the contrary, found it difficult to convey in words what were often the rich treasures of his mind. In conversation the German usually remains silent, merely conveying by an engaging facial expression his hidden desire to be loved. "Moreover," she recorded, "in France a person who monopolises the conversation is regarded as a usurper, surrounded by jealous rivals; he can only maintain his monologue by the brilliance and success of what he says. In Germany, such a person is regarded as the legitimate ruler over the attention of his audience. He therefore takes his time."

Yet in the end, says Madame de Stael, such bourgeois defects are of slight importance. We must overlook the clumsiness of the Germans, their lack of all military aptitude or ambition, their gross inefficiency of method. We must admire their "*Innigkeit,*" which, as Schlegel assured her, did not mean intellectual depth and vigor only, but also a certain special warmth of sensibility. Above all, says Madame de Stael, we must recognize them as the great imaginative minds of the century, the noblest idealists that Europe had as yet produced.

On reading Madame de Stael's *De l'Allemagne,* Heinrich Heine, who really did know something about German life and character, was irritated and even incensed. The venom with which he attacked the book may have been due to his personal hatred of Schlegel and his brother. Yet he certainly did feel that Madame de Stael, with her great contemporary influence, might mislead Europe as to the true nature of German idealism.

The gentleness, the *Gemütlichkeit,* of the German character was, so Heine insisted, a pathetic fallacy on the part of Madame de Stael. The impulse beneath all their *Innigkeit,* their concentration, and their hunger for knowledge, was not a noble impulse but "the irresistibly daemonic," the "*Unbezwingbar-dämonisches.*" Heine warned his European contemporaries that from the seeming idealisms of the followers of Kant and Fichte would be born a race "who will know no reverence for anything; who will brutally ravage with axe and sword through the soil of European life, rooting out all vestiges of the past." "Once Madame de Stael's idealists really get going," said Heine, "there will be played in Germany a drama, compared to which the French Revolution was an innocent idyll."

Four

This excellent type of civility did not, as I have said, set the pattern of behavior for all the Germanies or even for communities as a whole. It was a standard adopted by the upper middle class in certain areas only. The eastern provinces still regarded themselves as the bulwark of Graeco-Roman civilization against the Tartars: there the high military ideals of the Teutonic Knights still prevailed. In the Rhineland, in Bavaria, even in Würtemberg, a Latin lightness had come to animate the solid Tacitean virtues of the Germanic tribes. The Prussians were always a restless race and I imagine that, even in its sleepy days, Berlin was a nervous town. I have been assured by those of my German friends who share my interest in the subject that the best specimens of *Gemütlichkeit* are to be sought for, in the period between 1840 and 1880, in the smaller towns of Saxony, Thuringia, Mecklenburg, Hanover and Schleswig-Holstein. It was there and then that was achieved this admirable fusion between the domestic affections, a sentimental approach to Nature, solid comfort, and a lively, if not very adventurous, interest in the arts.

The highest level of this bourgeois culture was reached, I have been assured, by the great commercial societies of the Hanseatic towns. These patrician burghers, these senator-merchants, were as exclusive and proud as any of the Venetian magnificoes. For them trade, sound business methods and honorable gain were both the badges of gentry and the necessary function of a virtuous man. By them a son of one of the great trading houses who displayed no taste or aptitude for his hereditary profession was regarded as foreign, effeminate, a wastrel and a disgrace. Their world was rich, pious and dull.

One of the greatest of modern German writers, Thomas Mann, has in his early novel *Buddenbrooks* provided a complete picture of Lübeck society in the nineteenth century. He describes three generations of these patrician merchants. There is the grandfather, who still retains his eighteenth century deportment, his Voltairean skepticism, and who laughs aloud when he hears his son being taught the catechism. There is the father who carries on the business through the mid-century, unperturbed by the revolutions of 1848, not very imaginative about his children, and profoundly affected by the Evangelical movement. There is the son Thomas who, anxious not to deviate from ancestral ways, finds it increasingly difficult to cope with the brisker methods of upstart competitors and who wears himself to an early death by fussing over his family, his business and the burden of his senatorial duties.

Throughout these eighty years the center of the Buddenbrook family was the old house in the Mengstrasse, with its seventeenth century hall and staircase, with its offices on the ground floor, its warehouses in the courtyard, and upstairs a suite of reception rooms, hung with French tapestries and large landscapes in oil. There was a garden attached with an elaborate summer house, where the family gathered on June evenings, smoking and sewing while the ships hooted in the harbor and in the intervals of silence could be heard the far sigh of the Baltic Sea.

It is the memories of his Lübeck boyhood, between 1880 and 1890, that Thomas Mann vividly conveys. The household consists of a governess-companion, a man servant, a cook and two maids. Frau Senator Buddenbrooks personally supervises the kitchen and the young ladies of the family are expected, with neat little feather brushes, to help with the housework. There was Herr François Knaeb, who gave lessons in dancing and deportment in the drawing room of Frau Consul Hustede. The Buddenbrooks did not mix in county society; in fact the girl Antonie had never even met a member of the nobility until she was over eighteen. Their circle consisted of the Lübeck commercial patricians, Senator Möllendorpf, Doctor Overdieck, Consul Kistenmaker. They were extremely pious, holding family prayers morning and evening, and once a week a drawing room meeting with readings from the Bible. The main meal of the day was after business hours at four o'clock in the afternoon. The Buddenbrooks were known in Lübeck for their ample hospitality. When invited to the old house in the Mengstrasse one could be certain of having a good square meal, "*ein nahrhaftes Bissen,*" and Frau Consul would provide the excellent

Plettenpudding, consisting of raspberries, macaroons and custard. After the meal, the women would be conducted to the "Landscape Room" where they would sew and chat and sometimes play some music. The men would retire with their cigars to the billiard room. At ten o'clock tea would be brought in and the company would reassemble. At half-past ten the guests would say goodnight and calm would descend over the city of Lübeck. It was a worthy life.

It does not seem, however, that Thomas Mann looks back upon his Hanseatic years with an affection more lively than that which we invariably experience when we remember ourselves at the age of sixteen. The society of Lübeck is represented as heavy, proud and mean. When Herr Permaneder appears from Munich, he is at first regarded as "South German" and thus "a little too easy mannered." When Antonie Buddenbrooks marries Herr Permaneder and goes to live in Bavaria she is acutely wretched. It is not only that she is shocked to discover that the name of Buddenbrook arouses no sense of awe in Bavarian ears; it is that she finds the South Germans lacking in energy, dignity and self-respect. They do not possess the seriousness of the Hanseatic Senator nor are they imbued "with the same fanatical respect for human feelings." How could Antonie Buddenbrook feel at home in Munich "where they eat cake with a knife and the very princes speak bad grammar"?

These Baltic manners, with their high level of seriousness, although they furnish a noble example of a middle-class community at its most distinguished, do not recall to me those vestiges of *Gemütlichkeit* which I myself so much admired and enjoyed. I feel closer to Tonio Kröger, who although a member of the Lübeck patrician family, had Latin blood in his veins. With his soft brown eyes he was ill-adjusted to Lübeck ways; he drifted away from the stark north to the lands where the orange and the lemon scent the air; Thomas Mann, I feel, is also fonder of Tonio than he ever was of Senator Möllendorpf.

Five

I prefer to choose my example of *Gemütlichkeit* from one of the several families with whom I lived when studying German forty-five years ago. Shall I take old Frau Bürgermeister Lahmeyer of Hanover, with her two dear daughters Lilli and Ermine? Shall I take Professor Gregorovius of Frankfurt and his wife, the Frau Professor, a woman of profound sensibility? Shall I take little Herr Heindt of Hildesheim, one of the few Germans whom I have ever seen to smoke a long pipe with a painted porcelain bowl? No, I shall take Herr Baumeister Ehrlich and Frau Baumeister Ehrlich of the little town of Blankenburg in the Harz.

Herr Ehrlich had spent his life in the planning department of the Leipzig City Council from which function he had retired at the age of sixty-five. He must also have been in private practice as an architect, since he had saved sufficient money to buy a plot of land on the outskirts of Blankenburg and there to construct a little villa of his own design. The Ehrlichs were in comfortable circumstances and only received paying guests into their home because their boy, Kuno, was away working in a bank in Brazil; his room was empty, and they enjoyed the company of the young.

Herr Ehrlich had, while at Leipzig, come under the influence of Henri Van De Velde and the Bauhaus Dessau at Weimar. The entrancing novelty of Art Nouveau had not, however, eaten very deep into his soul, since the villa he built for himself at Blankenburg was Tyrolean, even Swiss, in feeling, with wide eaves and a long balcony running outside the windows of the bedroom floor. Over the balustrade of this balcony would hang throughout the morning the huge red feather quilt, or *Decke,* together with the coverlet, or *Steppdecke,* from the conjugal bed. The only evidences of the Van De Velde influence were the ash trays in the *Herrenzimmer* and an abominable standard lamp in the *Wohnzimmer* representing a maiden of unnatural slimness with scarabs in her hair clasping the leaves of a nenuphar.

We had four meals during the day, beginning with *Morgenkaffee* at eight o'clock, at which I, being English, was given eggs and toast. At one o'clock came the *Mittagessen* which was a heavy meal, enjoyed with slow formality. When it was finished, we said *Mahlzeit* to each other, and the Herr Baumeister retired to bed until the *Nachmittagskaffee* which took place at four o'clock. The day was concluded by *Abendessen* at seven o'clock, which consisted of tea, cold ham and sausage, cheese and pumpernickel, ending with beer. Thereafter the Frau Baumeister would sit down at the piano and play Greig. Sometimes, in an ageing voice, she would half hum and half sing her girlhood songs. She would give us a low rendering of *Ich grolle nicht,* and when she came to the passage about the *Diamentenpracht* her eyes would flash with anger and her voice rise in scorn. Her husband, smoking his cigar in his armchair, would beam at her with devotion and respect.

Often she would take a book from the shelf and read aloud to me in a low voice that never irritated. It was not the usual things that she read to me, but poems and plays that were then new and perhaps startling. I can still recall her reading aloud *Der Tor und der Tod* of Hofmannsthal and repeating twice over the line about the Gioconda—"*Dem Prunk der traumeschweren Augenlider.*" She was a cultivated woman, and did not adopt a bleating tone when she read aloud.

After tea, in the cool of the evening, the Herr Baumeister would ask me to accompany him to the town. He was a slow and breathless walker and conversation was not continuous. He would take me to his *Stammlokal,* a small wine shop in the market place, where he would order a bottle of Steinberger which we drank in green glasses. He would tell me about the Franco-Prussian war; of how well he had acquitted himself at the battle of Weissenberg and how he had been wounded at Mars-la-Tour. He would tell me about his student days and the girl he had known at Nordeney and how, when the Crown Prince Frederick visited Leipzig, it had been he who had handed upon a velvet cushion a golden key. He was not a man who was resigned to getting old and he loudly regretted the opportunities that he had allowed to slip past him as leaves in the wind. He would then order a second bottle and sigh deeply.

"You can have no idea," he would say, "how quickly life passes. It seems but yesterday that I was young as you are. We imagine that we can turn the pages slowly, one by one, pausing at each paragraph. But it is not like that, believe me. The pages are caught by a gust of wind, a hurricane, and they flutter in a rush through our fingers. It is so strange, so strange, *so merkwürdig.*" A tear would come into his eye.

One late afternoon as we sat there a group of boys and girls crossed the little square returning from some expedition in the hills. The boys were dressed in shorts, their shirts were open at the neck and their sleeves were rolled high. "What beauty there is in all that!" he exclaimed, "look at those necks like swans, those powerful forearms. When I was a boy we had to wear trousers and laced boots and collar and tie. What beauty! What beauty!" Again a tear would gather in his eye, but it did not seem to me at all ridiculous that the old man should want to be a Wandervogel. I felt sorry, because he was old and corpulent and liked things that were simple and young. Then, very slowly, we would walk back for our *Abendessen*.

Sometimes, at breakfast, a letter would arrive from Brazil, a letter from Kuno. I would swallow my coffee quickly and retire to my room. They would keep their letter until the Herr Baumeister also had finished his coffee and had lit his cigar. Then they would walk across the little garden with its two kobbolds and its two glass balls to the summer house. They would read the letter with their heads close; then read it again. Then they would sit hand in hand together, talking about their Kuno and his prospects in Sao Paulo:

Papa Fittig, treu und freundlich
Mama Fittig, sehr gemütlich,
Sitzen, Arm in Arm geschmiegt. . . .

The lines of Wilhelm Busch occurred inevitably; but I never found the Ehrlichs comic. I felt that they expressed a gentle honorable style with which to end their lives.

I was not, I think, a disappointment to the Herr Baumeister, since I would listen to his stories, was quite prepared to take seriously the etiquette of drinking and toasting (what he called his "*Bierkomment*"), tried to learn Skat, and was delighted when he kept on assuring me that I should grasp at every pleasure while still young. But I was a grave disappointment to the Frau Baumeister. In the first place, to her mind, I was suffering from undernourishment. I can still hear her worried words: "*Na, Sie sind wirklich ein schwacher Esser! Sie können doch unmöglich satt sein!*" And in the second place, during the three months I lived with them, I never became seriously ill. How she longed to take my temperature, or lay on poultices, or rub my chest with camphorated oil as if I had been an *ersatz* Kuno! How she longed for me to confide in her the deep unhappiness of my inner soul, the disappointment of my love, the harshness of the world! I was a satisfactory guest in many ways, punctual in my payments, quite tidy in my habits, industrious and sober. But I lacked a secret sorrow. The Frau Baumeister would sigh wistfully when she thought how delightful a large secret sorrow would have been!

No, I do not laugh at the Ehrlichs. They were decent folk. They represented all that was best in that rare type of civility—*Gemütlichkeit.*

Chapter 12
Respectability

—◦◦◦—

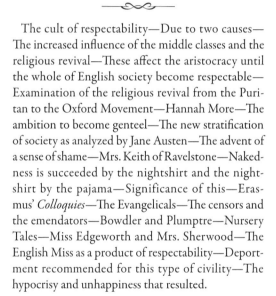

The cult of respectability—Due to two causes—
The increased influence of the middle classes and the
religious revival—These affect the aristocracy until
the whole of English society become respectable—
Examination of the religious revival from the Puritan to the Oxford Movement—Hannah More—The
ambition to become genteel—The new stratification
of society as analyzed by Jane Austen—The advent of
a sense of shame—Mrs. Keith of Ravelstone—Naked-
ness is succeeded by the nightshirt and the nightshirt by the pajama—Significance of this—Erasmus' *Colloquies*—The Evangelicals—The censors and
the emendators—Bowdler and Plumptre—Nursery
Tales—Miss Edgeworth and Mrs. Sherwood—The
English Miss as a product of respectability—Deportment recommended for this type of civility—The
hypocrisy and unhappiness that resulted.

One

"THE PASSION FOR respectability," writes
Mr. Peter Quennell, "is of recent growth."
It was a phenomenon which first became

apparent in the last two decades of the eighteenth century, which reached its maximum development between 1840 and 1885, and which thereafter declined gradually until today it has ceased to be obtrusive. The standard of conduct, the set of values, established by this passion produced many complicated situations, much new material for the moralists and novelists, and considerable personal unhappiness. The type of civility it created is not to be praised.

Although it exercised a potent influence in the United States, France, Scandinavia, Germany and Holland, the cult of respectability is best examined in its purely English manifestation. In Scotland it was from the first associated with such serious qualities as effort, self-denial and learning; in Ireland it invariably became frayed round the edges; it was in southern England that it acquired its trimmest shape.

The triumph of this new ideal can be ascribed to two major causes. The first was the rapid expansion during the nineteenth century of the middle and lower-middle classes. The second was the religious revival inaugurated by Wesley and concluding with the Oxford Movement. These two events combined to create a new and intricate stratification of society, an exaggerated sense of shame, and a theory of deportment which was artificial and harsh.

It would be incorrect to say that the development and triumph of this new type of civility were due to the decline in power of the land-owning class. The social

influence of the English aristocracy remained operative until 1918, or even 1946, long after their political
privileges had been curtailed or abolished. In that they
never became an exclusive caste, and always preserved
good manners, they constituted a not unwelcome and
not unpopular élite.

The British aristocracy avoided becoming a closed
corporation, in the sense that the Venetian oligarchs or
the Egyptian priesthood were closed corporations. The
peerage was continuously being refreshed by the admission of new members from the other classes. In the reign
of Henry VII there were only twenty-nine temporal
peers: in that of Henry VIII only fifty-one: in that of
Queen Elizabeth I only fifty-nine. It was the Stuarts
who started to inflate the order. James I created sixty-
two fresh peers. Charles I fifty-nine, Charles II sixty-
four. Between 1760 and 1820 as many as 388 commoners
were admitted to the House of Lords. The new creations
between 1820 and 1912 numbered 476. The peerage
ceased to be the preserve or sanctuary of an hereditary
order and became a sort of paddock in which retired
politicians could browse at ease. Nor was the House of
Commons itself immune to aristocratic influence and
infiltration. In spite of Reform Bills, agitators, radicals
and pamphleteers, as many as 108 members of the Lower
House were, as late as 1860, the sons of peers.

Government, moreover, has always been that of the
unchosen many by the chosen few. The experiment in
pure Democracy made by the Greek city-states ended

in such disaster that it has never again been attempted. What has changed is, not the principle that in every generation it is only a small minority that is fit to rule the majority, but the method by which this élite is recruited and trained. The hereditary or aristocratic method, however illogical in theory or fortuitous in operation, has in practice proved not infrequently more welcome than recruitment by assumed merit. It may even be, as I have already mentioned, that an élite chosen on the hereditary principle arouses less competition, and therefore less jealousy, than one recruited by more arbitrary methods of selection. But if a popular aristocracy, such as that which existed in England in the eighteenth and nineteenth centuries, is to retain influence, it must be careful of its manners. On the whole, whatever Cobbett may have said, the English land-owning class during those two centuries were good at this: "They played their part," writes Arthur Ponsonby, "with unobtrusive dignity. By their endeavor to avoid wounding the susceptibilities of their fellow men they gained their admiration and in some cases their affection."

It was not therefore owing to any decline in the influence of the upper classes that the age of respectability was born and prospered. It was the bourgeois who, during the Victorian period, in England as in Germany, set the tone: respectability spread from the lower levels upwards: by 1850 the whole of England had become middle-class.

Two

Concurrently with this upsurge of a vast and self-assertive bourgeoisie, there occurred a startling revival of theology and religion. Puritanism had always been endemic in England, although until the seventeenth century its influence remained local and sporadic. With the coming of the Roundheads it rapidly acquired the force of a class, and even a political, creed. "The bigotry of Puritanism," wrote Buckle, "has left a living sting which still corrodes the very heart of the nation." To him it was this poison that destroyed the old high spirits of the British people. "There perhaps never was," he wrote, "a country in which was to be found so much splendor and so little gaiety as in England." The fallacy was preached that it was possible to make men and women virtuous by law. Under the "rule of the saints" theaters and even maypoles were abolished and the military were empowered to enter private houses to ensure that the Act of 1640 making adultery a capital offense was not being evaded, or that the Sabbath was being properly observed. Inevitably the Puritans, with their nasal voices and their self-righteous ways, became unpopular. They were accused even of hypocrisy, an accusation which, although fully understandable, was not always fair. Samuel Butler in *Hudibras,* a poem which Charles II would murmur to himself as he walked slowly in Spring Gardens, slashes the self-complacency of the Puritans with lusty venom and especially their tendency to:

> Compound for sins they are inclin'd to
> By damning those they have no mind to.

Puritanism did not die with the Restoration. The "Society for the Reformation of Manners" was founded in 1692 and provided itself with a Vigilance Committee which employed spies, informers and even *agents provocateurs*. Both Swift and Defoe denounced these snoopers as hypocrites who, while bullying the poor and nagging at the middle classes, ignored the debauchery of the rich and titled. Yet it is from the end of the seventeenth century that date the first earnest stirrings of a social conscience. The "Society for the Promotion of Christian Knowledge" was constituted in 1698 and almost immediately began to found charity schools and to direct contemporary attention to the need of popular education. It was this new spirit of responsibility that induced Addison, from 1711 onward, to preach the refinement of manners and consideration for the unfortunate. Robert Raikes of Gloucester followed with his invention of the Sunday Schools. Finally a revivalist of genius appeared in the person of John Wesley.

On the death of Wesley in 1791, heathenism returned for a short while to England. The Church almost reverted to the condition which Bishop Butler had denounced in 1736. "Christianity," he had remarked, "has now become a principal subject of mirth and ridicule." Bishop Butler did not foresee the great flame that John Wesley was so shortly to kindle or that, after a temporary reaction, the Evangelicals would receive from Wesley's hand a torch that was to smoke and flicker for some eighty years.

The extremist exponents of this second religious revival were Lady Huntingdon and her chaplain George Whitefield. The latter held the doctrine that "a certain number are elected for eternity and these must and shall be saved. The rest of mankind must and shall be damned." The Calvinistic idea that man was in any case destined for perdition had led many people to suppose that, if one is bound whatever one does to burn in hell, it is well to enjoy meanwhile such pleasures as are provided upon this sinful earth. The theory of the antinomian school, namely that since God's grace is boundless one was certain to be pardoned hereafter however much one might have sinned in life, also exercised a weakening effect on morals. The Evangelicals of the more moderate school sought to inculcate a sense of personal responsibility, less pessimistic than that of Lady Huntingdon, less deleterious than that of the Antinomians. They held that the essence of the Gospel teaching was the belief that salvation can come through faith in the atoning death of Christ. They knew that the influence of the established Church had decayed owing to indolence and neglect; they succeeded in inspiring the younger clergy with a sense of immediate responsibility and a remarkable new vigor. They reminded all classes of the community of the shortness of life, the certainty of Judgment, and the hope of Redemption.

The most active and respected of the Evangelicals were the men who gathered round John Venn, the rector of Clapham. The Clapham Sect comprised such men of ability and influence as Henry Thornton, the member for Southwark, Zachary Macaulay and William Wilberforce. They founded Bible societies, they held meetings, and they flooded the length and breadth of England with evangelical tracts. In 1844 as many as fifteen million tracts composed and issued by the Clapham sect were distributed throughout the country. The success of the evangelical movement was immediate, wide and deep.

One of the most effective of the many propagandists of the religious revival was Hannah More. In her *Thoughts on the Manners of the Great,* written as early as 1809, she contended that it was not enough for high society to be smart and clever; it must also be good. "Mere decorum of manners," she wrote, "without a strict attention to religious principle is a constant source of danger to the rich and great." People who accorded no more than a conventional tribute to religion were regarded as perfectly respectable. This was a mistake. "Ananias and his prevaricating wife," writes Hannah More, "were perhaps well esteemed in Society." Even quite virtuous members of the nobility and gentry were apt to err in little things. Why should they engage the services of a hairdresser on a Sunday? Has he not also "a soul to be saved"? How can such people tolerate a vice that has but "newly crept into polished Socicty," namely attendance at Sunday concerts? How can any hostess who has been religiously trained indulge in "the daily and hourly lie of *not at home*"? Hannah More and her friends worked without pause or even hindrance. In the end they triumphed. "It is a singular satisfaction to me," Hannah More was able to write in 1825, "that I have lived to see

MODESTY

such an increase of genuine religion among the higher classes of society."

These were fine achievements. The Evangelical movement undoubtedly did immense good to the Anglican Church and to all sections of the community. But it had its faults. The Evangelicals, believing as they did in the validity of all Bible statements, had a weakness for the gift of prophecy. Even the more sensible of their number would suppose at moments that such events as the French Revolution, the Reform Bills, or the cholera epidemic were portents of the Great Tribulation ordained to precede the Second Coming. They were strict Sabbatarians, feeling that Sunday should be marked by "an absence of secular thoughts." They forbade their adherents to play games on Sundays, or to indulge in such diversions as painting, needlework, riding, or music, other than the singing of hymns. They repudiated the theater, described a pack of cards as "the Devil's prayer book," denounced light reading as a "misappropriation of time," and condemned such "highly seasoned Corruption" as the poetry of Byron and "his compeers in sin and infamy." Lord Shaftesbury, who disapproved of the racecourse, was miserable when, being Minister in attendance at Windsor, he was ordered to accompany the Queen to Ascot. Lord Mount Temple got into disgrace with his fellows for attending a fancy dress ball at Buckingham Palace. For some reason which I have been unable to fathom the Evangelicals approved of shooting, but thought hunting a wicked indulgence. All the old country pastimes and ceremonies were condemned as pagan survivals, which indeed they were. "Evangelicanism," writes George Eliot in *Middlemarch,* "has cast a certain suspicion as of plague infection over the few amusements which survived in the provinces."

From the theological point of view it may be that the Evangelicals had centered too exclusively upon the doctrine of Justification by Faith. A less pragmatic interpretation of the ways of God to man had become inevitable. *Tracts for the Times* came to rob the Evangelicals of part of their self-assurance and something of their unity. To most of them, however, the Oxford Movement seemed the work of the devil. When many of the leaders of that great movement seceded to the Church of Rome, the Evangelicals rejoiced in no Christian spirit and with ugly *Schadenfreude.* Thereafter the whole evangelical movement, which had brought such benefit to the Anglican Church, declined from a missionary and revivalist movement into the Low Church Party.

But by then they had established respectability as the aim and idol of the English middle classes.

Three

The money put into circulation by the Industrial Revolution brought with it, as I have said, a rapid increase in the number of English families who

regarded themselves as genteel. Until then people had
envisaged society as divided into three main categories of upper class, middle class and lower class. As the
middle class expanded proliferously, the cells began to
divide, and strange new fissures were observed. Instead
of taking for granted the station into which they had
been born, men and women began to be self-conscious
about it and competitive. Human vanity then operated
to create a fresh and elaborate stratification. Everybody
wished to rise into the category above them, or at least
to differentiate themselves by shibboleths, possessions
and pretences from the category believed to be immediately below. Swift had already remarked that:

> So, naturalists observe, a flea
> Hath smaller fleas that on him prey;
> And these have smaller fleas to bite 'em
> And so proceed ad infinitum.

The intricacy of these new gradations were classified
by that gifted woman, Miss Jane Austen. In *Persuasion*
she devotes space to an analysis of the shades of social
difference that separated Mrs. Musgrave from her sister Mrs. Hayter. In *Sense and Sensibility* Miss Austen
says of the two Miss Steeles: "Lucy was certainly not
elegant and her sister not even genteel." It caused pain
to her heroines if these minute distinctions were either
not recognized or regarded as immaterial. It shocked
Emma to realize that Mr. Elton, while "so well understanding the gradations of rank below him," should fail

to observe that she herself was his social superior "both in connection and mind." Frank Churchill, although of the best county category, was so cheerful that he appeared blissfully unaware that some people were genteel whereas others were not. "His indifference to a confusion of rank," Miss Austen tells us, "bordered too much on inelegance of mind." To our ideas Frank Churchill is about the only really gentlemanlike hero in Miss Austen's novels, most of them being either snobs or prigs. Even the awful Mr. Elton appeared at first "quite the gentleman himself and without low connections," and Mr. Weston, who was really a nice man, was hampered in Emma's eyes by the fact that he "was born of a respectable family" who only "for the last two or three generations had been rising in gentility and property." We do not understand the atmosphere of nervous class-consciousness in which during that period the bourgeois existed.

However much Miss Austen may have disliked "the yeomanry," her contempt for commerce was even more acidly displayed. Thus the Coles of Highbury were to her "of low origin, in trade, and only moderately genteel." In *Pride and Prejudice,* which was written as early as 1796, the insufferable Darcy remarks that a girl who has one uncle who is a small attorney and another who lives in his business premises in Cheapside, suffers from disadvantages which are bound "materially to lessen her chance of marrying men of any consideration in the world." When Mr. Gardiner, Elizabeth

Bennet's offending uncle, actually appeared: "The Netherfield ladies would have had difficulty in believing that a man who lived by trade, and lived within view of his own warehouses, could have been so well bred and agreeable." Yet for all their frightful class consciousness, for all their contempt for commerce, the ladies of Miss Austen's world were mercenary: they loved money as such. "A poor Honorable," comments Mary Crawford in *Mansfield Park,* "is no catch."

What they could not stand were "low connections." When little Fanny Price is torn from her raffish home at Portsmouth to become the snubbed inmate of Sir Thomas Bertram's mansion, he warns his family in advance that "we must prepare ourselves for gross ignorance, some meanness of opinions, and very distressing vulgarity of manner."

It is customary to attribute such remarks, as well as the blatant cruelty of so many of Miss Austen's heroes and heroines, to her delicious sense of humor and to her genius for irony. The society which she depicts is mean and competitive, almost wholly uninterested in intellectual, spiritual or aesthetic values, and wastes time, energy and even passion upon the meaningless subtleties of social status. Miss Austen was assuredly justified in directing against such empty folk the arrows of her satire. I should feel better satisfied did not an identical materialism, a similar feline worldliness, reveal themselves from time to time in Miss Austen's own letters to her sister. Her published correspondence leaves behind it an uneasy suspicion that she was not always intent on caricaturing the vulgarity of others: that sometimes she reveals her own. She has, none the less, provided posterity with an incomparable analysis of the stratification of English upper-middle and lower-middle society at the time of the Industrial Revolution. The type of civility she depicts was undistinguished, heartless and base.

Four

The doctrine of respectability, as I have indicated, and as Miss Austen abundantly proved, arose mainly from economic causes. Good society was suddenly invaded by legions of the newly rich: the snobbishness of the period was predominantly a defense apparatus. But there were other and more interesting influences operating less blatantly and altering the care-free eighteenth century view as to what was seemly and what was not. Prominent among these secondary causes was a morbid preoccupation with the sense of shame.

So wide, so sudden, was the onrush of this social worry that it could completely transform an individual's conception of good manners during his, or her, own life-time. As early as 1782 Mrs. Thrale noted with surprise that Addison could describe a lady of breeding confessing that she was suffering from stomach ache. Such a solecism had by then become impossible at Streatham. "How great a change," writes Mrs. Thrale, "has been wrought in female manners during these few years!" An even more vivid example is provided by Walter Scott's great-aunt, Mrs. Keith of Ravelstone, with whom he had stayed for a happy month when a little cripple of six years old. When over eighty Mrs. Keith wrote to him asking him to procure for her the novels of Aphra Behn. He replied that he would do so if she really wished, but that the writings of Aphra Behn were not "quite proper reading" for a lady. Mrs. Keith replied that she well remembered that when a girl she had found these novels delightful and that she much desired to read them again. Dutifully, Scott obtained the volumes and sent them off to Ravelstone. When Scott visited his great-aunt she pushed the books towards him exclaiming: "Take back your bonny Mrs. Behn and if you will take my advice you will put them in the fire." She then made the following revealing commentary:

> I found it impossible to get through the very first of the novels. But is it not very odd that I, an old woman of eighty and upwards, sitting alone, feel myself ashamed to read a book which sixty years ago I have heard read aloud for larger circles consisting of the first and most creditable society in London.

Yes certainly it was very odd.

Dr. Norbert Elias, in his *Prozess der Zivilisation,* asserts that our present inhibitions about the facts of life and the functions of the body are recent inventions, unconnected historically with Calvin's doctrine of original sin. He dates the growth of *Schamgefühl* from the end of the sixteenth century; contends that it reached its climax in nineteenth century Europe and that with the advent of sport and sunbathing it has declined. He points out that it was customary in the Middle Ages for two or three men to share the same bed stark naked together when spending the night at an inn: as late as 1774 De La Salle mentions the practice as one that was only then becoming rare. Elias points out that the use of nightgowns came in with forks and that it was when people ceased to experience the acute *Schamgefühl* associated in the nineteenth-century with beds and bedrooms that they replaced the ugly and ridiculous nightgown by the more elegant pajama. He quotes from an American magazine of 1936 in which the pajama is condemned as a symbol of decadence and effeminacy. "Strong men," runs this article, "wear no pajamas. Theodore Roosevelt wore a nightshirt. So did Washington, Lincoln, Napoleon, Nero and many other famous men." The point may appear irrelevant, but it is useful to be reminded that the cult of respectability is not unconnected with the sense of shame, and that this in its turn is among other things associated with bed-shame, nightshirt-shame and pajama-pride.

In the Middle Ages, again, the facts of life were not hidden from little boys and girls. They were expected to troop with the rest of the family into the bridal chamber and to watch the bride and bridegroom being put to bed. They were accustomed to hear of brothels, mistresses and bastards and came to regard such matters as part of everyday life. Today, owing to our inhibitions, we do not possess even the vocabulary in which to instruct boys and girls about the sexual functions. To a mother in the Middle Ages, or of the Renaissance, it would have seemed wrong as well as silly to tell lies to children regarding the birth of babies. Nobody could have accused the great Erasmus of being at all interested in pornography, yet his *Colloquies,* which were composed with the avowed purpose of "the instruction of children," and which were dedicated to the nine-year-old son of his own publisher, might today be classed by the Public Prosecutor as obscene literature. The hero, Sophronius, visits a brothel and is taken by the harlot, Lucretia, to her room. He develops inhibitions and expresses the fear that they might be seen or heard. "But," Lucretia expostulates, "But, lovey duck, not even a gnat could see us. Why this dawdling (*Ne musca quidem, mea lux. Quid cunctaris.*)?" Sophronius replies that God and the whole company of heaven can see them and, with this reflection he abruptly leaves the room. A cautionary tale of this nature would have seemed to the sixteenth-century parent both delicate and profitable. Yet to Mrs. Sherwood, authoress of *The Fairchild Family,* such realism would have appeared misplaced.

The sense of shame was thus among the many tributaries that came to swell the great river of bourgeois respectability. There were other and more sensible contributions.

Five

By 1803 piety had become fashionable and even the most cultivated members of society had begun to say grace at meal times and to kneel daily in the library together with the cook, butler, footman and house-maids in the domestic ceremony of family prayers. The lovely morning ritual of the sacrifice to the Lares and Penates in the presence of all *familiares,* was restored in England shortly after the nineteenth century was born. What were the subsidiary causes that induced society to forget the smiles of Lady Bessborough, Lady Melbourne and the Duchess of Devonshire, to forget how thoroughly they had enjoyed the wide good humor of their beloved Charles James Fox, and to condemn as "careless levity" all the laughter that had echoed through the galleries or across the lawns? I have already mentioned the infection of bourgeois ideas of respectability, the powerful spread of evangelicanism and the resultant appearance of a new and most unhealthy sense of shame. There were other secondary causes and symptoms.

We, in our shockproof generation, are unimaginative regarding the profound moral reaction occasioned by the excesses of the French Revolution. The disturbing logic of Thomas Paine frightened all literate classes of society and led to a spate of anti-Jacobin pamphlets to which Hannah More was not slow to accord her righteous prestige and flowing pen. It became the habit to contrast British "seriousness" with French frivolity, and British "principles" with French atheism. Many quite eupeptic Whigs began to imagine that in some way the horrors of the Revolution were the penalty imposed by God upon a self-indulgent nation. Whig principles remained articles of faith and doctrine; but if they were not to degenerate into Jacobin heresies they must be controlled by Protestant observances and insular good sense.

The Evangelicals were quick to profit by the moral panic that the Revolution caused. Sunday observance was revived and the idea became current in the provinces and even in Mayfair that all forms of gaiety were forms of levity, and that levity, as they now knew, inevitably led to impiety, the subversion of all rules of correct conduct, the fierce farce of revolutionary tribunals, and the grunting, grinding, the flap and crash, of the guillotine. In 1787 William Wilber force had induced King George III to issue a Royal Proclamation condemning vice. He thereupon founded his "Proclamation Society" to which a Vigilance Committee was attached on the old Puritan model.

In alliance with the Evangelicals came the "educators," of whom the most active and prominent were Mrs. Trimmer and Hannah More. Periodicals such as the *Eclectic Review* could denounce the poetry of

Byron as "such as no brother could read aloud to his sister, no husband to his wife." Even the *Christian Observer,* a less immoderate organ of the Clapham Sect, which was edited by Zachary Macaulay, disapproved of young people reading novels, dancing, or attending the theater. Beside the "educators" there appeared a worser breed, namely the expurgators, the emendators, the censors and the reformers. The *Family Shakespeare* of Thomas Bowdler appeared in 1818. But the worst expurgator of them all was James Plumptre, who in 1828 issued a bowdlerised version of *Robinson Crusoe,* and who outdistanced his master in not merely omitting improper passages but actually inserting elevating sentiments of his own. Thus the concluding lines of the song in *Cymbeline* run, in the original version composed by Shakespeare:

> With everything that pretty is,
> My lady sweet arise.

The Reverend James Plumptre realized that such language was unsuitable; he therefore altered the words to run:

> With everything that pretty is,
> For shame, thou sluggard, arise.

It was not the doctrine of abstinence and early rising only that James Plumptre, Fellow of Clare, Cambridge, so coldly advocated; he also introduced into the songs of Shakespeare lines of his own invention furthering the gospel of work. Thus Shakespeare's lines:

> Under the greenwood tree
> Who loves to lie with me,

were transformed by the Rev. James Plumptre into:

> Under the greenwood tree,
> who loves to work with me.

It did not occur to these emendators that they were committing forgery and printing lies. Their pudency quickly infected the reading habits of the period, the manuals of deportment, and the tone of the many seminaries for the instruction of young ladies which multiplied throughout the land. Even nursery life was changed by this sudden Puritanism. The happy, if often alarming, fairy stories that had survived from the remote past were replaced by cautionary tales such as *The Parent's Assistant* and the Rosamund stories of Maria Edgeworth, or the *Fairchild Family* which Miss Martha Butt, who became Mrs. Sherwood, composed in 1818.

The lesson which Miss Edgeworth (who was quite a jolly woman in real life) sought to inculcate was the utilitarian doctrine that ultimate happiness is preferable to immediate satisfaction. With this in mind Rosamund's hard and ignorant mother on two occasions exposes her child to death by blood poisoning in order that she may learn that well-fitting shoes are preferable to purple jars or that sweet briar is not as gentle as it smells. In the *Fairchild Family* there are two instances of cruelty, parental or providential. Henry aged six, having eaten a forbidden fruit, is locked up alone in an attic without food or drink for some ten hours. Augusta Noble, having disobeyed her parents, is visited with divine vengeance, being burnt alive. It is not, however, the horror stories in Mrs. Sherwood's book that render it repulsive so much as the molasses of self-satisfaction in which it is drenched. Mr. Fairchild had originally been destined for the church, but owing to chest trouble his enunciation became so poor that it was realized that his sermons would be inaudible. He therefore retired on a small income to the country where he did nothing whatsoever except reprove his children. Finally he inherits the large fortune amassed in India by a nabob brother and goes to live in righteousness at "The Grove," near Reading. The Fairchild children—Emily, Lucy and Henry—were not only very very good, but also "vastly genteel." They were aware, even at the age of six, that "their hearts were naturally sinful." They devoted much attention to improving this hereditary condition. "Oh Mamma, Mamma!" exclaims Lucy, "how unhappy wickedness makes us!" "Oh Papa!" exclaims Henry, "I do not wish to have my own way as I had this morning. I am now quite sure that it does not make people happy to have it." Such were the insufferable children who set the tone of nursery life from 1800 until 1885.

Six

The product of this complacency, of this worship of respectability, was that fraudulent and misshapen type of civility; the English Miss. Already Keats of all people had written of "the milk-white lamb that bleats for man's protection" and Tennyson was to repeat this unhappy figment in frequent poems and in his idolization of the "meek unconscious dove." The early nineteenth century débutante was expected to eat little, faint with facility, and blush at sight. "To be able," writes James Laver, "to go into a decline was almost a necessity for the contemporary heroine." They therefore aged quickly. "A woman of seven and twenty," says Marianne in *Sense and Sensibility,* "can never hope to feel or inspire affection again."

In the days of the Pastons and the Verneys, in the days of Queen Elizabeth I, the women of the family were gay, lusty and well-occupied. With the coming of bourgeois sensibility it was considered inelegant for a girl to be concerned with anything but her "accomplishments," meaning thereby music of a sort, painting of a sort, dancing and some acquaintance with foreign languages. They were not expected to move about very much, and Emma, who although intolerable, was a healthy enterprising girl, had at the age of twenty-one never even seen the sea. They were not encouraged to take exercise. When Elizabeth Bennet walked three miles in muddy weather to Netherfield, both Miss

Bingley and Miss Hurst considered her conduct displayed "a most country town indifference to decorum." Although they knew it not, these young women seated with their embroidery beside a brisk fire of sea coal, had been reduced to the status and quality of odalisques.

Here again we may find a reaction against the French Revolution and especially against Mary Wollstonecraft's *Vindication of the Rights of Women,* which was published in 1792. Horace Walpole, whose refinement was feminine in type, was so shocked by this work that he referred to its author as "a hyena in petticoats." In 1809 Hannah More wrote *Coelebs in Search of a Wife,* a work which, more than any other, created the model of "the perfect woman nobly planned." Eight editions of this dreadful book were issued within two months. The hero—a virtuous, sexless and self-important young man—journeys in search of a bride. The first girl he meets possesses great physical attractions, but unfortunately he finds her reading *The Sorrows of Werther* and dismisses her as no good at all. The second girl has a charming nature, but lacks any deep knowledge of religion and wears "transparent and scanty clothes." Finally in Hampshire Coelebs encounters his Lucilia, who, although almost inarticulate and unbearably inert, spends her spare time in reading the Bible to the aged infirm. It is Lucilia who is chosen.

The manuals which ministered to this ideal were frequent and detailed. I shall quote from two of them only, which I happen to have in my possession. The first is entitled *The Female Instructor or Young Woman's Companion,* and was published in London in 1824. In the Introduction to this manual it is admitted that God meant the male to be superior, having granted him a more muscular body and "a mind endowed with greater resolution and more extensive powers." But the female, if she be not merely beautiful and accomplished, but also very good, "can bend the haughty stubbornness of man."

A girl should dress simply, should refrain from imitating "the fluttering votaries of that capricious dame called Fashion" and should eschew cosmetics, on the principle that a "false face may be supposed the covering of a false heart." She should cultivate "dignity without pride, affability without meanness, and elegance without affectation." She should "strenuously avoid anything that is masculine" both in her deportment and her dress; laughter should be moderate; all familiarity should be eschewed: great intimacies are both foolish and imprudent." She should never forget that "the principal beauty and basis of the female character is modesty," since there "cannot be a more captivating or interesting object than a young girl who, with timid modesty, enters a room filled with a mixed company. The blush which diffuses its crimson on her cheek, is not only the most powerful charm of beauty, but does honor to the innocence of her heart."

A girl should realize that she is not expected to talk much or loud. She must avoid babbling, telling improbable or unkind stories, or indulging in sarcasm. Although it is most desirable for a girl to mix with her social superiors, she must never succumb to "the vain ambition of being noticed by the great." She must choose with care the books she reads. Novels, even when they ostensibly serve a moral purpose, may contain passages which "are totally improper to be perused by the eye of delicacy." A girl may take "moderate exercise in the open air," but must remember that her primary occupation must be "to smooth the bed of sickness and cheer the decline of age." In seeking for a husband she should realize that, although wealth and rank are important, respect and even love should be present as well. She should not permit herself to start liking someone of the opposite sex: "Love should be no means begin on your part: it should proceed from the attachment of the man."

My second document is a collection of "Answers to Correspondents," published in the *London Journal* between 1855 and 1862. A young lady enquires whether she would be right to present a curate who is leaving for another parish with a pair of braces that she has embroidered. The editor suggests that it would have been better if she had spent her time on something that might be sold for the benefit of the poor. "Presents to clergymen," he concludes with some asperity, "are at best ambiguous acknowledgements of their sacred services." A correspondent asks whether it would be an act of impropriety on her part to embrace her fiancé when saying goodbye. She is advised to reserve such endearments until after marriage. "Ladies," writes the editor, "should never presume too much on the forbearance, honor or delicacy of unmarried gentlemen. Men are apt to jump at the most startling conclusions." The *London Journal* contends that it is improper for married women to receive visits from gentlemen in the absence of their husbands. Such visitors know that in asking to be received they are committing a breach of etiquette and must thereby be condemned as "very vulgar or very designing." The odalisque ideal is sturdily maintained: "All poets," writes the *London Journal* mendaciously, "and all prose writers are agreed on one point, and that is that a delicate reserve, a rosy diffidence, and a sweetly chastened deportment are precisely the qualities in a woman that mostly win upon the affections omen."

Many Victorian young ladies did I suppose struggle to conform to this exacting model. The only one of them whom I knew personally was my grandmother, who died in 1919 in her hundredth year. There was nothing meek, or unconscious, or dove-like about my grandmother. She was a vigorous and intelligent old lady who bullied her family, bullied her servants, bullied the vicar, bullied the local tradesmen, bullied her neighbors and was universally respected and beloved. I asked her once whether in her youth she had shared and practiced these proprieties. She said that she had practiced them, that she now thought them idiotic, and that at thc time they had rendered her gawky, unhappy and actually ill. She told me that her contemporaries had been told that Brummell had broken off his engagement when he discovered that his fiancée liked cabbage and that Byron had mentioned that it made him sick to see a woman eat. The early nineteenth century maidens would thus starve themselves in public and then get their maids to bring wads of cake and ham and chicken to their bedrooms. "It was all most unpleasant" said my grandmother. "I much wish that I had been young at some other period of history."

Is there any more that need be said about the type of civility produced by the worship of respectability? There is no more that need be said.

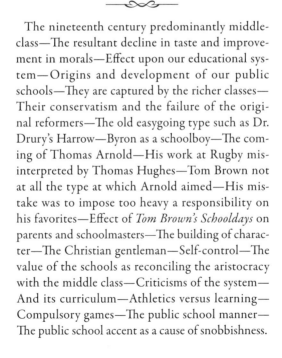

Chapter 13
Tom Brown

The nineteenth century predominantly middle-class—The resultant decline in taste and improvement in morals—Effect upon our educational system—Origins and development of our public schools—They are captured by the richer classes—Their conservatism and the failure of the original reformers—The old easygoing type such as Dr. Drury's Harrow—Byron as a schoolboy—The coming of Thomas Arnold—His work at Rugby misinterpreted by Thomas Hughes—Tom Brown not at all the type at which Arnold aimed—His mistake was to impose too heavy a responsibility on his favorites—Effect of *Tom Brown's Schooldays* on parents and schoolmasters—The building of character—The Christian gentleman—Self-control—The value of the schools as reconciling the aristocracy with the middle class—Criticisms of the system—And its curriculum—Athletics versus learning—Compulsory games—The public school manner—The public school accent as a cause of snobbishness.

One

THE CULT OF the respectable, although an English specialty, was never an English monopoly. In every European country with the exception of Russia, the Industrial Revolution led to an expansion of the numbers and influence of the middle classes. In Germany a massive *Bürgertum* had long existed and had produced the excellent if sedative type of civility that I have examined under the heading of *Gemütlichkeit*. In Belgium and Holland, even in Italy, even in Spain, a commercial and professional class arose which had inherited little from the old Burgundian, Renaissance or Castillian traditions. In Scandinavia solid communities were established, inspired by the conventions that form the background of Ibsen's ingenious dramas. And in France, under the monarchy of Louis Philippe, a heavy middle block asserted itself which, although less greedy and materialistic than it became under the second Empire and the third Republic, was dull, dowdy and intent on gain.

This new stratification of society did not in every country assume identical or simultaneous form. Yet the types of civility created in Europe by the Industrial Revolution displayed common features. Hitherto, as I have said, the middle classes had admired and therefore imitated the manners of the court; during the nineteenth century it was the bourgeois who created the tone of behavior for the whole community. The conventional standards which they established led to hypocrisy among those who conformed; and to extreme, often histrionic, eccentricity among those to whom discipline was repugnant. Admittedly the bourgeois introduced many material conveniences, such as good drainage, water closets, baths and armchairs. "Comfort," writes Clive Bell in his study of *Civilization,* "came in with the middle classes." Yet they also rendered utilitarianism fashionable and by despising the useless they robbed mankind of grace. Under their domination aesthetic taste disappeared abruptly from Europe; the individual craftsman became the factory hand; and the calamity occurred that the half century which witnessed the most extensive building in all history coincided with the fifty years during which, for the first and I trust last time, architectural taste and invention perished in Europe. Norman Shaw was nearly thirty years of age when Charles Barry died; yet what atrocious damage was done to our cities in the interlude when the authority of the latter had waned and before the influence of the former became active. Even Mr. John Betjeman could scarcely deny that the mid-nineteenth century, in spite of its great achievements in other areas, created wider, more expensive and more durable ugliness than any other epoch in the known history of mankind.

The bourgeois society dominant throughout Western Europe from 1830 onwards was, in its cult of respectability and its indifference to aesthetic values, remarkably uniform. In England, however, during those three generations a unique phenomenon was evolved in the shape of the public school boy. As a type, he has not as yet been successfully imitated in any foreign country. His pattern of behavior furnishes an interesting confirmation of the theory that evolution is the result of intention, although not the result intended. It is customary to describe the development of the public school spirit as the product of organic growth. It would be more accurate perhaps to define it as a quite natural result of inattention. It was inertia rather than constructive energy that produced the public school boy or, as he would have been defined in 1840, "the Christian gentleman."

As an ideal he was unique and may be obsolescent. But as a phenomenon he is interesting in that, at his best, he represents a rather grubby reversion to the Greek ideal of Lysis or Charmides. There was nothing banausic about him since he was a child of the rich: between the ages of nine and seventeen he was withdrawn from female influence and his instruction entrusted to males; he mixed on easy terms with his contemporaries, competing with them in sport and games; he was supposed to achieve an equal balance between music and gymnastics: and from time to time, in the form of chapel sermons and private tuition, he could absorb the wisdom of his elders. Yet to the Greek mind the slight importance attached at an English public school to intellectual attainments and aesthetic interests would have appeared barbaric; the fagging, bullying and fighting that figure so largely in our school stories would to an Athenian have seemed illiberal; in the gymnasium that stood beside the spring of Hermes there would have been no such bloodstained battle as that between Tom Brown and Slogger Williams; Hippothales would have been able to protect Lysis more effectively than Tom was ever able to guard Geordie Arthur.

The American investigator, Dr. Edward Mack, has defined these peculiarly English institutions as "those nonlocal endowed boarding schools for the upper classes which are termed Public Schools." Until 1840 there were only seven schools in England which came even roughly within this definition, namely Winchester, Eton, Harrow, Shrewsbury, Westminster, Rugby and Charterhouse. None of them had originally been founded for the education of rich children. Winchester was endowed in 1382 by William of Wykeham as a boarding school for prospective secular priests. Eton and Westminster were also established mainly in the interests of the Church. Shrewsbury was a local undertaking, having originally been financed by the burgesses of the town. Until the sixteenth century Harrow and Rugby were little more than local grammar schools. In each of these establishments, provision was made by the founders for the free education of impoverished scholars. Thus under their original statutes Eton and Winchester had to provide for seventy scholars and Westminster for forty. The headmaster was at the same time permitted to receive and educate fee-paying boys. In the days when it was customary for the sons of the rich to be as it were apprenticed to the houses of great nobles, ecclesiastics or statesmen, this privilege was but rarely exercised. When later it became fashionable for upper class boys to be educated at home by private tutors and thereafter to receive a final polish by spending a year or more abroad under the supervision of some bear-leader, the public schools were still regarded as unsuitable for boys of noble birth. Locke was hostile to these schools and as late as 1729 Swift could contend that a public school education was valueless to those whose parents could afford private tuition. But already, by the middle of the seventeenth century, a change had set in. Parents discovered that private tutors were not always virtuous or welcome and that their boys all too often returned from the Grand Tour with dissolute habits and mincing ways. Swift, in his *Essay on Modern Education,* had contended that to send boys to public schools was an unwise proceeding since "by mingling the sons of noblemen with those of the vulgar you engage the former in bad company." The parents discovered that the company kept by their sons at Venice or Padua was worse than that which they might encounter at Winchester or Eton. Thus gradually, from 1650 onwards, the privilege originally given to headmasters to receive fee-paying boys in addition to endowment scholars was abused to the point when the rich boys outnumbered the scholars by six to one.

Great headmasters, such as Dr. Busby of Westminster, acquired a reputation in society and a situation arose when the parents of poor scholars hesitated to send their boys to a public school, where they would be overwhelmed and bullied by the sons of the rich. This tendency was increased by the third Act of Uniformity of 1662 which in effect forbade Dissenters to teach at all. Thus the scholarships fell more and more into the hands of patrons who distributed them to their dependants. The intentions of the original founders were distorted by vested interests and resultant corruption. Money was diverted from the free education of scholars to more general purposes, foundationers were obliged to make some monetary contribution to their maintenance and instruction, and favoritism was exercised in the bestowal of free places. Thus by the middle of the eighteenth century Christ's Hospital was the only institution that really deserved the name of Charity School. It was this departure from original intention that produced the public school of the nineteenth century with its unique combination of privilege and harshness. It was a system which had not been applied since the distant days of Lycurgus. It is not surprising therefore that it should have produced a unique pattern of behavior in boy and man.

It must be remembered that the great public schools as we know them today did not always possess the eminence, the esteem, the sanitation, and the high social value which they now so rightly enjoy. Eton, with its rich endowments and its privileged university scholarships, has always been unequalled in the production of boys possessing self-assurance, adaptability, tidy hair and clothes, *sprezzatura,* and outward appearance of refinement. Winchester with its ancient tradition of politeness and learning has never ceased to inspire non-Wykehamists with amused, but quite reverential awe. Harrow, before 1721, was little more than a country grammar school until the suspicion that Eton had become a breeding ground for Tories and Jacobites, and the wholly undeserved suggestion that Westminster was unhealthy, induced the Whig oligarchy to send their sons, not to the ancient Thames-side institutions, but to the upstart on its hill.

However much these original seven schools may through the last two centuries and a half have differed from each other in their character and fortunes, they did possess one thing in common, namely a dislike of reform. Such changes as have been introduced into our public school system have come from younger schools, such as Uppingham in the 1860s, Oundle in the 1890s and Stowe in our own century. The older institutions preferred to move like majestic glaciers one inch a year. Arnold's Rugby was, as we shall see, a striking, and perhaps unfortunate, exception to this golden rule. His two predecessors in the work of reform, lacked his obstinate fanaticism. John Russell, who became headmaster of Charterhouse in 1811, adopted the two abominable experiments of getting the senior boys to teach the little boys, on the Lancastrian system, and of abolishing the custom of fagging. For some fifteen years Russell was hailed as a great educational reformer and the numbers at Charterhouse rose to 640. It was then found that the little boys were not respectful to the intellectually eminent among their contemporaries and that the abolition of organized fagging led to promiscuous bullying. By 1830 the numbers at Charterhouse and the repute of John Russell had declined.

Samuel Butler was more successful at Shrewsbury. He insisted upon the most rigid discipline and imposed the humanities upon his boys by a system of rewards and punishments. He retired in 1836 having in the thirty-eight years of his headmastership restored to Shrewsbury its reputation of hard work and sound scholarship. His boys when they went to the university competed brilliantly with those who came from more fashionable but easy going schools. The reforms of Samuel Butler, unlike those of John Russell, were educational rather than institutional. In that they affected the intellectual standards of the school rather than its customs they did not arouse the enmity of parents, assistant masters, or boys. It was Thomas Arnold of Rugby who, by his insistence on moral tone, changed the whole conception of English public school education, infected even Winchester, Eton and Harrow, and created the type of Christian gentleman who was during the nineteenth century so deeply admired, not in England only, but also in Scotland and Wales. Thomas Arnold, who has been misrepresented by such writers as Hughes and Lytton Strachey, merits a section to himself.

Two

It is a matter of regret to me that Lord Byron, in whose intricate character reticence did not figure with any emphasis, has never told us much about his first two and a half years at Harrow. We know that he was in a permanent state of rebellion; we know that he learnt small Latin and less Greek, but that he read deeply and widely in all those refreshing works that his masters did not wish him to read; we know that his friendships, especially those with younger boys of excellent family, such as Lord Clare and the Duke of Dorset, amounted to passions; and we know that most unexpectedly he played in the Harrow eleven against Eton in 1805. We suspect that as a small, lame and pidpodgy little boy, possessed of an impossibly vulgar and intrusive mother, he suffered much on his arrival. I doubt whether Byron ever consented willingly to be beaten or fagged. "I always," he recorded, "*hated* Harrow till the last year and a half." Yet when it came for him to leave the school, his distress was so deep that he was unable to sleep at night and that he experienced "one of the deadliest and heaviest feelings of my life."

What interests us most about Byron the Harrovian is the laxity with which his indiscipline, his truancy, his moodiness and his rebellions were regarded by the authorities. Miss Ethel Colburn Mayne, in what I still regard as the best of the three-hundred-odd biographies of Byron, makes the amusing suggestion that Dr. Joseph Drury, the headmaster, was "Byron's first conquest." Certainly Drury pampered him, soothed him, flattered him, encouraged him. Byron never lost his sense of gratitude and esteem for his old headmaster. This tempestuous shirker, this lazy rebel, who absented himself for hours lying on Peachey's tomb reading works on oriental travel would not for one instant have commended himself to Dr. Thomas Arnold. The Harrow of 1801–1805 was a very different and perhaps more civilized institution than the Rugby of 1828–1842. In that short interval occurred a revolution in the eighteenth century conception of a public school and the type of boy which it ought to produce. Thomas Arnold may have been a trifle mixed, and even confused, in his intentions. But we may be positive that never, even in his moment of greatest perplexity, would he have desired to produce a Byron. Charm was not his aim.

Thomas Arnold was appointed headmaster at Rugby in 1828 when he was thirty years of age. During his early years he was suspected by the boys of wishing to destroy school customs; those of their parents who were Tories were not quite happy regarding the orthodoxy of his theological opinions; those of the parents who were Whigs accused him of being too dictatorial and harsh. The Trustees of the school were alarmed by his obstinacy, his independence, and his habit of expelling boys whom he happened not to like. Within ten years he had disciplined the school by creating prefects in his own likeness; had tamed the Trustees; and had satisfied parents, both of the left and the right, that Rugby had become, as Carlyle wrote, "a temple of industrious peace."

Arnold possessed a complex character. He was but an average scholar, utterly insensitive to art, but formidable in his combativeness in the battle between righteousness and sin. He was naive and sensitive, obstinate and fierce, tyrannical and nervous. His purpose was to instill into boys something of his own moral earnestness. He was convinced that human beings, especially human beings of under thirteen years of age, were fundamentally wicked; they must be whipped for their own salvation and thereafter taught their moral responsibilities. He disliked the lower boys, since they were incapable of absorbing moral enthusiasm; he pressed them on too quickly, hoping that as premature adults they would spread moral influence throughout the school with something of his own missionary zeal.

With this in mind he did not seek so much to change the existing forms and customs as to infuse them with a new and higher spirit. He believed that to entrust a boy with responsibility when young gave him a "sense of corporate duty." Thus he legalized, organized and exploited the existing system of sixth-form dominance, fagging and beating. He introduced, but without much zest, some instruction in history, modern languages and mathematics into the old classical curriculum. He did not encourage science and a boy with real scientific interests, such as "poor Martin," was thought, and treated as, a freak. He did not really care for literature; he taught the classics as syntax and prosody rather than as a living expression of ideas. In his formidable sermons and through his band of prefects he sought to communicate his fervor to the lower boys. Yet perhaps his greatest achievements were the organization on a very firm basis of the prefectorial system and his creation of confidence between boys and masters.

How far did Arnold succeed? Certainly he inspired his senior boys with a strong sense of responsibility. Lord Shaftesbury always said that he preferred Rugby to Eton on the ground that it produced "more of the inward and not so much of the outward gentleman." Yet the defects of the method were that he forced boys to mature too early and that he turned them into moral prigs. As Bertrand Russell has written, the disadvantages of the Arnold system was that it "sacrificed intellect to virtue."

The real error of Arnold was, however, more personal. His strength of character, his very ferocity, were so compulsive that he acquired far too much influence over his favorite boys. His son Matthew could write of his "radiant vigor," of "his buoyant cheerfulness," of his being invariably "fervent, heroic and good." Yet his dominance was a that of a upas tree which casts a blight over those who linger too long beneath its branches:

> We who till then in thy shade
> Rested, as under the boughs
> Of a mighty oak, have endured
> Sunshine and rain as we might,
> Bare, unshaded, alone,
> Lacking the shelter of thee.

Matthew Arnold was a busy, strong-minded man, who confronted his own skepticism with buoyancy. Yet even on him there descended sometimes the sense of abandoned despair which affects those who have in boyhood relied too much on a personality for whom there were no intermediate shades between right and wrong:

> The Sea of Faith
> Was once too at the full, and round earth' s
> shore
> Lay like the folds of a bright girdle furl'd.
> But now I only hear
> Its melancholy long-withdrawing roar
> Retreating to the breath
> Of the night wind, down the vast edges drear
> And naked shingles of the world.

On Arthur Hugh Clough, a tenderer and less humorous character, the effect of Thomas Arnold was disastrous. Clough had been the prize school-boy, the best goalkeeper that Rugby has ever known, the devoted scholar, the missionary after Arnold's own heart. What did it matter if he was devoid of humor, of any aesthetic sensibility, and inclined to indolence? His consciousness of the unceasing battle between sin and righteousness was an abiding consciousness; he stalked the dormitories of Rugby angered and watchful, seeking to convey the great message of the headmaster (and what exactly was it?) to little boys. When he left Rugby he became involved in all the theological tortures of the time, "in storms that rage outside our happy ground." The light darkened, he left Oriel, and thereafter did practically nothing at all. Dean Stanley, Arnold's other prize pupil, was less of a collapse.

In his later age Clough realized that at Rugby his conscience had been overworked. He writes about "my strange distorted youth" and in the *Epilogue to Dipsychus* the elderly mentor is represented as decrying too much moral earnestness in the young. "They're all too pious" he exclaims. "It's all Arnold's doing. He spoilt the public school."

Three

It may be true that Arnold, in his dislike of wicked little boys, tried to render them good big boys before they were ripe for such a transformation. It may be true that he imposed upon his favorites a sense of moral purpose heavier than young minds or souls can stand. It may be true that he sent up to the university batches of moral prigs who were not always self-reliant enough to survive the merriment they aroused. But it is a mistake to assert that Thomas Arnold alone created the public school spirit of the nineteenth century. The man most responsible for that creation was Thomas Hughes, the hearty author of *Tom Brown's Schooldays.*

It is important to realize that Thomas Hughes was not the sort of Rugbeian whom Arnold either wanted or liked. Hughes, in his degradation of Arnold's faith into muscular Christianity, was not following the lessons of Rugby chapel, but those of Charles Kingsley and Frederick Denison Maurice. Hughes was too stupid a man fully to understand the mysticism that lay behind the Doctor's hatred of sin, still less his sense of intellectual adventure. Arnold would have strongly disapproved of any system of education which placed the cult of the body above the cult of the mind and soul. He would, quite rightly, have regarded *Tom Brown's Schooldays* as a caricature of all that he had wished to do, and almost succeeded in doing, at Rugby.

Tom Brown's father is represented as saying of his son: "I don't care a straw for Greek particles, or the digamma, no more does his mother. If he'll only turn out a brave, truth-telling Englishman and a gentleman and a Christian, that's all I want." Had Dr. Arnold heard that remark, he would have advised Mr. Brown to send his son to some other school. The head of Tom's house, young Brooke, is represented as saying that he would rather win two house matches than a Balliol scholarship. Had the Doctor heard young Brooke saying anything so idiotic, he would have fixed upon him the perplexed and furious stare which remained for so long in his pupils' minds. Hughes approved of indiscriminate combat. "Fighting with fists," he wrote, "is the natural and English way for English boys to settle their quarrels." Arnold would have been less patriotic on this subject. Hughes comments on the difficulty created for the prefectorial system by the fact that the boys who reached sixth form were often clever rather than muscular. He represents Arnold as asking young Holmes to beat a boy in Wharton's house, since Wharton himself was not sufficiently muscular to cause real pain. "Holmes," the Doctor, is represented as adding, "has plenty of strength. I wish all the Sixth had as much. We must have it here, if we are to keep order at all." Arnold would have disliked that passage. I much doubt also whether the Doctor would have listened with any enthusiasm to the relish with which young East describes the season's football on Big Side: "Why, there's been two collar bones broken this half and a dozen fellows lamed. And last year a fellow had his leg broken." I doubt even whether Arnold would have admired the robust, philistine, and combative Tom Brown or his passion for poaching and kicking balls. Yet Hughes' book immediately became a best seller.

It was admired by masters, assistant masters, fathers, prefects, and even mothers and sisters throughout the land. It set the tone for the new public schools which, in the second half of the century, were springing up all over England. It stabilized the pattern of what a healthy, truthful, plucky schoolboy ought to be. How valuable was the type of civility thereby produced?

The aim was not the transmission of knowledge, or even the training of the intellect, so much as the building of character. It was assumed that the boys would bring with them from home the rudimentary instincts of courage, loyalty and leadership. To these chivalric virtues would be added the ecclesiastical virtue of humility. But it would not be the masters who would teach this modesty, but the boys themselves, often by processes that were humiliating and harsh. The idea was that a boy achieved self-reliance by overcoming obstacles. In place of the conception of self-development in a congenial environment there was the conception of self-conquest in an atmosphere which might prove most uncongenial. On the moral plane, this conception was akin to Alain's intellectual ideal of *la difficulté vaincue*.

The virtues of loyalty and truthfulness were much recommended. One of Thomas Arnold's most lasting achievements was, as I have said, to break down the distrust and animosity that had existed between boys and masters. He invariably believed what a boy told him, so that in the end it became bad form, or unsporting, to tell the Doctor a lie. Loyalty again was elevated above the ordinary levels of caste loyalty to become loyalty to the school itself. It was regarded as essential in after life to express affection for one's old school. Only very exceptional people, such as the Duke of Wellington and Shelley, dared to confess that they had hated Eton: Gladstone contended that his schooldays had been the happiest of his life and Thackeray, who had in fact been bullied at Charterhouse, became sentimental about it in his later age. Sydney Smith was one of those rare instances of a man who, although he had been a success at Winchester, spoke of it for ever after with uninhibited dislike. Such loyalty is all too often either a regret for lost boyhood or a deliberate form of belief. Yet the public school system did certainly teach boys to be loyal to each other, not to tell tales, not to take mean advantages and to be fair. These were valuable lessons.

A further quality inculcated by the Tom Brown tradition was that of self-control. It is convenient to reduce personal violence to a minimum and to subject the overt expression of the passions to some automatic discipline. In the later half of the nineteenth century the advocates of the public school spirit contended that this self-discipline should extend to all expressions of feeling whatsoever. Although it had been considered effective rather than unmanly for such public heroes as Pitt, Fox, Nelson and even Wellington to cry in public, tears began about 1850 to be regarded as ungentlemanlike. This prohibition was not, until 1900, universally accepted. Lord Houghton, when told of the death of Lady Waldegrave, burst into a fit of unrestrained weeping. Tennyson used to sob passionately when reading *Maud* and expected his audience to do likewise. I have myself seen such men as Curzon and Churchill cry, quite quietly, but very hard. Yet the theory became established that to display emotion was a feminine, or provincial, or foreign, thing to do.

There is a passage in Tom Moore's *Memoir on Sheridan* which makes me wonder whether it was really the muscular Christianity of Hughes and Kingsley that first taught the upper and middle classes not to reveal their emotions in public:

"The natural tendencies," writes Moore, "of the excesses of the French Revolution was to produce in the higher classes of England an increased reserve of manner, and, of course, a proportionate restraint upon all within the circle, which have been fatal to conviviality and humor and not very propitious to wit,—subduing both manners and conversation to a sort of polished level, to rise above which is often thought to be almost as vulgar as to sink below it."

At its worst, this doctrine of self-control and reticence may have led to insensitiveness or at least impassivity. But at its best, it produced a calm reflective manner by which stupidity was concealed and modesty mingled with self-assurance. It cannot be dismissed as a wholly negligible component of good manners.

From the more practical aspect, the Victorian public schools did serve to bridge the gap between the old territorial aristocracy and the second generation of industrialists. It is questionable whether had the antagonism between the landowners and the new middle class persisted after 1840 the Victorians would ever have been able to cope with their social and economic problems.

Even Gibbon, who can scarcely be regarded as a typical schoolboy, contended that the system was that "best adapted to the genius and constitution of the English people." "In a free intercourse," he wrote, "with equals, the habits of truth, fortitude and prudence will insensibly be matured." The severest critics of the system will admit that none of our experiments in other educational methods has as yet proved successful. The idea of allowing a boy to develop his own talents and temperament naturally, as had been advocated by Jean-Jacques Rousseau and essayed by such educationalists as the Edgeworths, Thomas and Roland Hill, or Joseph Lancaster, have not for long proved successful in our soil or climate. We have always preferred Tom Brown.

Four

The public school system and the type it produced were perfectly adapted to the social conditions of the eighteenth and nineteenth centuries. The governing classes were provided with a constant supply of young men, uniform in manners, indistinguishable in intellect or character, and prepared to defend their caste privileges against internal and external proletariates. Sensible people, such as Trollope and Walter Bagehot, took it for granted that government could only be exercised by the select few and that this elite should be composed of "gentlemen." But they both believed in what they called a "fluid" society in which boys from middle class homes could become gentlemen once they were sent to the right school. The public school was regarded as a melting pot in which the rich industrials could be fused with the old aristocracy by somewhat drastic means. Bagehot entitled the method "removable inequality."

Yet there were other nineteenth century critics who assailed the whole system for its narrowness and brutality. The cult of manliness benefited the muscular many to the grave damage of the intellectual few. The prefectorial system, in those days, was less frequently effective in suppressing bullies than it was in suppressing originality. Such gifted men as Froude, Lewis Carroll, Dolben, Fitz-James Stephen, and J. A. Symonds all suffered when at school from the pressure of uniformity. They complained that they were not given any opportunity to develop their own temperaments, talents, or tastes. Sydney Smith, in an article in the *Edinburgh Review*, denied that the roughness of public schools was in fact a good foundation for after life. A boy was exposed to cruelty out of proportion to anything that he would be obliged to endure as an adult. The masters found it convenient to leave to the prefects the maintenance of order, but their avoidance of responsibility often had calamitous results. "This neglect," wrote Sydney Smith, "is called a spirited and manly education." The *New Monthly* asserted that our public schools "were models of instruction in arbitrary power and abject slavery." "I am no friend," wrote Southey, "to public schools. Where they are beneficial to one they are ruinous to twenty." Trollope's most pleasant recollection of his school days was an occasion when he thrashed a boy so mercilessly that he had to be taken home. Thackeray's criticism of Eton was more detailed:

> There are at this present writing 500 boys at Eton, kicked and licked and bullied by another 100,—scrubbing shoes, running errands, making false concords and (as if that were a natural consequence) putting their posteriors on a block for Dr. Hawtrey to lash at: and still calling it education. They are proud of it—good heavens!—absolutely vain of it; as what dull barbarians are not proud of their dullness and barbarism? They call it the good old English system.

The prefects also came in for criticism. William of Wykeham had provided that there should be eighteen seniors to maintain discipline and to report misdeeds. Henry VI established sixteen praepostors at Eton. The prefectorial system, which is of such immense convenience to masters, was systematized at the end of the eighteenth century by such men as Dr. Goddard of Winchester and Dr. Drury of Harrow, long before Arnold created his Apostles of the Sixth. Fagging was also attacked, but often defended. "At Eton," writes Thackeray, "a great deal of snobbishness was thrashed out of Lord Buckram and he was birched with perfect impartiality. He was caned several times with great advantage for not sufficiently polishing his master Smith's shoes."

The exclusive teaching of Latin and Greek, which was regarded as valuable, partly because they were difficult languages and therefore good for the brain, and partly because they were useless and therefore precious factors in "a liberal education," did not in the nineteenth century command universal approval. The tradition of the great Erasmus lingered long in our academies and Locke could write: "Latin I look upon as absolutely necessary to a gentleman." The Benthamites, on the other hand, urged more utilitarian subjects and contended that even science should figure in the curriculum. Cobbett, as might have been expected, denounced the classics as "serviceable to monks and friars only." Thackeray when at Athens anathematized the very stones for all the misery they had brought to little boys. And even Byron, who in fact owed much to the *Satires* and the *Ars Poetica,* wrote rude things about the Horace of his Harrow days.

More serious were the criticisms that the cult of athletics produced a type of civility that was in fact barbaric. The Rev. F. W. Farrar, for instance, when a master at Harrow could echo what, although not realized at the time, was the purest Arnold doctrine. "By God's blessing," he wrote, "we have in large measure ennobled and purified the once unhealthy moral atmosphere of our public schools." He spoke with warm approval of "the deeply encouraging growth of Christian character" since Arnold's days. Yet he contended that "this mania of muscularity has its share in the hunger-bitten poverty of our intellectual results." He profoundly regretted "that a boy should spend *all* his energies and *all* his admiration on the attainment of those corporeal attributes in which, let him do his best, the brute and the savage will beat him still."

MUSCULAR CHRISTIANS, 1879

Obviously young males must be given some opportunity for discharging their physical energies. In the
twelfth century they indulged in sham battles, water-
quintain, boar fights and bull-baiting. In the sixteenth
century the manuals recommended tennis in moderation, horsemanship, fencing, swimming, archery and
hawking. Football was regarded as a vulgar exercise, but
it was urged that every little boy should be instructed
how to play chess. It was not until the nineteenth century that games became compulsory and figured as
an organized element in the structure of every school.
Thenceforward a boy was deprived of the ability to
choose his amusements. By about 1870 athletics had
replaced learning as the central aim of English education. Thenceforward schoolboys were not able to follow
their own inclinations or to develop their own tastes:
uniformity settled down upon the woods and playing
fields as a thick grey cloud; house matches and house-
colors became the center and object of interest and
ambition. The masters themselves were infected by this
philistinism; to them also games seemed more admirable than individual talent or high standards of scholarship. Most assistant masters became Tom Browns.

I do not think that these processes, given contemporary conditions, produced a wholly valueless type of
civility. It taught boys how to obey and how to command. If they had been too pampered or spoilt at
home, it did provide them with humble thoughts and
some ability to face the crudities of adult life. It was,

of course, hard on the athlete, whose sudden glory was exposed to the sad law of diminishing returns. It was bad for the second-rate schoolmaster. But the intellectual, if he possessed any authentic talent at all, was pruned by the process into subsequent florescence. And the prefectorial and fagging systems, including corporal punishment, did preserve boys from that sense of "personal honor" (which is little more than a morbid preoccupation with youthful dignity) that has caused so much unhappiness and worry to foreign adolescents.

Moreover, if the public schools did not consciously teach manners, they did assuredly produce a manner, whether it was the sleek insouciance of Eton, the eager courtesy of Winchester, the affable clumsiness of Charterhouse, or the slick urbanity of Harrow. It may be that both the system and the type it created have become irrelevant. I remain convinced that the insistence of the public schools upon gentleman-like, rather than courtly, qualities, and their success in transmitting these qualities to the State schools and the poorer classes, rendered them factors in civilization which should be much esteemed.

My main criticism of the public school system is that it has served to emphasize class differences. As Arthur Ponsonby has pointed out in his book *The Decline of Aristocracy,* a German parent had to decide whether his boy should go to a *Gymnasium,* a *Realgymnasium* or an *oberrealschule:* a British parent decided which of the many luxury schools he could afford. Ponsonby considered that the educational segregation of the rich from the poor had had a damaging social effect, being "the strongest factor that exists in fostering class jealousy and exclusiveness." He contended that a boy leaves his public school "saturated with class prejudice." Arthur Ponsonby's book was published in 1912, at a date before two wars and the triumph of socialism had changed the structure of our society. Today class distinctions have been modified by the impoverishment of the rich and the self-assurance acquired by the Trades Unions and the Labor Party as a result of a long and highly successful exercise of power. The level of education provided by State and local schools is today equal to that given by the most expensive institutions: our universities are attended mainly by undergraduates who do not come from wealthy homes. Moreover, now that all men and women are obliged to earn their living, and that National Service assists the fusion of classes, the old segregations are less rigid and may become less apparent. Yet the accent, most unfortunately, persists. One can detect by the accent of Frenchmen and Germans from what provinces they originated, but not to what social class they belong; in England the several layers of society are as it were labeled by intonation. This may still create snobbishness on the one hand and lack of self-confidence on the other. Yet in the future this defect may be removed when we all speak English as beautifully and uniformly as they do upon the BBC.

Chapter 14

The Need for Change

—⤜∽⤛—

Civilization a process rather than a condition—The inevitability of change—Examples of this—Salutations—Methods of address—Fashions in language and pronunciations—Thus civility varies always both in space and time—Incivility on the other hand may assume permanent form and produce permanent types—The coldly discourteous—The bore—The snob—Good behavior has always been the work of a minority—Even in a classless community differences of taste and interests are bound to develop—If the British lose their own tradition they will probably adopt the American model—They will then need to recall the European types of civility if they are not to become standardized, vulgar or dull.

One

IN CONSIDERING GOOD behavior I have followed the system of examining types of civility evolved by successive European societies. This more or less chronological method has the advantage of giving some measure of concentration to a theme which, if grouped under subject headings, such as "Family Relationships" or "Cleanliness and Sanitation," obscures the all-important truth, on which Dr. Norbert Elias and others have insisted, that civilization is a continuous process and not a sequence of detached phenomena. I should not wish to leave the impression of a few isolated pictures: the picture of Charmides banging his music master on the head, the picture of Bertrand de Born thrumming his mandoline below his mistress" window, the picture of the Chevalier de Méré scribbling social stratagems. It is not the Catholicism of good manners that is important so much as their incessant variations in space and time. In order to emphasize their transitory quality I shall, in this concluding chapter, adopt the alternative method of subject headings. I shall illustrate the transience of good form by examining three of its most recurrent manifestations, namely methods of salutation, forms of address, and clique jargon and pronunciation.

Professor Østrup has made the interesting suggestion that the raising of the right hand in greeting, thereby assuring an advancing stranger that we are both amicable and unarmed, is so primitive as to date back to Cro Magnon times before the period of any organized religion. He contends even that it was these prehistoric salutation movements that were developed by the early shamans and the later prophets into gestures of prayer. It is true that the ancient Egyptian formula of salutation by raising the hands to the shoulders with the palms opened outwards can still be recognized even in the simplest village mosque; and that the Assyrian convention of self-abasement— "I eat the dust beneath your feet"—still lingers in the stylized Arab gesture of sweeping the dust from the floor and carrying it to lips, or in the Persian phrase of abject apology, *gel mikhoram*.

The raising of the hat, in the days when people still wore hats, is a well known survival of the custom of raising the visor in the presence of a lady or a friend. Conversely, as Herodotus assures us, the old Achaemenids never appeared bare-headed: even in my own day, it was regarded as indecorous for a Moslem to be observed in public without his turban, his fez, or his tarboosh. I have seen elderly hodjas tumble off their donkeys and search frantically for their turbans before rising to their feet.

The kiss as a form of salutation has been resorted to variously in different countries and at different times. Members of reigning European families always embrace other Royalties in public, even if they loathe them horribly, or have never met them before. If they wish to kiss a friend, they do so in the privacy of their own apartments. This is a most ancient distinction. Herodotus tells us that the Persians of his day attached elaborate significance to this kissing ceremony. Equals kissed each other on the lips: near-equals on the cheek:

inferiors greeted superiors by prostration. Constantine Porphyrogenitus, in his manual on etiquette, devoted pages to discussing who kissed whom and where— whether on the head, breast, hands, lips or cheek. Foot-kissing was a gesture of immense antiquity. In Egypt it was rated as a rare privilege to be allowed to kiss the foot of Pharoah. Diocletian, the Dalmatian shepherd boy, dealt a final blow to Roman *gravitas* by introducing foot-kissing into imperial receptions: from him it descended to the Carolingians and so to the Papacy. In Greece, as we should expect, this ugly gesture of abasement was regarded as illiberal and unrefined: you should lightly touch the chin of a superior and then kiss your own hand. In this graceful manner did Thetis intercede with Zeus on behalf of Achilles. In Japan it was regarded as good form to turn the back on a member of the Royal Family or a Prime Minister, indicating thereby that he was too glorious to be viewed front face. Such a posture would have been misinterpreted at Windsor or Schönbrunn.

The Polynesians, the Malays, and the Eskimos greet each other by smelling or sniffing: this gesture of courtesy is called "rubbing noses." The Andaman islanders and the Australian aborigines adopt a wholehearted embrace, such as that of the grizzly bear. The Israelites bowed—and for all I know may still bow—seven times to the ground. The elaborate greeting ceremonies of the Chinese entailed many years of initiation and practice. In Rome, as Martial recounts, the ceremony of kissing became such a nuisance that it was gradually discarded. Parents, when they kissed their children, held them tightly by the ears. In my own lifetime the convention of kissing has altered much. When I was a young man, to kiss any female other than a very close relation was regarded as a gesture of espousal; today debutantes are kissed openly by their male friends with glacial impartiality.

In France, as in Austria, the practice of kissing in public (unless it be the long ecstasy of embrace indulged in by oblivious lovers in the Underground) is confined to the empty and unsanitary formula of kissing a lady's hand. "*La France,*" writes André de Fouquières, "*reste le bastion du baise-main.*" It also remains the last fortress of the handshake. The French cultivate the limp, perfunctory, inattentive handshake known as the '*poignée de main parlementaire.*" It is practiced, not in the Palais Bourbon only, but among colleagues in Government departments, insurance offices, clubs and railway stations. It is an impersonal, inattentive almost dismissive, gesture, which for us recalls Shakespeare's rebuke to those who greet their friends "like a fashionable host that slightly shakes his parting guest by the hand." Our English inhibitions against all forms of gesticulation may end by abolishing movements of greeting; we shall meet and part in future with nothing more than a stylized grunt.

Two

Complicated variations can be observed also in methods of address and especially in the use or abuse of Christian names. Until the early nineteenth century, when sobriquets such as "Mama" and "Papa" were introduced, children would address their parents as "Madam" or "Sir," as "My Lady" or "My Lord." In *Moll Flanders,* which was published in 1722, even siblings avoided the use of Christian names when addressing each other and would prefer to say "sister" or "brother." Towards the end of the eighteenth century a sudden change occurred: the gods and goddesses of Whig society began to call each other "Charles" or "William." Tom Moore, writing in 1825, notes that one of the strangest transformations that he had observed in recent decades was the disappearance of the old habit of "men of high station" calling each other by their Christian names. This happy convention seems not to have survived the death of Charles James Fox. Thus Byron, who regarded himself (quite wrongly) as representative of the very cream of Whig Society, never addressed his friends by anything but their surnames, not even Lord Clare whom he had loved at Harrow, not even the young Duke of Dorset who had been his fag, not even John Cam Hobhouse who had been his intimate at Cambridge and who remained his closest friend until he died. In *Coningsby,* which purports to describe the highest Tory society of 1832, the young men never use Christian names when speaking to each other, although in *Tom Brown's Schooldays* it is "Harry" and "Geordie" all the time. In my own youth, had I been addressed by my Christian name at my private or even my public school, I should have blushed scarlet, feeling that my privacy had been outraged and that some secret manliness had been purloined from me, as if I had been an Andaman islander or a Masai. And I do not believe that even Sydney Smith ever dared to call Lady Holland "Elizabeth."

Yet how different from the gay Devonshire House circle, and the sentimental intimacy of Charles James Fox and his friends, was the tightness in such matters observed and expected by the characters in Jane Austen's novels! Even when happily married, the Woodhouse daughters continued to call their father "Sir." Emma denounced as "vulgar familiarity" Mrs. Elton's reference to Mr. Knightley as "Knightley;" she herself, we may assume, continued to refer to him as "Mr. Knightley" even when they had been husband and wife for many years. Mrs. Elton on one occasion committed the enormity of referring to Miss Fairfax as "Jane Fairfax." "Heavens!" exclaims Emma, "let us not suppose that she dares go about Emma Woodhousing me!" Anne Elliot in *Persuasion* continues to address her old school friend as "Miss Smith." In *Mansfield Park* Mrs. Norris never speaks of or to her sister except as "Lady Bertram;" it is as "Mr. Bertram" that dear little Fanny Price continues to refer to her cousin, after she has been living as a member of the family for nine years. It is strange that a convention, as rigidly enforced in one class of society at a given period, should have become established so suddenly and then so suddenly have disappeared.

In my own lifetime, as I have said, the feeling about Christian names has changed completely. My father would never have used the Christian name of any man or woman who was not a relation or whom he had not known for at least thirty years. My aunt called her husband by his surname until the day of his death. It was in the reign of Edward VII that the use of Christian names first became fashionable, and even then it was surrounded by all manner of precautions and restrictions. Today to address a man by his surname might appear distant, snobbish, old fashionable and rather rude. Members of the House of Commons, and even of the House of Lords, will today address each other by their Christian names even when totally unaware of what their surnames may be. I am often amazed by the dexterity with which actors, bandleaders, merchants, clubmen and wireless producers will remember to say "Veronica" or "Shirley" to women to whom they have not even been introduced. This engaging habit derives, I suppose, from the United States: from the belief cherished by the citizens of that Republic that all men, as all women, are created equal and that these gambits of intimacy form part of the pursuit of happiness, the necessity of seeming "folksy," and the essential requirement of avoiding anything suggestive of patronage. It is an inflationary, and therefore vulgar, habit none the less.

Three

In every society, as I have said, a certain type of civility is first evolved by a minority and thereafter imitated by smaller or larger sections of the community as a whole. The élites who have perfected their own pattern of behavior resent this imitation and tend to invent a clique language and pronunciation whereby to segregate themselves from those outside. This has always happened.

Thus De Callières writing at the end of the seventeenth century, had already noticed that the language of society differed in tone and expression from that of the town. "You know," he says, "that the bourgeois speak quite differently from us." A bourgeois, for instance, will say "*je vous demande excuse*" instead of "*je vous demande pardon;*" "*un mien ami*" instead of "*un de mes amis;*" or "*je le l'ai*" instead of "*je l'ai.*" Strange also was the alteration in court accent caused by the Italians imported by Catherine de Medicis. The "*ois*" in words such as "françois" was changed into "*ais.*" Words such as "*moi*" or "*roi*" were pronounced "*mé*" and "*ré;*" the short *o* became *ou,* so that "*chose*" was pronounced "*chouse*" and "*Rome*" as "*Roum.*" It was at this period regarded as smart to say "*j'étions*" or "*je venions*" in place of "*j' étais*" or "*je venais.*" The French have always been particular about the elegant as well as the precise use of language, and in the nineteenth century all manner of manuals appeared under the generic title of *Ne dites pas.* From these we learn that it was regarded as vulgar to say "drink coffee" rather than "take coffee" and that instead of saying "*j'ai lu dans le journal*" one should say "*j'ai lu sur le journal.*" In England, where the language of society changes as quickly as an April morning, we have been less fussy. In France, this clique or aristocratic language spread downwards during the eighteenth century and became the national language: in Germany the language of the educated was formed, less by court circles, than by universities and men of letters.

A similar change between one generation and another can be noted in the pronunciation at any one time considered elegant. I have already remarked that the Whigs said "Lonnon" for "London," "Room" for "Rome," and "goold" for "gold." In the sixteenth century a woman of fashion was supposed to turn a short *o* into an *a*, saying "a pax on it" for "a pox on it." As late as 1818 such words as "influential" or "lengthy" were ridiculed as "Americanisms." Lord Chesterfield was shocked by Dr. Johnson pronouncing the word "great" as we pronounce it today. "Only Irishmen," he sneered, "*say grate.*" Thackeray represents his fops as unable to pronounce the letters *s* or *r*. "Ever theen us on pawade?" enquires an officer in the Household Cavalry. Thackeray, again, gives us the refined cockney of 1840 in the form of a footman asking his master: "Wawt taime will you plase have the cage, Sir?" We cannot but feel that the jaunty cockney of Sam Weller was both better observed and more accurately rendered.

Even in a single generation such changes in the intonation and the vocabulary of the exclusive can be observed. I had a great-aunt who said "yaller," "orfice" and "layloc": Lord Curzon, who for some strange reason favored a Derbyshire accent, would always talk of "directing a letter," where I should have said "addressing": and those who wished to be regarded as belonging to the Edwardian set would drop the final "g" in such words as "fishing" or "shooting." The Cambridge intellectuals of my period would give emphasis to unstressed syllables or prepositions, saying "CIVilization," or "too boring FOR words." The bright young things of the "twenties had their own delightful jargon and accent. And I suppose that today at the universities the more decorative personalities adopt a way of speaking wholly different from that used by Newman or Froude.

Such changes in manners extend of course beyond the three illustrations that I have chosen. In France it is still regarded as ill-bred to keep the hands in the pockets when addressing a lady, even as in Germany it is rude to cross the legs when seated in a railway carriage or a tram. In Australia the guests are supposed, if well educated, to keep their hands below the tablecloth until the hostess herself has started to eat. In France it is customary, when one has consumed a boiled egg, to crush the shell down into the egg cup, a practice which at Eastbourne would be viewed as odd. In Australia oysters are washed in fresh water before being served, thus depriving them of that salt taste so much appreciated by the customers of Wilton's or Driver's. In France, although not in the United States, it is regarded as good form to drink wine at meals and not to light a cigarette until the last course has been finished. In Russia and Central Europe it was customary to tip the footman, the butler and even the hall porter when dining in a private house: in Israel, as I have been assured, it is considered bad manners to tip anyone at all. In England, among the young men and women of the present punctilious generation, it is thought proper to send a letter of thanks to one's hostess after a dinner or a ball; in France the Collins, or *lettre du château,* is only sent when one has stayed more than one night in a house. In the United States, as distinct from England, it is less intimate to begin a letter with "My dear" than with "Dear." I have been assured by French friends who have studied the subject that differences in deportment and conventions can be detected as between the several provinces. Casual greetings, they tell me, are more effusive in Alsace than they are at Lyons; in the latter you have but a distant, dismissive, wave of the hand: in the former you get the full glory of the *bürgerlicher Grüss.* Nor should we ourselves contend that the forms of courtesy observed at Brighton are identical with those expected, especially on Sundays, at Dundee.

Such variations could be multiplied indefinitely. I have, I trust, said sufficient to demonstrate that, however admirable may have been the successive types of civility which different ages and countries have produced, there exists no such thing as an absolute or stable pattern of good behavior. The society manners of one generation become the provincialisms of the next. "Good form" is, I am glad to say, but a relative expression, applicable only to a certain class of society, at a certain period and in a certain country. Yet what is interesting is that, although types of civility are transitory, types of incivility are recurrent and seemingly immutable. Good manners change from generation to generation: bad manners, like suffering, "are permanent, obscure and dark; and share the nature of infinity."

Four

Unconscious rudeness must always be forgiven, since it may proceed from shyness, lack of practice in the social graces, panic, absent-mindedness, impatience, astigmatism, a bad stammer, hunger, acute illness, love, a secret sorrow, deafness, or just ordinary fear. We should be tolerant also of that form of deliberate rudeness which is the result of sudden rage. Few things are more agreeable than the spectacle of a man who loses his temper: we should be grateful to such people for providing us with moments of often unsullied delight. Invective also is an attractive form of verbal activity, nor do I really mind when a person gives way to a temporary but quite healthy desire to insult. The Romans called the surrender to this desire a *convicium* and were amused rather than shocked when Trimalchio in his cups called his wife a sheep's head and a bitch. Orientals, who have little reflective capacity, and thus no gift for irony, indulge brilliantly in the direct invective. Their purpose is not permanently to humiliate the timid or the inferior: among intelligent people such outbursts leave no rancour behind and are quickly forgotten. Invective is often tumultuously, but seldom meanly, unkind. It is the passionless, the calculating, form of bad manners which is so deeply to be condemned. It is the parasitic types of incivility, as represented by the bore and the snob, that are the true enemies of human intercourse. Before I end I must examine cold discourtesy, the bore and the snob.

Cold discourtesy is the sign of a conceited, and therefore discontented, nature. Those afflicted with the miserable habit of calculated bad manners are seeking to compensate for their own self-hatred, or to increase their own self-esteem, by exposing others to humiliation or unease. They are the men and women who will either ignore, or draw attention to, the socially incompetent or the shy. Who, in the presence of some stranger, will introduce the names of people, or discuss subjects, that are entirely outside the circles of his acquaintance or knowledge; who will exploit the advantages of their wealth, position, or conversational powers without consideration; to whom the solecisms of the inept are a source of rancid satisfaction; and who will display icy inattention when the uninteresting dare to speak. Tactlessness is generally no more, as Theophrastus wrote, than "a painful failure in the sense of occasion." But intended tactlessness is worse than insult or irony, being the slyest of all forms of social cruelty.

Fortunately such creatures are malevolent and therefore rare.

Two types of incivility which are indestructible and eternal require closer examination. The bore, for instance, has throughout the centuries preserved the distinction of his species. Wrote Aldous Huxley:

> A bore is a person who drills a hole in your spirit, who tunnels relentlessly through your patience, through all the crusts of voluntary deafness, inattention, rudeness, which you vainly interpose—through and through, until he pierces to the very quick of your brain.

The primary characteristic of the bore is insistence. This takes the form of long-windedness, garrulity, and a refusal to permit us either to speak ourselves, or to listen to the conversation of others. A bore, who can be tolerable when you are alone with him, becomes intolerable in company, since he will not admit that the remarks of other people can ever be more interesting than his own. This symptom was observed by Theophrastus some two thousand two hundred years ago: "Garrulity," he writes, "is irrelevant talking; or talking at length and without reflection. The garrulous man will sit beside someone whom he does not know and begin to praise his own wife, or tell the story of a dream he had the night before, and then relate dish by dish what he had for dinner. As he warms to his business, he will remark that the younger generation have not the manners of the old, that the price of wheat has fallen, that there seem to be many foreigners in town, or that the ships will be able to put to sea after Dionysia. He will tell of what is being discussed in Parliament and even relate the speeches which he himself was wont to make when a member of the Assembly."

Petronius uses the word "*molestus*" to describe a bore and in the Ninth of his *Satires* Horace has left the most famous portrait of the species that has ever been composed. "You are, I know, terribly anxious to get rid of me," remarks the bore who had accosted him while strolling in the Via Sacra, "I see that clearly. But it's no use, I'll stick to you: *usque tenebo*." "How by the way is Maecenas?" the bore asks him as an opening gambit. Even when Aristius Fuscus appears, Horace is unable to detach himself. Finally the bore is summoned as a witness in an adjoining courtroom. "It was Apollo who saved me." Horace concludes—*sic me servavit Apollo*.

The words *usque tenebo* might indeed be assumed as the universal motto of the bore species. Their desire to prevent the escape of their victims assumes physical form. Plutarch noticed that one of the unmistakable signs of a bore is his insistence on physical contact, on button-holing. "He will seize hold of a fold in your cloak," writes Plutarch, "or touch your beard, or dig his shoulder into your ribs." It is strange that this obnoxious symptom should have distinguished bores for all those thousands of years. But there are other, almost equally distressing, signs.

It is not merely that a bore is long-winded; he is also touchy. He knows that he is a bore, yet he persists. Unfortunately, he detests the company of other bores, can recognize them immediately, and will avoid them as the plague. He enjoys reminiscences, coincidences and stories about imaginary circumstances and encounters. Wisecracks are a specialty of bores and I have met men in American club cars who will tell stories as long as the freight trains that trundle across the prairies through the night. The bore is irrelevant in that he will forget the point or concentration of his narrative to wander down bypaths and into hidden coppices. He indulges also in unnecessary precision, wishing to fix names and dates that have little bearing on his discourse. "It must," he will inform one at dictation speed, "have been in October '53—no it can't have been then because we were in Copenhagen—it may have been early in November—anyhow it doesn't matter, and to cut a long story short. . . ." He also much enjoys repeating Stock Exchange jokes of the "have you heard this one?" variety. "Clergymen," Vyvyan

Holland has remarked acutely, "are seldom boring, unless they belong to the gaitered classes. This is accounted for by the fact that, as they do not tell improper stories, they are forced to adopt more subtle forms of wit." Finally, the bore is invariably a nice man. Were he not kind, and virtuous, and honorable, we should not experience, as we do, both irritation at his insistence and remorse at our own unkindness. He leaves us, when he does leave us, feeling, not angry only, but ashamed.

Snobs also are a permanent element in human society. I suspect that Thersites was a snob at heart and would have been servile enough if invited to dine by Agamemnon. Theophrastus has an excellent word for snobbishness: he calls it μικροφιλοτιμία, meaning thereby both "a vulgar desire for distinction" and "attaching importance to unimportant things." In our own language, and still more so in the French language, the word "snob" has had a strangely fluctuating history. Originally used to designate a cobbler's assistant, it came to be applied by Cambridge undergraduates to what at Oxford used to be called "townees." In the nineteenth century it described both those who were second rate or pretentious and those who viewed the nobility with undue desire. Today, if it means anything, it means the effort on the part of an individual to enhance his own position by avoiding the society of his social inferiors and by cultivating the society of the rich and powerful. In extreme cases it takes the form of being ashamed of dowdy friends or relations and taking overt pride in acquaintance with Cabinet Ministers, film stars, press lords, dukes and members of the Royal Family. As such it is so painful that the crude word "snobbishness" has been softened into the euphemistic diminutive "snobbery." Thus disguised it does not sound quite so bad.

In my young days the term "snob" was applied exclusively to those who yearned for, or boasted of, the friendship of the great. In the series of papers contributed by Thackeray to *Punch* in 1846 which were subsequently published in his *Book of Snobs,* this meaning had not yet been isolated from other aspects of the genteel. Thackeray tells us that when he was at Cambridge the term had ceased to be applied to those who were not members of the university and had been extended to include the poorer and less elegant undergraduates who were shabbily dressed, worked hard at their books, and "walked two hours on the Trumpington Road every day of their lives." Yet he can say of General Sir George Tufto that: "His manners are irreproachable generally; in society he is a perfect gentleman and a most thorough snob." He can say also: "Stinginess is snobbish. Ostentation is snobbish. Too great profusion is snobbish. Tuft-hunting is snobbish." Occasionally he employs the term to signify no more than unjustifiable social pretension. "The jays," he writes, "with peacocks' feathers are the snobs of this world." At one moment he seems to be attacking aristocratic exclusiveness: "I am sick," he writes, "of

Court Circulars. I loathe hautton intelligence. I believe such words as Fashionable, Exclusive, Aristocratic and the like to be wicked, unchristian epithets that ought to be banished from honest vocabularies." At another moment he appears to be assailing, not the upper, but the middle classes. "It is," he writes, "among the respectable, the Baker Street, class of this vast and happy Empire that the greatest profusion of snobs is to be found." At yet another moment he satirizes the stratification of classes according to which each individual despises someone below him. Thus the Duchess of Battleaxe is contemptuous of her neighbor in Belgrave Square, Lady Croesus, who in her turn despises Mrs. Seeley, who despises Miss Letsam, who "never ceases to rebuke the impudence of Suky the maid who wears flowers under her bonnet like a lady." "The word snob," Thackeray concludes, "has taken a place in our honest English vocabulary. We can't define it perhaps. We can't say what it is any more than we can define wit, or humor, or humbug. But we know what it is. . . . I can bear it no longer, this diabolical invention of gentility, which kills natural kindliness and honest friendship."

Today, as I have said, we use the word "snobbish" to describe two forms of vanity. The first is the desire not to be seen associating with undistinguished people. The second is the desire to be seen associating with distinguished people. The former is certainly offensive, since it is harsh openly to disavow members of one's own family or the friends of one's youth. The latter possesses a certain charm. To love and desire the elegant or the eminent is surely a symptom of fastidiousness and taste. To me it seems romantic to yearn to be identified in the minds of others with the more powerful or decorative products of the human race. It may be true, as Vyvyan Holland has said, that the snob is often a bore, even as the bore is often a snob. Yet what I should define as "subjective snobbishness" is surely quite a noble form of aspiration. It is for this reason that I have always regarded *Twelfth Night* and *Le Bourgeois Gentilhomme* as disagreeable plays.

Five

Those who have had the patience to read this book to the end may be wondering why, when the Classless State is about to be created, I should have devoted so much time to patterns of culture created by minorities. It may seem strange that certain small sectors of a society should have been taken as representing the society as a whole. It may even have been thought snobbish of me to use such offensive terms as "upper class," "middle class" or "lower class." I do not see, however, how I could, with any gainliness, have applied to fifth-century Athens or the court of Urbino such deft phrases as "higher-income brackets" or "non-manual lower grades."

The fact is that, although I consider equality of opportunity an ideal of social justice, I do not believe that all the citizens of an alert community can, even by the most ruthless economist, for long be rendered identical in possessions, intelligence or physique. Differences of temperament, which as I have shown exist even among hens, will create among human beings differences of taste and desire. It is generally agreed that in any society it is a minority only (whether it be hereditary, elective or co-opted) which is fit to govern. Similarly it will be a minority only that will mould the manners of the future. "Groups," writes Clive Bell, "of highly civilized men and women are the disseminators of civility." "Culture," writes Werner Jaeger, "is simply the aristocratic ideal of a nation increasingly intellectualized." "*Toute civilization*," writes Ernest Renan, "*est l'aeuvre des aristocrats*" Whatever may be the ultimate effect of the distribution of incomes and the Butler Act, I doubt whether the British people will ever be rendered uniform, or whether the citizens of London will ever slouch along their pavements like mumbling Muscovites, displaying no variations of spirit or demeanor. I suppose that even in the Soviet Union some divergence can be detected between the student who has just left the University of Moscow, having enjoyed the luxury and high intellectual excitement of that garish skyscraper, and those who have received their education in the more drab universities of Tiflis or Irkutsk. Even if we British lose our aristocratic tradition, even if we forget all about the public school manner, even if baseball supplements cricket as a national game, there will always be those who take an interest in the subtleties of human relationships and those who take no such interest. It will be the former and not the latter who set the pattern of good behavior.

The question is rather what shape will this pattern assume? I do not foresee that the social habits of this island will ever be imitated from those of the French, the Germans, the Australians, the Dutch, the Trobrianders, or the Portuguese. I imagine that it will be the American model which will in the end impose itself on the English-speaking world.

When I say "American" I do not mean of course that abominable type of civility, to the presentation and propagation of which the film industry in the United States devotes so much trouble and so many million dollars. Nor have I in mind the type of social American who lives in New York or Paris. I am not thinking either of the lonely, homesick American whom we encounter on his travels abroad, and who is apt from lack of self-assurance to render his manners too emphatic. I am not referring to American big business which is to me wearisome and incomprehensible. Still less do I have in mind the political manager who encourages the fiction that it is unprofitable to differ from the average; that it is un-American to manifest intellectual or aesthetic distinction or to be interested in thoughts or feelings that are beyond the range of the common man. The best heads America possesses have always been her eggheads. The type that I esteem is that lauded in my first chapter and in Chapter 8, namely the calm scholar who preserves all that is most venerable in the tradition of the founding fathers.

I fear that it is inevitable, with the wider distribution of wealth and instruction, that we ourselves shall lose something of our rich eccentricity. If the Welfare State is not to become uniform, and therefore dull, we must keep in our memory the diverse types of civility which with such difficulty have been created in our European past. Nor need we ever forget that civilization is something more than social justice, something more than security, but also the enhancement of pleasure, the love of loveliness, the refinement of relationships, and the embellishment of life.

Index

E

F

G

R

S